SUPREMELY PARTISAN

SUPREMELY PARTISAN

How Raw Politics Tips the Scales in the United States Supreme Court

James D. Zirin

ROWMAN & LITTLEFIELD
Lanham • Boulder • New York • London

Published by Rowman & Littlefield
A wholly owned subsidiary of
The Rowman & Littlefield Publishing Group, Inc.
4501 Forbes Boulevard, Suite 200, Lanham, Maryland 20706
https://rowman.com

Unit A, Whitacre Mews, 26-34 Stannary Street, London SE11 4AB,
United Kingdom

Distributed by NATIONAL BOOK NETWORK

British Library Cataloguing in Publication Information Available

Library of Congress Cataloging-in-Publication Data
Names: Zirin, James D., author.
Title: Supremely partisan : how raw politics tips the scales in the United States
    Supreme Court / James D. Zirin.
Description: Lanham, Maryland : Rowman & Littlefield, 2016. | Includes bibliographical references and index.
Identifiers: LCCN 2016016520 (print) | LCCN 2016016740 (ebook) | ISBN
    9781442266360 (cloth : alk. paper) | ISBN 9781442266377 (electronic)
Subjects: LCSH: United States. Supreme Court. | Political questions and judicial power—United States. | Judicial review—United States.
Classification: LCC KF8748 .Z57 2016 (print) | LCC KF8748 (ebook) | DDC
    347.73/26—dc23
LC record available at http://lccn.loc.gov/9781442266360

∞ ™ The paper used in this publication meets the minimum requirements of
American National Standard for Information Sciences Permanence of Paper
for Printed Library Materials, ANSI/NISO Z39.48-1992.

Printed in the United States of America

To Marlene

CONTENTS

FOREWORD

The United States Supreme Court has the last word on the meaning of the Constitution in our political system. In a real sense, the Constitution is what the Court says it is. But what the Court says has changed greatly over the years. In 1896, for instance, the Court announced in *Plessy v. Ferguson* that the "separate but equal" racial segregation of railroad cars was constitutionally acceptable, but in 1953, in *Brown v. Board of Education*, it rejected that doctrine. In 1986, in *Bowers v. Hardwick*, it held that the Constitution allowed states to criminalize same-sex sexual activity, but in 2003, *Lawrence v. Texas* reversed *Bowers*. Even at any given moment there are typically sharp divisions among the Justices on important questions of constitutional interpretation: of the decisions just listed, only *Brown* was unanimous.

How can these disagreements be explained? The simplest theory starts with the premise that the Constitution prescribes clearly correct answers in all cases. Some Justices faithfully adhere to those solutions and others seek instead to advance their own political agendas.

This was basically the position of Justice Antonin Scalia, and his aggressive advocacy in its favor has exerted an enormous influence on the public's perception of the Court and the Constitution. Unfortunately, that influence is largely negative because the position is wrong. It takes no more than a quick glance at the words of the Constitution to see that it does not, in fact, contain specific answers to every question that might arise. Instead, the Constitution frequently speaks in majestic generalities. Equal protection, due process, the freedom of speech—

these are general concepts. The drafters of those words explained them in terms of broad notions of fundamental fairness and justified distinctions rather than arbitrary or oppressive discrimination. The ratifiers argued bitterly about which government acts would be forbidden and which allowed. It is not really possible to deny that on contentious constitutional questions there is some open space for argument, some indeterminacy, within which opposing positions are both legally plausible. So what determines the choices that Justices make?

One answer, also consistent with the Scalia model, is that when there is no answer, everyone acts like a politician. They advance the interests of their favored political party, or whatever policies they like, even when there is no constitutional basis for the choice.

Judges of course deny this. They claim to be umpires rather than players. As James D. Zirin puts it in this timely book, they "fall all over themselves saying" that when they decide constitutional cases, they are merely applying the law. But Mr. Zirin argues, to use the words of Justice Scalia, that this position is "pure applesauce." When it comes to certain highly charged issues such as homosexuality, abortion, affirmative action, illegal immigration, capital punishment, and guns, he contends, the opinions of the Supreme Court reflect the views of the Justices arising out of personal life experiences, gender, religion, or political predisposition: in short, identity politics.

It is true, almost as a matter of logic, that if law or the Constitution do not take judges all the way to an answer, something else must be at work. And it is also true, I believe, that life experiences and predispositions are in large part the something else that enters judicial decision-making. But how exactly does that happen, and what are we to make of it? I believe the picture is a complicated one.

First, some Supreme Court decisions—perhaps most notably *Bush v. Gore*—are hard to explain in any terms other than partisanship. Those decisions are justifiably condemned. But not all decisions, not even all of the controversial and divisive ones, are driven by partisan politics.

Instead, what determines a Justice's position in many cases is better described as either a constitutional (not a political) ideology, or a general worldview. There have been divisive cases in recent years, for instance, about the scope of federal legislative power. The Justices clearly have commitments and preconceptions about this issue, but those commitments and preconceptions are part of their constitutional interpretation. Some Justices think that the Founding and the original Constitution struck a particular balance between state and federal authority and that the Court should try to preserve that. Others think that the Reconstruction Amendments, the Thirteenth, Fourteenth, and Fifteenth, forever altered that balance, so that the Founding conception is no longer part of our Constitution. That is ideology, maybe, but it is still rooted in an understanding of the Constitution.

Justices also differ on the question of how much they trust judges—how willing they are to commit difficult choices to the judiciary rather than the political process. Justice Scalia had a very dim view of judicial capacity to settle hard moral questions; Justice Kennedy has much more confidence in it. Justices differ similarly on how much they trust the executive branch to take action in the name of national security without judicial oversight. Here, Justice Thomas is probably the most deferential. The liberals are less so, and Justice Scalia charted a compromise position, varying his trust depending on whether the action was directed at American citizens or not. Again, these are not narrow partisan differences. They reflect in part the Justices' weighing of underlying values—liberty vs. security, for example—and in part their faith in the men and women who make up the different branches of our government. The Justices are not always consistent in these views from case to case—and when they are inconsistent, we might suspect that partisanship is present—but to the extent that they are consistent, partisanship is not the driving force.

Last, the Justices differ in their understanding of general facts about the world. How much of a threat is in-person voter fraud? How hard is it for people to get the kinds of identification required by voter-ID laws? Are abortion protesters interested in thoughtful communication or intemperate harassment? Can Southern states be trusted not to attempt to disenfranchise minority voters? Are blacks, women, and the LGBT population fundamentally the same as straight white males, or are they different in ways that might justify differential treatment? These are the questions on which important recent constitutional cases have turned. Answers to them tend to correlate with political ideology—which is why the votes of the Justices do too—but they do not come directly from it. More likely, these underlying views about the world produce both political ideology and votes in constitutional cases.

Where do underlying views come from? They're informed by research and the arguments of parties in particular cases, of course, but they're shaped first and foremost by life experience. That means that a Justice's background, race, and sex will affect his or her constitutional judgments. But does that make them partisan, or the product of identity politics in a negative sense?

In this book, James Zirin makes the argument that the answer is yes. He examines the personal factors that influence judges through a wide-ranging and detailed study of Justices and cases. He suggests that such influences are generally illegitimate, that they make the Supreme Court "a political court." I tend to think that instances of true partisanship are the exception rather than the rule, that most decisions can be explained in nonpartisan terms as the product of influences judges may properly take into account. But regardless of which view readers accept, they will benefit greatly from reading this book. It will deepen their understanding of the Court at a time when concerns of partisanship and identity politics undeniably overwhelmingly drive the nomination process. All Americans should pay close heed.

> **Kermit Roosevelt** is a professor of constitutional law at the
> University of Pennsylvania Law School and the author of
> *The Myth of Judicial Activism* and the novels
> *In the Shadow of the Law* and *Allegiance*.

INTRODUCTION

What I care most about . . . is that we want this institution to maintain the position . . . where it is not considered a political branch of government.
—Ruth Bader Ginsburg

When the nine Justices of the Supreme Court of the United States meet each day to take the bench, each shakes hands with each of the other eight—a total of 36 handshakes. This tradition, which has existed since the late nineteenth century, is said to signify shared purpose. Yet the symbol of unity is belied by the fact. The Court is deeply divided along partisan lines, and its decisions frequently reflect the polarization of American society.

The death of conservative Justice Antonin Scalia on February 13, 2016, plunged the Supreme Court further into the epicenter of partisan politics. It is an election year, and the statements of the presidential candidates about who should serve on the Court, and who should not, reflect how politicized the third branch of government has become.

President Obama called Scalia "one of the towering legal figures of our time," but did not attend his funeral. Scalia was the darling of the conservative nursery. He was the bristling sparkplug of a bare conservative majority on the Court. Voting consistently against abortion and gay rights, affirmative action, and environmental regulation, he also voted for personal gun rights and capital punishment. He famously stated that "Judges have been known to be . . . politically partisan." Merrick Garland, the venerated chief judge of the D.C. Circuit, whom Obama promptly appointed as Scalia's successor, would be unlikely to adhere to Scalia's hardline, right-wing positions on these issues that so bitterly and deeply divide the nation.

Scalia's passing gave Obama a moment of constitutional reflection as well as political calculus. Republicans enjoyed a 54-vote majority in the Senate, and it would take 60 votes, a coalition of Democrats and moderate Republicans, to override an eventual filibuster. So if the Senate Republicans were to vote along straight party lines, the Garland nomination would appear to be beyond the rainbow. It may well have been Obama's bet, however, that if the Republicans were to reject such a spectacularly qualified nominee as Garland, they would appear obstructive and irresponsible, causing them to lose the Senate, and perhaps leaving a Democratic president with an additional appointment even more liberal than Garland. For the Republicans, it could well be a lose-lose scenario.

Senate Majority Leader Mitch McConnell, like most of the Republican candidates, called on Obama to kick the nomination over to the next president, saying that Senate Republicans would not even meet with Garland or hold hearings on the nomination. McConnell contended that Scalia's successor should be selected by the American people, a spurious position, which ignores that the Constitution says the Justices are selected by the president, not the people, and that if selected by the people because the people elect the president, then Obama is still the president in office selected by the people. Nice try, Mitch! As a lawyer, Obama has been trained to respect precedent. Despite Senator Ted Cruz's misleading claim that we have an eighty-year history of "not *confirming* a Supreme Court Justice in an election year,"[1] the historical record does not reveal any instance since at least 1900 where the Nation left a seat open on the Supreme Court until after the election.[2] In 2010, Chief Justice John Roberts had chastised both parties in the Senate for blocking judicial nominees on partisan grounds. So with Republican Senate leaders vowing to block any nominee, Obama correctly stated that the constitutional "responsibility to nominate and confirm is bigger than any one party, they are about our democracy."

In the exercise of his constitutional responsibility, Obama nominated Garland, a Jew with deep family ties to the Democratic Party,[3] a former Brennan clerk, and a distinguished lawyer and jurist. There was nothing in Garland's centrist liberal background to suggest he would share Scalia's hardline conservative views. The specter of identity politics haunted the president's calculus. The last two times around, Garland was at the top of the president's shortlist. Yet, Obama passed over Garland for two women, one a Latina, Sonia Sotomayor; and the other, Elena Kagan.

Prior to Scalia's death, the Court consisted of six Catholics and three Jews—the first time in its 226-year history that it was 100 percent minority. There were no evangelicals, and no traditional Protestants, three women (one of whom was Latino), and one African American. The composition of the Court cried out perhaps for some political rebalancing in making an appointment.

With Scalia's body hardly grown cold, the *New York Times* served up a delicious political stew of possible appointees said to be on the shortlist. Interestingly enough, although the original *Times* list shifted slightly, none of the five names was that of a white Anglo-Saxon Protestant male. In addition to Garland, there were four distinguished appeals court judges: Sri Srinivasan, an Indian immigrant; Patricia Millet, whose nomination to the DC Circuit in 2013 barely survived a Republican-led filibuster; Jane Kelly, a judge of the 8th Circuit in Iowa; and Paul Watford, an African American federal judge from the 9th Circuit in California. All, while presumably more liberal than Scalia, present a political profile of quintessential legal excellence that a moderate Republican Senator might find difficult to reject on purely party lines. Yet, although Garland appeared to be the most palatable to the Senate Republicans, they seemed determined to block his nomination.

The obstructive conduct of the Senate Republican leaders left the Court short-handed, and conjured the specter of 4-4 tie decisions. A tie leaves the judgment in place (the practical equivalent of an affirmance) and is of no precedential value.

Whether Garland is approved or not, 2016 will be a defining year in the Court's history. In addition to the Scalia seat, at least three vacancies may occur during the next president's term by reason of the retirement, in order of age, of Ruth Bader Ginsburg, Anthony Kennedy, and Stephen Breyer. So the Republicans have bigger fish to fry on the Court than just one seat. To contrast the polar ends of the political spectrum, the administration of Donald Trump would obviously appoint a very different kind of Justice from that promised by Hillary Clinton. The future of the Supreme Court figures as a key issue in the presidential campaign.

Senator Kirsten Gillibrand (D-NY), herself a lawyer, has deep concerns about the composition of the Supreme Court. She told her constituents, "Whenever anyone asks me why the 2016 election matters, I tell them the same thing: The future of the Supreme Court hangs in the balance. Up to four justices could retire during the next president's term. And if we want progressives like Justices Ginsburg, Kagan and Sotomayor on the bench, we *must* ensure we have a Democratic Senate confirming nominees in 2016."

The 2016 presidential campaign requires us to form an educated guess as to what kinds of Justices the respective candidates will appoint if they are successful. What will be their criteria for appointment? What are the candidates' views about ethnic and religious balance on the Court? Who will be the new Justices be?

In the second Republican presidential debate on September 17, 2015, Senator Ted Cruz, a former Supreme Court law clerk, referring to the appointments of David Souter by George H. W. Bush and John Roberts by George W. Bush, expressed a raw frustration that conservatives "keep winning elections" but don't "get the outcome we want" on the Supreme Court. Donald Trump called on the Senate to "delay, delay, delay" confirming any Obama appointee as Scalia's successor. From a Republican president, we might expect a Justice more in line with the "originalist" doctrines of Scalia or Clarence Thomas, using a skewed recitation of American history to weigh in on the side of guns; or, as Trump put it, willing to "punish" women or their doctors over abortions; or to narrow gay rights or affirmative action; or to approve capital punishment as consonant with Christian tradition; or to affirm the growing, and for some alarming, presence of sectarian religion in public life. [4]

From Clinton, we might expect the opposite—another female Justice to replace Ginsburg, the oldest of the Justices. After all, Ginsburg herself said, "When I am asked when will there be enough women on the Supreme Court? And I say 'When there are nine.' People are shocked. But there'd been nine men, and nobody's ever raised a question about that." Hillary might well appoint more liberals of whatever gender and ethnicity to replace Ginsburg, or Kennedy or Breyer, the next oldest Justices, and more ethnic and religious minorities to replace any other vacancies that might arise. The possibility of an openly gay Justice is not unthinkable. Since the Supreme Court is a lifetime appointment, the president elected in 2016 will have the power to shape the direction of the Court for long after he or she leaves the Oval Office.

This book is about the problematic fashion that the Supreme Court has come to use partisan politics to administer justice in many of its cases. And, according to Gallup, as the Court has become increasingly partisan, public confidence in its decisions has ebbed. This is a serious problem.

I intend to take a fresh look in an election year at the irrefutable fact that, despite protestations to the contrary, the Court has become a supremely partisan court, rapidly making policy choices right and left on ideological bases that have nothing to do with law or the Constitution. The Senate flap over the appointment of Scalia's replacement demonstrates that what we have created is a politicized judiciary with both sides uncertain of its direction. In the second Republican presidential debate of September 16, 2015, Cruz charged that the Justices have become so liberal, "we have an out-of-control Court."[5] Liberal pundit Jeffrey Toobin, however, predicted in the October 2015 Term, a "coming liberal disaster" with the "conservatives on the court poised for a comeback."[6] Toobin made his prediction before Scalia's unexpected death and possible replacement with a liberal Justice.

Since this book will be read (and hopefully enjoyed) by lawyers and non-lawyers alike, the sophisticated reader will forgive me if I present a few background facts at the outset, well known to many and perhaps not so well known to all. The Supreme Court is the court of last resort, the umpire of the Constitution. It has arrogated to itself the power to declare acts of the Executive or of the Congress or of the several states unconstitutional. Federal law trumps all state legislation since the Constitution and laws of the United States are "the supreme Law of the Land."[7] The iconic Justice, Oliver Wendell Holmes, said that striking down an act of Congress "is the gravest and most delicate duty that this Court is called on to perform."[8] It should not be done lightly. But this has been done all too often in recent years by both liberal and conservative Justices interpreting the Constitution to conform to their partisan views.

The Constitution did not expressly give the Court this awesome power. Chief Justice John Marshall seized it in 1803, and Chief Justice John Roberts reaffirmed it when he was appointed in 2005. The Court, as expounder of the Constitution, has tremendous influence over what we are and where we are going as the greatest multicultural society on the planet. Stanford Law professor Thomas C. Grey observes that the Constitution "has been, virtually from the moment of its ratification, a sacred symbol, the potent emblem . . . of the nation itself."[9] And Abraham Lincoln famously said, "What is the framework under which we live? The Constitution of the United States."

The Constitution is virtually impossible to alter. Amendment requires the vote of 2/3 of the Congress and 3/4 of the states. It has been amended only seventeen times in the more than 224 years since the first ten amendments were ratified in 1791 in the Bill of Rights. The Constitution exists not only to provide a "framework" of government, but also to protect minorities from the tyranny of the majority and the bureaucratic excesses of government, or, to use the famous words of Brandeis, "the right to be let alone—the most comprehensive of rights and the right most valued by civilized men."[10]

There is rarely one way to interpret the vague, and often conflicting, language of the Constitution. Some provisions are quite clear. When it says there shall be two senators from each state, it would be hard to give the statement anything other than its traditional interpretation. And of course, such a case would never reach the Supreme Court. But when the issue invokes the powerful values lurking in the shadows of the Due Process, Equal Protection, or Cruel and Unusual Punishments Clauses, the conflicting ideas of the Religion Clauses (freedom of religion; separation of church and state) of the First Amendment, or the separation of powers between the Executive and the Congress, we have for most of our history depended on the Supreme Court to tell us what the law is.

We like to imagine the Court as a pillar of liberty: the eloquent dissents of Holmes and Brandeis that later became the law; the Warren Court, unanimously ending school segregation, unanimously invalidating state curbs on miscegenous marriages,[11] unanimously establishing the right to counsel for the indigent accused, providing for Miranda warnings to those in custodial interrogation, and extending rules requiring the state courts to exclude illegally seized evidence even though, as Cardozo famously said, the "guilty may go free because the constable has blundered."[12] The Warren Court rendered liberal decisions in over 70 percent of the cases to come before it.

The Supreme Court post-Warren, however, has been largely conservative as it has been for most of its history. It has continued to be so to the hour of Scalia's death. The mainstream media, notably the *New York Times*, have seen the Court as inching to the left this past term. Adam Liptak suggests the shift is sparked by a disciplined liberal left wing.[13] Court commentators cite the poster child 6-3 decision in *King v. Burwell*,[14] upholding Obamacare for the second time, the 5-4 decision *Obergefell v. Hodges*,[15] finding a constitutional right to same-sex marriage, and the 5-4 decision in *Walker v. Texas Division, Sons of Confederate Veterans*,[16] allowing Texas to reject specialty license plates bearing the Confederate flag. In all three cases, a Republican-appointed Justice or two voted with the four liberals to achieve a majority. But don't fool yourself. Liberals have not prevailed uniformly. Business groups last term won 12 out of 22 cases in which they faced individuals or the government. The Roberts Court, true to its conservative DNA with Scalia in harness, repeatedly found for business in preference to the consumer, the stockholder, the employee, and the union. The Court has given the government the benefit of the doubt in close criminal cases; it has found against those detained without a hearing at a time of national emergency. It has sounded the virtual death knell for affirmative action, gutted voting rights legislation, chipped away at reproductive freedom, permitted Christian prayer at public meetings, and reaffirmed the death penalty. David A. Strauss, a Supreme Court practitioner and law professor at Chicago, states, "It's still a conservative court—just not as conservative as some had hoped, and some had feared." But Scalia's successor may well cause the conservative ideology of the partisan Court to turn on a dime.

To be sure, the Court in the October 2014 Term rendered liberal decisions in 56 percent of its cases.[17] But many of these "liberal" decisions are of scant precedential value, being 5-4 or 6-3 split decisions, with the Justices dividing sharply along partisan lines. The frequency of split decisions and ideological voting blocs causes many to question the Court's authority as a court of law. The public reaction to a Supreme Court decision will probably depend on one's own political conviction. Liberals may rejoice when the Court delivers a strained interpretation upholding a progressive piece of legislation such as Obamacare or finds an unstated right of "decency" in the Constitution that would validate the modernistic concept of gay marriage. They may cheer for the solidarity of the Democratically appointed "Four Horsemen" (Ginsburg, Breyer, Sotomayor, and Kagan), today's ironbound liberal voting bloc, on a host of politically charged issues as they confront the conservative majority.[18] In the October 2013 Term, Justices Ginsburg, Sotomayor, and Kagan voted together at least 93 percent of the time.[19] Conservatives may revel in 5-4 victories upholding the death penalty, invalidating voting rights legislation, curtailing campaign finance limitations that would adversely impact Republicans, upholding gun rights, limiting affirmative action, narrowing abortion rights, or siding with business interests. They may remember fondly Scalia's irreverently defiant and often amusing antics as he sarcastically railed at his liberal colleagues or against the Court itself.

When the Court deviates from a judicial role, and seeks to legislate from the bench, upholding statutes that it likes, striking down others when it disagrees with the legislative purpose, and proving quick to find new "fundamental rights" in the Constitution's Due Process Clause, it courts the "possibility of judicial emasculation by way of popular reaction against constitutional review by the courts."[20] This was the path the Court's slave-owning majority took in the infamous *Dred Scott*[21] decision, invalidating the Missouri Compromise and affirming the property rights of slaveholders. This was the approach of the conservative majority during the four decades of the discredited *Lochner* era, named for *Lochner v. New York*, which spanned the forty-year period from 1897–1937, when the Court repeatedly used substantive due process to strike down economic or social legislation it deemed unwise.[22] And this was the path of the liberals this past term in the gay marriage decision, with a big assist from conservative Justice Anthony Kennedy.

The *Dred Scott* decision led to the Civil War, and the decisions of the forty-year *Lochner* era led to Franklin Roosevelt's Court packing bill—a move that fortunately died in the Senate as it would have destroyed the independence of the judiciary. Prior to 2010, with the possible exception of the *Lochner* era, which we treat more fully later on, studies show that voting patterns of the Justices were thought of as nonpartisan. But of late, in major policy-charged decisions, the voting of the Justices has been largely along partisan lines.

In a memorable dissent in *Dred Scott*, Justice Benjamin Robbins Curtis stated that when the "fixed rules which govern the interpretation of laws [are] abandoned, and the theoretical opinions of individuals are allowed to control" constitutional interpretation, "we have no longer a Constitution; we are under the government of individual men, who for the time being have power to declare what the Constitution is."[23] Justice Curtis resigned from the Court over the *Dred Scott* decision, the only Justice in history to have resigned over a matter of principle.

At the moment, as we face a presidential election, the American people are deeply polarized not only about economic and social issues, but also about American power, and how it should be exercised in the world. As the people are polarized, so is Congress. So are those in our top think tanks and universities. And so, not too surprisingly, has been the Supreme Court.[24] Read any 5-4 or 6-3 decision of the October 2014 Term. That was the typical face of the Supreme Court until February 13, 2016, when Scalia unexpectedly passed from the scene.

It has become fashionable to think of liberals on the Court as "judicial activists"; conservatives as practitioners of "judicial restraint." The Justices on both sides of the debate, however, are often inconsistent in approach and result. When they like statutes of Congress or the state legislatures, they are restrained in "deferring" to the elected lawmakers. When they don't like the laws the elected legislatures have passed, they freely strike them down. The very conservatives who deferred to Congress when it came to the Defense of Marriage Act or the "United States Policy with Respect to Jerusalem as the Capital of Israel," or to some of the state legislatures when it came to gay marriage, were unwilling to do so when it came to monitoring "bad actor" states under the Voting Rights Act or to Obamacare. The liberals came down the opposite way: Voting Rights and Obamacare, defer to Congress; Defense of Marriage and Jerusalem, don't defer. Kennedy, the swinger, went both ways, voting with the liberals to ride roughshod over the policies of Congress when it came to the Defense of Marriage Act, the Voting Rights Act, Congress's declaration of policy on the Jerusalem statute, and the policies of the thirty-four state legislatures that had not seen fit to endorse gay marriage, but voting with the conservatives to defer to the legislatures on other issues such as limiting reproductive rights where he approved of the outcome.

The respective factions are also remarkably inconsistent when it comes to presidential power. When the president was George W. Bush, conservatives were willing to defer to him on detention in Guantanamo. When the president was Barack Obama, conservatives were unwilling to defer to him on whether Jerusalem was part of Israel. [25]

Court decisions are often not sourced in the Constitution or the law, but in the personal views of the Justices. And their background, education, and life experience undoubtedly inform their policy choices, with among the most pungent ingredients of the stew being ethnicity, gender, religion, and, most often, the political views of the presidents who appointed them.

Who is on the Supreme Court makes a tremendous difference. We saw this when in 2006 Samuel Alito, an extreme conservative Catholic, replaced Sandra Day O'Connor, a moderate conservative Protestant, and the Court lurched to the right in a decision upholding the federal partial birth abortion statute, in effect overruling a 5-4 decision invalidating essentially the same statute made only seven years before. [26]

In this book I shall treat the historical WASP, Catholic, Jewish, African American, and female seats on the Court; the real meaning of the constitutionally mandated no religious test for office; and the origins and evolution of partisan Supreme Court appointments that have led to the present Court being 100 percent minority, and largely conservative. I treat the jurisprudence of two extraordinary Justices, John Marshall, the prescient Chief Justice who elaborated the principle of judicial review, and Oliver Wendell Holmes, who, among other things, steered us on our free speech course of "freedom for the thought we hate." I also profile separately the lives of certain partisan Justices: Ginsburg and Sotomayor. And I reserve separate chapters for the high priest of the partisans, Antonin Scalia, and his acolyte, Clarence Thomas. I find Scalia, on whose legacy and jurisprudence we may now venture a preliminary retrospective, to be a fascinatingly colorful figure, more Catholic than the Pope, who filled what I call the "eccentricity seat" because his "originalism with a nuance" doctrine had a tremendous intellectual impact on the Court's current thinking.

I also select a number of recent cases, all, in my view, decided on partisan lines. These were all 5-4 or 6-3 policy decisions with the votes of the Justices being largely predictable long before briefs, oral argument, or submission. In each of these cases, neither the text, structure, nor original understanding of the Constitution was dispositive, and I argue that the Court came to its judgment based on the personal ideologies of the Justices and not on legal sources.

The Court's dramatic polarization in recent years is a recipe for uncertainty, governmental dysfunction, and declining confidence in what, in my view, is the greatest of our institutions. And this has not been fully appreciated by most otherwise well-informed Americans. Many will conclude that a deeply partisan Supreme Court imperils "Equal Justice under Law," the four powerful words engraved on the west pediment of the Supreme Court Building in Washington, and that it is not the correct path for the United States of America. Others, perhaps less cynical, may differ.

Notes

1. Transcript of ninth Republican debate held in South Carolina February 13, 2016. Available at http://time.com/4224275/republican-debate-transcript-south-carolina-ninth/. Cruz's claim that Kennedy was both appointed and confirmed in 1988 was flat out wrong. Ronald Reagan appointed Justice Kennedy in November 1987, and the Democratic controlled Senate confirmed him two months later in 1988, an election year.

2. By Amy Howe, "Supreme Court Vacancies in Election Years," SCOTUS Blog, February 13, 2016. Available at http://www.scotusblog.com/2016/02/supreme-court-vacancies-in-presidential-election-years/.

3. Garland's wife is the granddaughter of Samuel I. Rosenman, counsel, speechwriter and close confidant to Franklin Delano Roosevelt.

4. As will be seen, I argue that "originalism" is really elegant window-dressing for a decision heavily freighted with political ideology.

5. Transcript of September 16, 2015 debate of the Republican candidates for president. Available at http://www.washingtonpost.com/news/the-fix/wp/2015/09/16/annotated-transcript-september-16-gop-debate/#.

6. By Jeffrey Toobin, "The Coming Liberal Disaster at the Supreme Court," *The New Yorker*, September 1, 2015, available at http://www.newyorker.com/news/daily-comment/the-coming-liberal-disaster-at-the-supreme-court.

7. U. S. Const., Art. VI, cl. 2.

8. *Blodgett v. Holden*, 275 U.S. 142, 148 (1927) (Holmes, J., concurring).

9. Thomas Grey, "The Constitution as Scripture," 37 Stanford Law Review 1, 3 (1984).

10. Dissenting opinion in *Olmstead v. United States*, 277 U.S. 438,478 (1928).

11. *Loving v. Virginia*, 388 U.S. 1 (1967).

12. *People* v. *Defore*, 242 N.Y. 13, 24–25, 150 N. E. 585, 588–89 (1926).

13. See Adam Liptak, "Right Divided, a Disciplined Left Steered the Supreme Court," *New York Times*, June 30, 2015. Available at http://www.nytimes.com/2015/07/01/us/supreme-court-tacks-left-with-push-from-disciplined-liberals.html?_r=0.

14. 576 U.S. (2015).

15. 576 U.S. (2015).

16. 576 U.S. (2015).

17. A "Term" of the Supreme Court runs from October to June of the next year. For example, the October 2014 Term consists of cases heard and decided from October 2014 to June 2015.

18. The first group of "Four Horsemen" on the Supreme Court were the anti-Roosevelt conservatives in the 1930s: Van Devanter, Butler, McReynolds, and Sutherland. With the requisite gender neutrality, I have applied the term "Four Horsemen" to the liberals on the present Court: Breyer, Ginsburg, Sotomayor, and Kagan as well.

19. Adam Liptak, "Three Justices Bound by Beliefs, Not Just Gender, *The New York Times*, July 1, 2013. Available at http://www.nytimes.com/2013/07/02/us/bound-together-on-the-court-but-by-beliefs-not-gender.html.

20. John Hart Ely, *Democracy and Distrust* (Harvard, 1980), 47–48.

21. *Dred Scott v. Sandford*, 19 How. 393 (1857).

22. *Lochner v. New York*, 198 U.S. 45 (1905).

23. *Dred Scott, supra*, at 621.

24. See, e.g., Devins, Neal and Baum, Lawrence, "Split Definitive: How Party Polarization Turned the Supreme Court into a Partisan Court" (May 2, 2014). William & Mary Law School Research Paper No. 09-276. Available at http://ssrn.com/abstract=2432111.

25. Compare *Hamdan v. Rumsfeld*, 548 U.S. 567 (2006), with *Zivotofsky v. Kerry*, 576 U.S. ___ (2015).

26. *Gonzales v. Carhart*, 550 U.S.124 (2007).

I

WHAT THE SUPREME COURT IS SUPPOSED (AND NOT SUPPOSED) TO DO

We are under a Constitution, but the Constitution is what the Judges say it is.
—Chief Justice Charles Evans Hughes

Every student of high-school civics knows well that there are two political branches of government: the Congress, where the majority rules, is elected by the people, and makes the laws pursuant to certain enumerated powers; and the president, who is elected by the electoral college, and usually by a majority of the people, carries out the laws, and attempts to lead the nation from a "bully pulpit." Both of these political branches of government are expected to be partisan and reflect the views of the political base that elected them.

Least understood is the Supreme Court, which, as an institution is composed of many moving parts. In this chapter, I will try to elaborate the appointment process, how Justices get to the Court, judicial independence, the process of judging, the nature of the Court's docket, the quality of its opinions, the role of the law clerks, and the doctrinal and partisan divide that have polarized the Court: in short, what make this supremely partisan court tick.

The president with the advice and consent of the Senate appoints the Supreme Court Justice, who is unelected. The Court of nine consists of an elite cadre of lawyers. They are supposed to be independent of politics. The article of faith is that the judiciary is supposed to interpret and apply the laws—to tell us what the laws are, not to function as a super-legislature.

Presidents make Supreme Court appointments from their own party 85 percent of the time. In the recent past, Republican presidents appointed a few moderate conservatives, notably, John Marshall Harlan and Potter Stewart appointed by Eisenhower, Lewis Powell (a lawyer's lawyer) appointed by Nixon, and Sandra Day O'Connor appointed by Reagan. In more recent years, Republican presidents appointed five conservative Justices: Scalia by Reagan; Kennedy and Thomas by George H. W. Bush; and Roberts and Alito by George W. Bush. Democratic presidents appointed the four sitting liberal Justices: Ginsburg and Breyer by Clinton, and Kagan and Sotomayor by Obama.

In making nominations, presidents have passed over a number of our greatest jurists. An eminent English Justice of the Supreme Court of the United Kingdom, an admirer of American jurisprudence, told me once, "Learned Hand and Henry Friendly are two of the greatest American judges of the 20th century never to have been nominated to the Supreme Court."

Prospective Justices must answer a detailed questionnaire probing almost every aspect of their personal and professional lives. They are vetted by the American Bar Association, investigated by the FBI, and grilled by the Senate Judiciary Committee in searching confirmation hearings.

Justices are supposed to be appointed on the basis of their skill as lawyers. "[W]hether they reflect the policy views of a particular constituency is not (or should not be) relevant."[1] Unfortunately, it has been very relevant. Since 1789, 112 men and women have interpreted our Constitution. The exclusive preserve for most of its 227-year history of white Anglo-Saxon Protestant males, it is only in the last century that traditional politics has drawn such deep water in Court appointments. The profile and complexion of the nine-member Supreme Court has shifted dramatically in the past fifty years. Since 1953, there have been twice as many Republican appointments. As we have seen, some Republican appointees, such as Warren, Brennan, and Souter, have turned out to be liberal to the surprise and dismay of the presidents who appointed them. The votes of Democratic nominees, with the possible exception of Byron White, have been far more predictably liberal.

Occasionally, there are major surprises. Franklin Roosevelt repaid a political favor to Hugo Black, a Dixiecrat Senator from Alabama. Roosevelt said that he wanted a "thumping, evangelical New Dealer" on the Court. This was the litmus test of the Depression years. Black's record in Alabama was an issue in his confirmation. He had been a member of the Ku Klux Klan, and his background also bespoke strong anti-Catholic views. Although Black's record on civil liberties is tarnished by his opinion for the Court upholding the internment of American citizens of Japanese descent during World War II,[2] he was unbending in his absolutist approach to constitutional jurisprudence. He famously said, "When the Constitution says 'Congress shall make no law abridging the freedom of speech . . .' it means *no* law!" Black served on the Supreme Court for thirty-four years, rendering many decisions favorable to African American criminal defendants and other political dissenters. He frequently joined Justice William O. Douglas in dissenting opinions, arguing that all of the constitutional guarantees of the Bill of Rights were binding on the states. The majority of the Court later on largely accepted Black's view.

In the 1950s, Eisenhower kept getting burned in his Court appointments. He named Earl Warren as Chief Justice of the United States. Warren, a conservative Republican, had a stellar record as a no-nonsense state court prosecutor, elected three times as governor of California. Paradoxically, as attorney general of California, Warren had been instrumental, during World War II, in the internment of American citizens of Japanese descent. Warren became the paradigmatic liberal Chief Justice, and the leader of the "due process revolution," completely remaking Constitutional jurisprudence in a series of transformative decisions such as ending school segregation throughout the country,[3] guaranteeing indigent defendants the Sixth Amendment right to counsel in the state courts,[4] and enunciated the rights of criminals in custodial interrogation.[5] Ironically, bumper stickers calling on Congress to "Impeach Earl Warren" became a conservative shibboleth leveled at a jurist who had been appointed by a Republican.

For all its liberalism in issues of race and defendants' rights, however, the Warren Court had a questionable record in the field of gender equality. In *Hoyt v. Florida*,[6] the Court unanimously upheld the conviction by an all-male jury of a woman who killed her husband with a baseball bat. Florida law at that time required jury service of men but not of women, for whom it was optional. Mrs. Hoyt contended that in light of the nature of the crime, women would be "more understanding or compassionate than men" in gauging the "quality of her act and her defense of temporary insanity." The Court saw nothing discriminatory in the Florida approach since "despite the enlightened emancipation of women from the restrictions and protections of bygone years, and their entry into many parts of community life formerly considered to be reserved to men, woman is still regarded as the center of home and family life."[7]

In a recess appointment just before the 1956 presidential election, Eisenhower appointed William J. Brennan, a state court judge from New Jersey. Ike expected that the appointment of Brennan, a devout Roman Catholic, would woo Catholic voters in the heavily Democratic Northeast. He also expected that Brennan would come down hard on criminal defendants, given his authoritarian Roman Catholic background. The next year, when Brennan proved to be unwavering in upholding individual rights, often favoring criminal defendants, minorities, the poor, and other underrepresented groups against the government, Eisenhower said that the Brennan appointment and that of Earl Warren had been "big mistakes," and that in the future he would pay more attention to ideology. Even though abortion was a sin according to the dictates of his Catholic faith, Brennan notably voted with the seven-Justice majority in *Roe*.

Presidents don't like surprises. In the second Republican debate in September 2015, both Jeb Bush and Ted Cruz said that, if elected, they would vet Supreme Court candidates even more thoroughly on their ideology than had happened in connection with the Souter and Roberts nominations. In 1990, Bush's father, George H. W. Bush, had appointed David Souter, a federal appellate judge from New Hampshire, after being assured by his chief of staff, John Sununu, also of New Hampshire, that Souter was a "slam-dunk," a dyed-in-the-wool conservative. When senators couldn't get an answer out of Souter as to how he might vote on overruling *Roe*, liberals called him the "stealth candidate." Souter was confirmed, to the eventual dismay of the Republican right. George W. Bush nominated Roberts, with Cruz being one of the 78 senators voting to confirm. In the debates, both Jeb Bush and Cruz expressed disappointment in how Roberts has ruled, notably on Obamacare.

True to his conservative backers in his first year on the Court, Souter voted with Scalia close to 85 percent of the time. He voted with moderates Kennedy and O'Connor about 97 percent of the time. But he was faithful to the conservatives only "in his fashion." The turning point came in two cases in 1992: *Planned Parenthood v. Casey*,[8] in which the Court reaffirmed the essential holding in *Roe v. Wade*; and *Lee v. Weisman*,[9] in which Souter voted against allowing prayer at a public high-school graduation ceremony. In *Casey*, Anthony Kennedy considered overturning *Roe* and upholding all the abortion restrictions at issue in *Casey*. Souter considered upholding all the restrictions but still was uneasy about overturning *Roe*. After consulting with O'Connor, however, the three developed a joint opinion that upheld all the restrictions in *Casey* except for the mandatory notification of a husband while reaffirming the essential holding of *Roe*, that a right to an abortion is protected by the Constitution.

By the late 1990s, Souter began to align himself with the liberals on the court on death penalty cases, worker rights cases, criminal rights cases, and other issues. So while appointed by a Republican president and thus expected to be conservative, Souter became part of the liberal wing of the Court. Thereafter, conservative Republicans went on to look for more reliable indicators in judicial candidates.

Justices of the Supreme Court serve for life. Article III of the Constitution provides that "[t]he Judges, both of the supreme and inferior Courts, shall hold their Offices during good Behavior, and shall, at stated Times, receive for their Services a Compensation which shall not be diminished during their Continuance in Office."

The term "good behavior" is interpreted to mean that a Justice may serve for life, although he or she may resign or retire voluntarily. Therefore, recent calls for term limits for Supreme Court Justices are nonstarters since such proposals could not be accomplished without a constitutional amendment. The "receive for their Services" clause, like the "good behavior" clause, is intended to guarantee judicial independence. A Justice may also be removed by impeachment and conviction, but this has never happened in the history of the republic.[10] So anyone appointed to the Court may have a term of office only bounded by the grace of God.

Article III of the Constitution places the judicial power of the federal government in "one supreme Court" but leaves it to Congress to determine the size and responsibilities of the Court that sits at the summit of the federal judiciary. The Judiciary Act of 1789 established a Supreme Court of six with one Chief Justice and five Associate Justices. Congress required the Justices of the Supreme Court to preside with the local federal judges on the U.S. circuit courts that met in judicial districts throughout the nation, thus insuring that members of the highest court would participate in the principal trial courts of the federal judiciary and be familiar with the procedures of the state courts.

The size of the Supreme Court grew to accommodate the establishment of new circuits as the nation expanded. In 1807, Congress added a seventh Justice, and in 1837 an eighth and ninth Justice joined the Court. The Court reached its highest number of Justices in 1863 with the creation of a Tenth Circuit on the west coast and the appointment of a tenth Justice. In 1866, as an economy measure, Congress reduced the size of the Court to seven Justices, and provided that no vacant seats be filled until that number was reached. The number of sitting Justices fell to eight before an act of 1869 provided for nine Justices, one for each of the judicial circuits established in 1866. And the size has stood at nine to this day.

In the relatively few cases not having broad policy implications, the Justices do a pretty good job of being impartial arbiters of the dispute, analyzing the record, and applying facts to law—even when they disagree as to the disposition. Most, but not all, of the cases on the Court's docket involve constitutional questions. In the October 2014 Term, the Court considered such non-constitutional issues as whether Facebook posts are unknowingly threatening; whether a fisher could be prosecuted for destroying illegally caught undersized fish so they could not be used in evidence against him, in apparent violation of federal white-collar criminal laws, just as a businessman can be prosecuted for destroying relevant documents; whether someone is paying too much in state income taxes; and whether the federal government can subsidize individuals buying Obamacare in the thirty-four states that have refused to operate exchanges.

The Court, however, hears only the cases it wants to hear. It takes four votes out of nine to grant a Petition for Writ of Certiorari, or cert petition, the apparatus whereby somebody asks the Court for discretionary review, and the Justices tend to select cases for review that do have broad policy implications. Is the Court taking the wrong cases and letting the right ones go? The bottom line is that we have to trust them on cert. As Judge J. Harvie Wilkinson III, of the U.S. Court of Appeals for the Fourth Circuit, whose name had been mentioned in Republican administrations as a possible nominee for the Supreme Court, quipped, "If we cannot trust the Supreme Court's judgment in deciding what to decide, how can we trust its judgment in deciding what it has decided to decide?"[11]

The Court, one would think, should not stretch to decide such transformative issues as electing the president, deciding when life begins, regulating campaign finance in a way that defies Congress, conducting foreign policy, or finding an unstated "liberty" right to decency in the Constitution. But however unsuited it is for the role, it has done so determinedly—along partisan lines, often by narrow margins. The Justices are not supposed to be a political action committee. And when the Court's unelected Justices say by a vote of 5-4 or 6-3 that the Constitution means what they would like it to mean, what has occurred is what Scalia aptly called a judicial putsch.[12]

Those who think of the Supreme Court as a court of law, with its Justices functioning as Delphic oracles telling us what the law is, may take strong exception to my argument that the Supreme Court, when it comes to constitutional or other ideological issues, is a partisan body. Unfortunately for their argument, most Americans would agree with me. According to a mid-April 2012 Gallup Poll, 50 percent of Americans believed that the Court would decide the Obamacare case based on "their partisan political views," while only 40 per cent believed the decision would be made "on the basis of the law." In a March 2012 Bloomberg News poll, 75 percent believed that the Court's decision on Obamacare would be more "influenced" by "politics" than "based solely on legal merits."

Politics and polarization on the Court is nothing new. But the deep political divide of recent years is unprecedented. In the past, the great schism had been over laissez-faire economics. During the *Lochner* era, a period of about forty years of judicial activism during the early part of the twentieth century, the pro-business majority, often by 5-4 margins, consistently struck down on substantive due process grounds progressive measure after progressive measure on the state or federal level that it saw as infringing on economic liberty or the private contract rights of employers and corporations.

In *Lochner*, the Court, 5-4, invalidated a progressive New York law limiting the number of hours a baker could work each day to ten, and each week to sixty.[13] The majority opinion, authored by obscure Justice Rufus W. Peckham, is considered to be one of the worst in the Court's history. *Lochner* held that the law infringed on laissez-faire economic liberty. In a famous three-paragraph dissent, Holmes famously stated, "The Fourteenth Amendment does not enact Mr. Herbert Spencer's Social Statics."[14] Peckham, incidentally, nominated to the Court by President Grover Cleveland in 1895, enjoys the dubious distinction of being the last Justice nominated by a Democratic president to be confirmed by a Republican controlled Senate, and by voice vote—so there.

The *Lochner* era continued through Franklin Roosevelt's first term. Only in 1937 when Justice Owen Roberts, a staunch Republican, changed his partisan stance[15] and another dyed- in-the-wool conservative, Willis Van Devanter, retired, to be succeeded by Roosevelt appointee Hugo Black, did the *Lochner* era come to an end. In his confirmation hearings, Chief Justice John Roberts testified, "You go to a case like the *Lochner* case, you can read that opinion today and it's quite clear that they're not interpreting the law, they're making the law." Judicial activism is not unique to liberals. Often it is a case of "whose ox is being gored," with liberals in the 1930s calling conservative Justices judicial legislators, and conservatives in the 1960s calling the liberal Justices of the Warren Court by the same name.

In 1937, Roosevelt, recently re-elected to a second term, found the Supreme Court an annoyance. He felt that conservative "elderly" men dominated the Court, with six of the nine over the age of 70 (in point of fact, five of the nine were over age 75). Roosevelt's Republican predecessors had appointed seven of the nine. There was more to his annoyance than that. There had been a raft of decisions, some of them 5-4, invalidating many of his New Deal programs, which he deemed necessary to take the country out of the Great Depression. Roosevelt took these decisions as personal attacks. Ignoring that many of the New Deal statutes, like the Affordable Health Care Act in a later period, were poorly drafted and even more poorly defended, he embarked upon a "court-packing plan" designed to increase the size of the Court.

On February 5, 1937, Roosevelt unveiled his astonishing plan, known as the Judicial Procedures Reform Act of 1937—a broadside attack on the independence of the federal judiciary. The president would have the power to appoint an additional Justice, up to a maximum of six, for every member of the Court over the age of 70. He presented his justifications to the American people in his ninth Fireside Chat on March 9 in which he spoke of a "quiet crisis."

He argued that four years previously, the nation had been in a "great banking crisis." But when Congress enacted legislation to help remedy the problem by taking us off the gold standard, the Supreme Court upheld the measure "only by a five-to-four vote."[16] He argued that the "change of one vote would have thrown all the affairs of this great Nation back into hopeless chaos." He eloquently asserted that having averted a banking crisis, there was still "the need to meet the unanswered challenge of one-third of a Nation ill-nourished, ill-clad, ill housed."

He said that the Court "has been acting not as a judicial body, but as a policy-making body." It held the Railroad Retirement Act unconstitutional by a 5-4 vote;[17] it held the Agricultural Adjustment Act unconstitutional by a 6-3 vote;[18] it held the New York Minimum Wage Law unconstitutional by a 6-3 vote.[19] He quoted Chief Justice Charles Evans Hughes, an opponent of the Court-packing bill, who had stated the truism "We are under a Constitution, but the Constitution is what the Judges say it is."[20] FDR said, "We want a Supreme Court which will do justice under the Constitution—not over it. In our Courts we want a government of laws and not of men." Then came FDR's coda, "We have therefore, reached the point as a Nation where we must take action to save the Constitution from the Court and the Court from itself."

This was not Roosevelt's first attempt to undermine a federal judiciary composed mostly of Republican appointees. In 1933, he had authorized a "secret project" to remove the power of judicial review. When a 1935 Gallup Poll reported public disapproval of this approach, however, Roosevelt backed off to fight the Court another day.

Although the Democrats controlled both houses of Congress, the court-packing plan fell flat on its face. Roosevelt's own vice president, John Nance Garner, opposed the measure, as did many other Democrats. Bluff Harvard Law School professor (later dean) Erwin Griswold weighed in against the plan, testifying that there was no historical prec-edent for enlarging the Court on the grounds advanced by Roosevelt.

Impetus for the bill lost further political steam when in March 1937 Owen Roberts, a conservative Justice, reversed his anti–New Deal stance and voted with a liberal majority to uphold the Washington State minimum wage law.[21] Although history records evidence that Roberts had cast his deciding vote in the case two months before Roosevelt publicly introduced the court-packing plan, he did so the month after Roosevelt had won a re-election landslide. Whatever the evidence, pun-dits called Roberts's politically motivated vote the "switch in time that saved nine."

The court-packing bill was dead on arrival. The Senate Judiciary Committee, having failed at a compromise amendment, reported the bill adversely on May 18. The Committee's sizzling report, issued June 14, termed Roosevelt's plan "a needless, futile and utterly dangerous abandonment of constitutional principle . . . without precedent or jus-tification." Chief Justice Rehnquist has said of the Roosevelt 1937 Court-packing contretemps,

> [T]he Constitution provides for ultimate responsibility of the Court
> to the political branches of government. [Yet] it was the United
> States Senate—a political body if there ever was one—who stepped
> in and saved the independence of the judiciary. . . . [22]

Also, on May 18, 1937, Justice Willis Van Devanter, 78 years of age and an ardent conservative, announced his plans to retire at the end of the 1937 Term. This would give Roosevelt his first appointment to the Court, Dixiecrat Senator Hugo Black of Alabama. Indeed, between 1937 and 1941, Roosevelt appointed eight Justices, thereby creating a decisive majority favoring New Deal Legislation and pledged to repudi-ate *Lochner* era decisions.[23]

Are judges supposed to make the law or "discover" the law? Eng-land's William Blackstone, the great 18th century commentator on the common law, thought that the judge discovers the law, and does not make it. He and other judges after him in America viewed the law as like a vast unmapped continent, the mountains and seas of which are yet to be explored. Holmes, however, disagreed, ridiculing the Black-stonian view as seeing law as some "brooding omnipresence in the sky."[24] Holmes' philosophy was that the personal element in a great judge really matters; that law is more like a skyscraper under construction with judges in their own way and legislators in own their way gradually building new beams, making new laws to meet the needs of an evolving society.[25] Human beings, Holmes thought, build the law. "The life of the law," he famously said, "has not been logic: it has been experience."[26] He wrote, "The felt necessities of the time, the prevalent moral and political theories, intuitions of public policy, avowed or unconscious, and even the prejudices which judges share with their fellow-men, have had a good deal more to do than the syllogism in determining the rules by which men should be governed."[27] He argued that ethical values, as opposed to deductive reasoning, drive the law. As he later expressed it, "General propositions do not decide concrete cases. The decision will depend on a judgment or intuition more subtle than any articulate major premise."[28]

Who was right, Roosevelt or Holmes? Both sides are right, says Zechariah Chafee. "[T]he judges make the law out of what they discover, and that law is the will of the Justices trying to do that which is right."[29]

In the area of discovering what is the law, Judges are supposed to observe strict fidelity to precedent (lawyers call this *stare decisis*, meaning you stand by your decisions). All of the Justices would certainly agree on that. That is why almost all Supreme Court opinions are liberally peppered with citations to reported cases. In discovering applicable precedent, however, the Justices of the present Court go through a political process. They clash over what cases are applicable, what cases are distinguishable, what cases should be overruled, and heatedly over whether the decided cases having precedential value are to be exclusively U.S. cases, or whether they can include foreign law as well. Even on this basic question, the supremely partisan court is deeply divided. Four of the Justices—Kennedy and three of the four liberals, Breyer, Ginsburg and Kagan—believe that the Court may engage with foreign law for guidance in the modern era of globalization.[30] That means, "Let's see how the Brits or the French do it, just to see if it makes sense." The four conservatives, Roberts, Scalia, Thomas, and Alito, weighed in together on this issue, holding that the mere consideration of foreign law threatens our traditions of democratic self-governance.[31]

Every rule has its exceptions, and *stare decisis* is a custom often more honored in the breach than the observance. Chief Justice Roberts has said, "[D]epartures from precedent are inappropriate in the absence of a 'special justification.'" But the Court is free to reject *stare decisis*, overrule its decisions, and make new law. It did so when 58 years later it overruled the "separate but equal" holding of *Plessy v. Ferguson*[32] in *Brown v. Board of Education,* which ended school segregation.[33]

Brandeis said once, "The most important thing we do is not doing."[34] Some Justices think the power to overrule gives them carte blanche to abandon Brandeis's minimalist approach to constitutional interpretation. Some Justices think they can follow the precedents they like and overrule those they disagree with. Rejecting this idea, the fiery Justice Antonin Scalia said, "It seems to me that *stare decisis* ought to be applied even to the doctrine of *stare decisis*, and I confess never to have heard of this new, keep-what-you-want-and-throw-away-the-rest version."[35]

As the Court has become more partisan, the size of its plenary docket of cases heard and decided on the merits in the event cert is granted has diminished, while the number of cert petitions has soared to approach 10,000. In the October 1953 Term, the heyday of the Warren Court, the Court decided 113 cases culled from 1,131 cert petitions. In the early 1980s, it decided more than 150 cases annually. Now it is down to less than half that much. The Court has heard on average only 70 to 80 cases in recent years. By the 2013 Term, the number had fallen to 75; and in the 2014 Term the number had dwindled to 67, of which only 14 were deemed "major cases."[36]

What explains the Court's dwindling docket?[37] Many scholars have scratched their heads and ticked off a number of factors, such as Congress's elimination of mandatory jurisdiction in 1988, but the better view gauges that this factor played only a "miniscule role."[38] The most convincing theory is that the Court has become increasingly partisan, and that the conservative majority is reaching out for the ideologically freighted cases they really want to hear, with the liberals, knowing they will be outgunned if cert is granted, picking their battles for the major cases. As Professor A. E. Dick Howard of Virginia Law School, a former law clerk to Justice Hugo Black, elaborates in his superb article "The Changing Face of the Supreme Court,"

Studies have also found a correlation between a Court's degree of ideological homogeneity and the number of cases decided in a Term; over time, less homogenous Courts have taken on a docket that is twenty-five percent smaller than average. . . . The relationship between the continuing decline of the docket size and the Roberts Court's closely divided ideological makeup may offer support for this theory.[39]

While the number of cases decided continues to diminish, the verbosity of the Court's opinions has soared. According to data collected by two political scientists, James F. Spriggs II of Washington University and Ryan C. Black of Michigan State, the majority opinions of the Roberts court set a record for prolixity with a median length of 4,751 words. The study showed that the lengths of decisions, including majority concurring and dissent, also set a record with a median length of 8,265 words. In the Warren Court era, the median length of majority, concurring, and dissenting opinions was 2,000 words. The 5-4 decision in *Citizens United v. Federal Election Commission*[40] consisted of over 48,000 words, consuming 183 pages in the U.S. Reports, a tempting comparison with the Warren Court's decision in *Brown v. Board of Education*, with only 1,848 words occupying only 11 pages in the U.S. Reports. Long opinions are dangerous, according to Professor Edward H. Cooper of Michigan Law School. He has said, "The more things you say, the more chances you have to be wrong."[41] This is not always so. Short opinions can be dangerous too. Remember what the professors said about *Bush v. Gore*, with only 4,078 words consuming only 13 pages in the U.S. Reports. "By stopping the vote count in Florida, the U.S. Supreme Court used its power to act as political partisans, not judges of a Court of law."[42]

The Justices are apparently heedless of the advice of William Cullen Bryant, the nineteenth-century American romantic poet and long-time editor of the *New York Evening Post*:

Never use a long word when a short one will do. Call a spade a spade, not a well-known instrument of manual industry. Let a home be a home, not a residence; a place is a place, not a locality. Where a short word will do, you lose by using a long one.

The *Citizens United* decision was about the same length as *The Great Gatsby*.[43] As an aside, Gatsby happens to end with an originalist mantra: "So we beat on, boats against the current, borne back ceaselessly into the past." Chief Justice Roberts likes the past. Dissenting in the gay marriage case, he wrote, "[T]o blind yourself to history is both prideful and unwise." Then he quoted William Faulkner, "The past is never dead. It's not even past."[44]

Many lawyers believe that law clerks significantly influence the Court's judgments. Oliver Wendell Holmes, like the Justices of his day, had one law clerk, the most notorious of which was Alger Hiss. The clerk had little to do except to sit at the feet of the master. Holmes wrote out his own opinions, did his own legal research, and read every cert petition.[45] Things are quite different today. Lawyers have always harbored the suspicion that Supreme Court opinions are ghost written by the law clerks. Scalia said that his clerks almost always did the first draft of his opinions. The first draft must have borne little resemblance to the final since Scalia's unique writing style was unmistakable.

Law clerks typically share their bosses' political predilections. Scalia used to say he hired clerks who were "really smart people who don't necessarily have to share my judicial philosophy, but they cannot be hostile to it."[46] There is a case to be made that the Justices mostly hire only law clerks who share their political views. In the past ten years, the Republican appointees hired clerks who had first served Republican-appointed appeals court judges at least 83 per cent of the time. Thomas hired one from Democratic chambers, and Scalia hired none. On the left, Ginsburg, Sotomayor, and Kagan hired from Democratic chambers more than two-thirds of the time. Breyer, the exception, has chosen about evenly.[47]

Law clerks have much more importance than they used to. All have spent at least a year in a lower-court clerkship, and there are more of them than there were a decade or two ago. Justices wrote more in the old days because they had fewer clerks, and law had a writing culture. Today, legal writing may be more of a chore than anything else so to few clerks, much is delegated.

There have been roughly 1,900 law clerks to serve on the Court since the first was hired in 1882. Today, each Associate Justice has four law clerks, and the Chief has a fifth if he wants it. Six Justices in the modern era have themselves served as law clerks at the beginning of their respective careers: White to Vinson, Rehnquist to Jackson, Stevens to Rutledge, Breyer to Goldberg, Roberts to Rehnquist, and Kagan to Thurgood Marshall. Garland, whom Obama has nominated as Scalia's successor, was himself a clerk to Justice Brennan.

Law clerks have great power. As we have seen, cases to be heard by the Court are by grant of a writ of certiorari, which is a discretionary order to take the case. Most petitions for certiorari are denied. It takes a vote of four Justices to grant the writ, and the Court reviews the petitions for review based on a memorandum coming from a pool of law clerks that serves all the Justices. While the prior practice was for one clerk to each Justice to write a memorandum recommending that the writ be granted or denied, the practice today is a pool system where one clerk writes a memorandum for all Justices in the pool.

From the point of view of political decision-making in constitutional cases, the more there is delegation of opinion-writing to a team of highly qualified law clerks, the more the tendency of the Justices to decide cases based on political preference. "This is my policy inclination, let's see how it writes."

Doctrine is the engine that drives the Justice to decision. I view doctrine as a scholarly expression of raw partisanship. Originalists like Scalia and textualists like Clarence Thomas believe in a "dead" or a "durable" Constitution, which makes for less judicial discretion in deciding such cases. They look for meaning in the text and the original understanding of the document, and say they disregard what happened later. Full stop. At least they would have you believe that. Thomas has grown fond of citing Thomas Jefferson, who was in France in 1787, essentially sitting out the Constitution, but who now and then sent over a bench signal to the Framers. Thomas has quoted Jefferson as saying:

> Relieve the judges from the rigour of text law, and permit them, with praetorian discretion, to wander into its equity, and the whole legal system becomes uncertain. [48]

In addition, Thomas is an apostle of "natural law." The thesis of natural law is that the moral standards governing human behavior come from nature, not the rules of society or positive law. Accordingly, the Constitution cannot tolerate even a neutral stance on the issue of abortion, for example, since the "right to life" is endowed by the Creator and is an inalienable right secured by Jefferson's Declaration of Independence.

But, what about the outcome of the doctrinal thought process? Does anyone, liberal or conservative, wonder whether doctrine is leading them to a just, reasonable, and most importantly, desired result? Of course, they do. And when they do, they arrive at precisely the policy outcome that they wanted to bring about in the first place. Judge Posner of the Seventh Circuit calls these approaches "priors." Which doctrine is more likely to bring about the political outcome that the Justice wants? Originalism, textualism, natural law, or what Scalia disdainfully saw as "the Constitution means what I would like it to mean" approach of the liberals? Judge Posner sees the doctrinal divide this way:

> [O]ne school [Scalia and Thomas, being the hardline leaders] seeks certainty in text and disparages precedent, and the other [represented by the liberals] seeks certainty in precedent and disparages text.[49]

The paradox is that Scalia and Thomas used originalism to come to the interpretation of the Constitution that they would like. Thus it is easy for them to say that because neither abortion nor privacy nor same-sex marriage is mentioned in the text of the Constitution, there is no basis for a constitutional right to abort or marry someone of the same sex; or that because there was capital punishment, including the execution of infants and mental retards (now called those with intellectual disabilities) at the time of the Constitution, the death penalty is neither "cruel" nor "unusual" despite the force of changing times. So they would see no constitutional limitation on the right of a state to place legal obstacles between a woman and an abortion even in the first trimester. Conversely, if a state were to permit "abortion on demand" at any stage of gestation, it necessarily follows that Scalia (if he were with us) and Thomas would view such a law as sinful but constitutional. Why is it I am inclined to doubt it?

When it comes to expounding the U.S. Constitution, an eighteenth-century document of continuing vitality, Justices are supposed to use traditional tools of judicial analysis—text, meaning, original understanding, and decided precedents-- in John Marshall's words, " to say what the law is." But how do you apply an eighteenth-century document to the Internet, DNA testing, electronic surveillance, smartphones, video games, social media, gay marriage, affirmative action, whether capital punishment by lethal injection with or without an effective anesthetic is "cruel and unusual," and other societal and technical phenomena, undreamed of at the time of the Constitution, without some overarching philosophy as to where you are headed?

"Politics plays a really significant role in shaping our judicial system," writes Maya Sen, a political scientist at Harvard's Kennedy School of Government. She argues that this is because the appointing authority takes account of ideology in the judicial selection process. Sen concludes that the bottom line is a recent conservative flavor to the politicization of the courts. She notes that conservatives have worked hard to develop qualified judicial candidates with a rightist point of view, principally through the Federalist Society, a conservative organization active on law school campuses, before which Alito, Thomas, and Scalia have spoken.[50]

It is a certainty that Supreme Court Justices, even those of the highest intellectual quality such as the nine on the present court, tend to make political decisions. As Scalia observed, "[J]udges have been known to be . . . politically partisan."[51] Their religion, their professional training, or their personal life experience informs their political partisanship, like everyone else's.

What is a partisan decision? When, by reason of a change in personnel, the Court votes 5-4 to uphold a statute limiting late-term partial birth abortion without an exemption for the health of the mother, essentially overruling a 5-4 decision it had made seven years before, that is a partisan decision.[52] When the Court in 2013 votes 5-4 to strike down Section 3 of the Defense of Marriage Act, signed into law by Bill Clinton in 1996, that defined "marriage" as the "legal union between one man and one woman," that is again a partisan decision.[53] When the Court votes 5-4 in favor of a conservative organization to uphold corporate free speech in the context of campaign finance, the result being the reaffirmation of money as the source of political power, that is a partisan decision. When the Court votes 5-4, with three Jewish Justices dissenting, to approve a decade-old practice in a small upstate New York town to begin monthly town board meetings with prayers dominated by sectarian Christian idiom, that is a partisan decision.[54] When a five-Justice majority, consisting of five conservative Catholic Justices, holds that there is no violation of the constitutional boundary between church and state for an eight-foot metal cross to be maintained in a national park in honor of fallen war dead including non-Christians, that is a partisan decision.[55] When five Catholic male Justices find that a closely-held not-for-profit corporation can on religious grounds opt out of that portion of the Obamacare mandate covering the cost of a female employees using, if she wants to, certain drugs and devices that may possibly operate after the fertilization of an egg, that is a partisan decision.[56] And when the Court, 5-4, citing racial progress since 1965, guts the Voting Rights Act of 1965, intended to invite black voters into the political mainstream of a democratic society, that is a partisan decision too.[57] And these are but a few examples. Whatever the inspiration for these decisions, their partisan nature could not be clearer.

The Court historically has not covered itself with glory in the field of race relations either. In the nineteenth century, prior to the Civil War amendments to the Constitution, the Court, consisting largely of present or past slaveholders, time and again voted to sustain slavery. It epitomized its bigotry against black slaves, whom it deemed property, not people, in the infamous 1857 *Dred Scott* decision, penned by its first Catholic Justice, Roger Taney.[58] The decision may have been responsible for the Civil War. In *Plessy v. Ferguson*,[59] decided thirty-nine years after *Dred Scott*, and twenty-eight years after the Civil War amendments guaranteed every person the "equal protection of the laws," the Court held 7-1 that separate but equal school facilities passed constitutional muster. Following *Plessy*, there were fifty-eight years of judicially approved segregation before the Court unanimously overruled *Plessy* in *Brown*, stating that "separate educational facilities are inherently unequal."

Supreme Court Justices tend to vote on certain issues in accordance with religious or moral beliefs that do not come from text or precedent. They often appear heedless of Holmes's admonition that "nothing but confusion of thought can result from assuming that the rights of man in a moral sense are equally rights in the sense of the Constitution and the law."[60]

So we have it, a court of law in many cases, and a political court in many others with 5-4 decisions laced with ideology, a partisan divide, and diminished public confidence in the Court's legitimacy as the final interpreter of the law of the land.

Notes

1. Dissenting opinion of Scalia, J. in *Obergefell v. Hodges*, 576 U.S. (2015). Slip op. at 5.

2. *Korematsu v. United States*, 323 U.S. 214 (1944). Black later said he regretted his decision.

3. *Brown v. Board of Education*, 347 U.S. 483 (1954).

4. *Gideon v. Wainwright*, 372 U.S. 335 (1963).

5. *Miranda v. Arizona*, 384 U.S. 436 (1966).

6. 368 U.S. 57 (1961).

7. 368 U.S. 57 (1961) at 62.

8. Note 2, *supra*.

9. 505 U.S. 577 (1992).

10. Justice Abe Fortas resigned in 1969 in the wake of scandal involving his receipt of payment from a foundation controlled by convicted stock fraudster Louis Wolfson, who was seeking a presidential pardon.

11. By J. Harvie Wilkinson, III, "If It Ain't Broke," Yale Symposium on Supreme Court Case Selection Process. Available at http://www.law.yale.edu/documents/pdf/Clinics/Wilkinson.pdf.

12. *Obergefell v. Hodges*, U.S. (2015). Dissenting opinion slip op. at 6.

13. *Ibid.*

14. *Social Statics*, published in 1851, enunciated the libertarian political philosophy espoused by Clarence Thomas. Spencer argued for a "survival of the fittest" social Darwinism in which man is at his freest where there is a limited state.

15. *West Coast Hotel Co. v. Parrish*, 300 U.S. 379 (1937), upholding the constitutionality of Washington State minimum wage legislation. West Coast overruled *Adkins v. Children's Hospital*, 261 U.S. 525 (1923). Roberts had joined his conservative brethren the prior year in finding a similar New York State minimum wage law unconstitutional. *Morehead v. New York*, 298 U.S. 587 (1936).

16. Gold Clause cases: *Norman v. Baltimore & Ohio R Co.* 294 U.S. 240 (1935); *Nortz v. United States*, 294 U.S. 317 (1935); *Perry v. United States*, 294 U.S. 330 (1935).

17. *Railroad Retirement Board v. Alton*, 295 U.S. 330 (1935).

18. *United States v. Butler*, 297 U.S. 1 (1936).

19. *Morehead v. New York* ex rel. *Tipaldo*, 298 U.S. 587 (1936).

20. Speech before the Chamber of Commerce, Elmira, New York (May 3, 1907); published in *Addresses and Papers of Charles Evans Hughes, Governor of New York*, 1906–1908 (1908) at 139.

21. Compare votes of Justice Roberts in *West Coast Hotel C. v. Parish*, 300 U.S. 379 (1937) with *Morehead v. New York* ex rel. *Tipaldo, supra*.

22. By William H. Rehnquist, "Judicial Independence Dedicated to Chief Justice Harry L. Carrico: Symposium Remarks" 38 Univ. Rich. Law Rev. 579–96.

23. These were Black, Reed, Frankfurter, Douglas, Murphy, Byrnes, Jackson, and Rutledge who replaced, among others, Van Devanter (appointed by Taft), McReynolds (appointed by Wilson), and Butler and Sutherland (both appointed by Harding), the "Four Horsemen" of the *Lochner* era cases.

24. Dissenting in *Southern Pacific Company v. Jensen*, 245 U.S. 205, 222 (1917).

25. By Zecheriah Chafee, Jr. "Do Judges Make or Discover Law?" Proceedings of American Philosophical Society, Vol. 91 No. 5 (December 3, 1947), PP. 405-420 Available at https://www.jstor.org/stable/3143421?seq=1#page_scan_tab_contents, arguing that in at least five situations the choice between the two theories has "considerable bearing" on the outcome of litigation.

26. Oliver Wendell Holmes, Jr., *The Common Law*, Boston, Little Brown and Company (1881).

27. Oliver Wendell Holmes, Jr. *The Common Law*, New York: Little, Brown and Company (1881).

28. Dissenting in *Lochner v. New York*, 195 U.S. 45, 76 (1905).

29. Chafee, "Do Judges Make or Discover Law?" *supra* at 420.

30. In her confirmation hearings, Sotomayor testified she would not rely on foreign law. Nevertheless, 18 Republican senators, voting against her, expressed concern that she would. Whether she will fulfill her pledge to the Senate remains to be seen.

31. See *e.g.*, D. Farber, "The Supreme Court, the Law of Nations, and Citations of Foreign Law: The Lessons of History," 95 Cal. Law Rev. 1336 (2007); D. Seipp, "Our Law, Their Law, History, and the Citation of Foreign Law, 86 Boston Univ. L. R. 1417 (2006). Notably, Scalia when it suited his purposes, cited English cases of the period he considered relevant.

32. 163 U.S. 537 (1896).

33. 347 U.S. 483 (1954).

34. Quoted in Alexander Bickel, *The Least Dangerous Branch: The Supreme Court at the Bar of Politics*, New Haven, CT: Yale University Press (1986) at 71.

35. On *stare decisis* (adhering to judicial precedent): *Planned Parenthood v. Casey*, 505 U.S. 833 (1992) (dissenting).

36. From information appearing on the SCOTUS blog. Available at http://www.scotusblog.com/statistics/.

37. See e.g., Ryan J. Owens and David A. Simon, "Explaining the Supreme Court's Shrinking Docket," 53 W&M Law Rev. (2012); by Adam Liptak, "The Case of the Plummeting Supreme Court Docket," New York Times, September 29, 2009. Available at http://www.nytimes.com/2009/09/29/us/29bar.html.

38. Compare A. E. Dick Howard, "The Changing Face of the Supreme Court," August 10, 2014. 101 Virginia Law Rev. 231, 267 (2015). Available at http://www.virginialawreview.org/volumes/content/changing-face-supreme-court with Owens & Simon, *supra* note 6.

39. Howard, supra note 9.

40. 558 U.S. 310 (2010).

41. By Adam Liptak. "Justices Are Long on Words but Short on Guidance," *New York Times*, November 17, 2010. Available at http://www.nytimes.com/2010/11/18/us/18rulings.html.

42. 554 Law Professors at 120 American law schools (New York Times full-page ad January 13, 2001).

43. By Adam Liptak, "Justices Are Long on Words but Short on Guidance," *supra* note 36.

44. *Requiem for a Nun* (1951); *Obergefell v. Hodges*, 576 U.S. (2015), Slip op. at 22–23.

45. Catherine Drinker Bowen, *Yankee from Olympus*, New York: Little, Brown and Company (1944) at 379.

46. Interview with Justice Scalia by Jennifer Senior appearing in *New York Magazine*, October 6, 2013. Available at http://nymag.com/news/features/antonin-scalia-2013-10/.

47. By Adam Liptak, "The Polarized Court," New York Times, May 10, 2014. Available at http://www.nytimes.com/2014/05/11/upshot/the-polarized-court.html.

48. 9 Papers of Thomas Jefferson 71 (J. Boyd, ed. 1954).

49. Richard A. Posner, *How Judges Think*, Cambridge: Harvard University Press (2010) at 345. Posner wrote this in contemplation of the time when Justice John Paul Stevens, a Protestant, was still on the Court.

50. By Adam Liptak, "Why Judges Tilt to the Right," *New York Times*, February 1, 2015, at SR 6.

51. *Morrison v. Olson*, 487 U.S. 654, 730 (1988).

52. *Gonzales v. Carhart*, 550 U.S. 124 (2007).

53. *United States v. Windsor*, 570 U.S. (2013).

54. *Town of Greece v. Galloway*, 572 U.S. (2014).

55. *Salazar v. Bono*, 559 U.S. 700 (2010). Justice Stevens, a Protestant, Justices Ginsburg and Breyer, both Jews, and Justice Sotomayor, a Catholic, dissented.

56. *Burwell v. Hobby Lobby*, 573 U.S. (2014).

57. *Shelby County v. Holder*, 570 U.S. (2013).

58. *Dred Scott v. Sandford*, 60 U.S. 393 (1846). Taney was also the first Catholic Chief Justice.

59. 163 U.S. 537 (1896).

60. Holmes, *"The Path of the Law,"* 10 Harvard Law Rev. 457, 458 (1897).

2

IDENTITY POLITICS AND
THE PARTISAN COURT

I often think it's comical—Fal, lal, la!
How Nature always does contrive—Fal, lal, la!
That every boy and every gal
That's born into the world alive
Is either a little Liberal
Or else a little Conservative!
Fal, lal, la!

—W. S. Gilbert, *Iolanthe* (a favorite of Chief Justice Rehnquist)

The Supreme Court is afflicted by identity politics. Until the death of Scalia, the Court consisted of six Catholics and three Jews—the first time in its 226-year history that it had been 100 percent minority. No evangelicals, and no traditional Protestants. There are three women, and one African American. One of the women is a "wise Latina." Five are "baby boomers," having been born between 1948 and 1960. This represents a tectonic historical shift. Until 1988 there were no more than two Catholic or, save for a brief time, two Jewish Justices at once. And for most of the Court's recorded history, there was reserved a single Catholic seat or a single Jewish seat or a single female seat—or none at all.

Any individual appointed to the Court has received the ultimate professional accolade. For some, nomination personifies the American dream. In accepting Obama's nomination, Garland said that it was the "greatest honor of my life . . . the greatest gift I've ever received," other than his marriage and birth of two daughters. The Justices are exceptional people. Their competence and intellectual quality cannot be fairly questioned, but no one would argue that they are fairly representative of the American people. For example, there are only three women out of the eight Justices remaining after Scalia's death, while women comprise roughly 51 percent of the population; there is only one Latino, while census numbers disclose we are close to 20 percent Latino/Hispanic. And there are no Asians represented, although they represent roughly six percent.[1] None of the Justices had ancestors who came over on the Mayflower. For this odd mix of children of recent immigrants, blame the presidents of both parties.

The four Justices appointed by Republican presidents, Thomas, Alito, Kennedy, and Roberts, are rock-ribbed conservatives. Democratic presidents appointed the "Four Horsemen" liberals, Ginsburg, Breyer, Sotomayor, and Kagan. Kennedy, while generally conservative, is the "swing vote" on certain issues, notably gay rights. His pairings are more evenly distributed than any other Justice. And his vote is often decisive. He voted last term with the majority in most of the 5-4 decisions, whether liberal or conservative. He joins the liberals roughly 1/3 of the time when the Court divides along partisan lines.

So who are these judges who tell us what the law is? Are they, as Scalia put it, the intellectual "aristocracy"? We may want a government of laws and not of men and women, but it is men and women who call the shots and write the opinions that set policy for future generations. What has been the Justices' background and experience? How do they reach the awesomely weighty decisions they do, which help chart our course for generations? Although in the modern era, most of the Justices have had prior judicial experience in the federal courts of appeals, many have come from other professional experiences. Seven of the eight, like Scalia, came from the federal circuit courts (four alone from the DC Circuit), while the eighth, Kagan, previously served as dean of Harvard Law School, and later as solicitor general. A number of others, notably, Holmes, Cardozo, Brennan, and O'Connor, had prior experience as state court judges; others, Murphy, Black, and Warren, made their mark in the political arena. Brandeis came directly from the Bar, as did Powell; Frankfurter was a law professor. Jackson, like Kagan, served in the Department of Justice as solicitor general. Later, he was attorney general of the United States.

There is no statute or rule that requires a Justice of the Supreme Court to be a lawyer, but all 112 have been. While prior to Scalia's death the nine Justices had all gone to elite Ivy League law schools, as did Holmes and Brandeis (Roberts, Kennedy, Scalia, Breyer, and Kagan to Harvard; Thomas, Alito, and Sotomayor to Yale; and Ginsburg to both Harvard and Columbia), some of the most iconic Justices of the modern era attended lesser-known law schools (Warren, Black, O'Connor, Murphy, and Harlan). Another, Jackson, one of the greatest jurists ever to sit on the Court, never attended college, and failed to graduate from Albany Law School. Education, while not irrelevant, is a hazardous basis for predicting ideology or getting political mileage out of an appointment. Harvard Law School has an insignificant political constituency.

Three of the court's current Justices grew up in the ethnic neighborhoods of New York City, encompassing three of the five boroughs. They are Kagan, Manhattan; Ginsburg, Brooklyn; and Sotomayor, the Bronx (Scalia grew up in Queens). Two of the Justices, Breyer and Kennedy, come from California, although Breyer spent most of his professional life in Washington or Boston; one, Chief Justice Roberts, hails from Indiana; one, Alito, from New Jersey; and one, Thomas, from Georgia. All except Kennedy, however, spent their professional lives in the northeast corridor of the country.

The road to the Supreme Court is a hard one: for some, as will be seen, Brandeis and Thomas, harder than necessary. In the nineteenth century, the Senate rejected twenty-one Supreme Court nominees—seventeen of them on ideological grounds. During the twentieth century, the Senate rejected four nominees, all on ideological grounds, including Judge Robert Bork, an originalist of impeccable intellectual credentials, who was seen as taking an overly restrictive view of free speech, a right to privacy, and gender equality. Bork, a Reagan nominee, went down in flames in 1987 by a vote of 58-42 in a Democratically controlled Senate, an event which created the ridiculous impasse we see today over the Garland nomination.

The opinions of the nine lawyers on the Court profoundly affect our lives as they do the life of the nation. In the event of a Democratic victory, it is possible that the conservative Anthony Kennedy, now 79, may hang on and not resign within the next decade in the hope that a Republican will capture the White House in 2020 or 2024. Scalia's death at 79 was quite unexpected, and he had announced no plans to retire. After all, people are living longer nowadays. Oliver Wendell Holmes didn't retire until he was just short of his 91st birthday.

Modern presidents have flavored their appointments with Justices representing ethnic and religious minorities as part of the particular president's perceived need to accomplish "balance." It is a reflection of how politicians think about the world. There could be no other explanation for the pattern of "reserved seats"—Jewish, Catholic, and African American—which obtained historically following the appointment of Brandeis in 1916 (although the reserved seat concept has taken on relaxed contours in recent years). The quest for ethnic balance has actually created imbalance. The result is that the Court has become more, rather than less, polarized, more, rather than less, deeply divided, and more, rather than less, conservative.

The personal backgrounds and beliefs of ethnic and religious minority Justices should, one would suppose, make them especially empathetic to minority feelings of marginalization in a "majority rules" society. Yet, ironically, when it comes to issues of liberty at a time of national crisis, preserving the separation of powers, a level playing field in political campaigns, racial justice, religion, capital punishment, reproductive and other human rights, the Roberts Court, although 100 percent minority, has not covered itself with glory.[2] Is it a case of that's what the law is or is it a case of "last one in, close the door"?

The Roberts Court has denied recovery to those injured by generic drugs, restricted class actions brought on behalf of injured workers, favored arbitration of disputes authorized by non-negotiable form contracts drafted by suppliers of goods and services, expanded immunity from suit against government officials brought by prisoners deprived of their constitutional rights, generally protected business at the expense of consumers and employees, limited abortion rights, eroded the barrier between church and state, and seriously undermined voting rights and affirmative action.

Clarence Thomas, a hardline conservative, and the only African American on the Court, says he will vote to overrule any precedent, no matter how recent, that in his view is contrary to the Constitution. This would include *Roe v. Wade*[3] and cases upholding much of the New

Deal legislation. He believes that these cases impermissibly found "new" or unenumerated rights in the Constitution. Thomas ignores the doctrine of "super precedents" or "super-duper precedents"—precedents that cannot be disturbed. Circuit Judge Michael Luttig, long on Republican shortlists for a Supreme Court appointment, referred to *Roe v. Wade* as having achieved "super-*stare decisis*" in constitutional law because of its repeated re-affirmation by the Court.[4]

The term "super-precedents" resurfaced in the Roberts confirmation hearings in 2005 when the late Senator Arlen Specter of Pennsylvania, chairman of the Judiciary Committee, asked Roberts whether he agreed that certain cases like *Roe* had become "super-precedents or 'super-duper' precedents—that is, that they were so deeply embedded in the fabric of law they should be especially hard to overturn."[5]

In the hearings, Roberts never directly answered the question except to say that he agreed with the doctrine of *stare decisis*. He has said that the *Planned Parenthood v. Casey*[6] decision reaffirming *Roe* is itself "a precedent on whether or not to revisit the *Roe v. Wade* precedent." Chief Justice Roberts has said he doesn't want the Court to be viewed as a forum where "partisan matters would be worked out." Supreme Court Justices fall all over themselves in contradicting the popular perception that they are just partisan politicians in robes occupying red and blue chambers, but no one really believes them.

Identity politics is a major factor. We live in a world fond of psychoanalyzing the unconscious influences that mold and shape our opinions and conduct. The life experiences of blacks and Latinos may spawn differing attitudes toward civil rights, capital punishment, government surveillance, or affirmative action. Clarence Thomas certainly does. Suggesting that we should give up on school integration, he argues that black children don't learn any better sitting next to white children than they do sitting next to black children. Concurring in *Missouri v. Jenkins*,[7] he wrote,

> Given that desegregation has not produced the predicted leaps forward in black educational achievement, there is no reason to think that black students cannot learn as well when surrounded by members of their own race as when they are in an integrated environment.

The "beloved world" of Sonia Sotomayor, born to a dysfunctional Latino family in a Bronx housing project the same year as the decision in *Brown v. Board of Education*,[8] is seen through a lens dramatically different from that of a white male who faced less challenging barriers to entry in American society. Sotomayor's beautiful memoir, *My Beloved World*, indicates that her ethnicity, and all the challenges that go with it, are relevant to how she might judge. No wonder she believes it is the Court's role to defend the civil rights of "historically marginalized groups." But nowhere is this commendable role set out in the Constitution. And doesn't it take the sensibility of a member of a "historically marginalized" group to discover how deeply sewn that value is in the fabric of the document?

Sotomayor had previously made a pro–affirmative action statement that it was at Princeton that she first "began a lifelong-commitment to identifying [herself] as a Latina, taking pride in being Hispanic," and recognizing an obligation to help her community "reach its fullest potential in society."[9] Statements such as this caused her critics to accuse her of "identity politics." But in her 2009 confirmation hearings, Sotomayor promised the senators that she would "apply" the law not make the law.

Her pledge to the Senate notwithstanding, she has been in office true to her identity-based take on affirmative action and other issues. Personal experience will strongly bear on how an ethnic minority Justice might approach an issue like affirmative action. Both Thomas and Sotomayor say that they are personal beneficiaries of affirmative action. The difference is that Sotomayor believes it is necessary to insure racial justice, and Thomas says it is demeaning. Affirmative action is today on its last legs, about twelve years earlier than the 25-year reprieve Sandra Day O'Connor gave it when she decided *Grutter* in 2003.[10] If all forms of affirmative action are declared unconstitutional, it will be ironic indeed that Clarence Thomas, the successor to Thurgood Marshall, may well write the majority opinion.

On the bench, as in life, human beings do not easily escape the influence of where they come from or their deeply held religious beliefs. And their personal backgrounds inform their policy choices. As goes without saying, women see reproductive rights from a different perspective than men. Catholics and Evangelicals may differ with others as to what indeed is "our moral heritage" in their attitudes toward abortion, gay marriage, and family planning.

The Catholic Church has long had a vested interest in political decisions related to reproductive rights. At the 2009 memorial service for Teddy Kennedy, a Catholic bishop reportedly voiced his concerns to Obama about premium subsidies for abortion and birth control coverage in the proposed Affordable Care Act. He spoke of the opposition of the Church and, implicitly, conservative Democrats to a measure that included coverage for abortion and birth control. Such coverage was eliminated from the final bill. [11]

It cannot be a matter of mere textual interpretation that Scalia, like Clarence Thomas, a Catholic Justice, said he wanted to overrule *Roe v. Wade*, decided by a 7-2 majority, and that three other Catholic Justices (Roberts, Kennedy, and Alito) are tottering on the brink. It is safe to say that if *Roe* is overruled, at least four Catholic Justices will vote with the majority.

Recognizing that the Church's pro-life stance might be inconsistent with its approval of capital punishment, successive Popes have in recent years called for an end to the death penalty. In the year 2000, Pope John Paul II called for the abolition of capital punishment. In November 2011, Pope Benedict XVI called for an end to the death penalty as well. In October 2014, the present Pope Francis declared that he was against the death penalty. Pope Francis also called for the abolition of life sentences without parole. The Church's latest stance might pose a moral dilemma for Catholic Justices who have consistently voted to uphold the death penalty or even life imprisonment. The Constitution not only permits *but expressly authorizes* the death penalty. [12] No moral dilemma for Scalia, a vigorous death penalty advocate, who said his religion required him only to consider seriously the Pope's death penalty stance since the Pope was not speaking *ex cathedra*. Scalia asserted he had considered the Pope's edict, and rejected it.

Jews are supposed to be sensitive to protecting the rights of unpopular minorities—a value inherent in the Constitution. As Ginsburg put it, "Jewish Justices have viewed the law as the protector of the oppressed minority, the loner." [13] They might sympathize more deeply with criminal defendants as Kafka did in *The Trial*. But this was not typically true of Justice Frankfurter, who as a law professor advocated against the perceived injustice of the Sacco and Vanzetti case in Massachusetts, but as a Justice voted with the wrong-headed majority in *Korematsu v. United States*,[14] the Japanese internment case, even lobbying Justice Murphy to do the same.

But it is often dangerous to generalize as to what elements are mixed in a Justice. Their votes have often been counterintuitive. William J. Brennan voted with the seven-man majority in *Roe* although his Catholic faith informed him that abortion was a sin. Jews may be seen as more sensitive to the rights of the scorned and rejected in society, the "forgotten man at the bottom of the economic pyramid."[15] Yet Frankfurter, as noted above, voted with the majority in *Korematsu*, one of the worst decisions in the Court's history. Catholics and WASPs are supposed to have a preference for a more authoritarian and ordered societal regime. Yet in the case of the Japanese internments, one Catholic (Murphy) joined with two Protestants (Owen Roberts and Jackson) in dissent.

It was a white Protestant male, Justice Robert Jackson, writing for the Court in the school compulsory flag salute case, to reaffirm the Court's commitment to protecting the marginalized from the tyranny of the majority:

> [T]he compulsory flag salute and pledge requires affirmation of a belief and an attitude of mind. . . . If there is any fixed star in our constitutional constellation, it is that no official, high or petty, can prescribe what shall be orthodox in politics, nationalism, religion or other matters of opinion or force citizens to confess by word or act their faith therein.[16]

Many share the cynical belief that the Catholics or African Americans or Jews or women on the Court may vote too predictably on certain issues. The evidence, however, does not fully bear this out. As Justice Kennedy said, the notion that all members of a certain group think alike is "demeaning" as it is patently absurd.[17] As he put it, "[I]t cannot be entertained as a serious proposition that all individuals of the same race think alike."[18] Consider Clarence Thomas, who prefers natural law to affirmative action. The same would apply to religion or gender. I argue here only that when it comes to interpreting socially loaded issues under the Constitution, identity politics, informed by ethnicity (race, religion, gender), background, and life experience of the Justices, like anatomy, may well often be destiny. It is not that John Marshall was wrong when he said, "The Government of the United States has been emphatically termed a government of laws, and not of men."[19] It's that laws must be created, executed, and interpreted by men and women, and it is here where politics enters the equation.

In his confirmation hearings, Roberts implicitly repudiated identity politics in decision making. He famously gave an odd response to Senator Schumer's question as to "what kind of Justice John Roberts would make." He said that he would be an objective "umpire" calling "balls and strikes," and not a pitcher or a batter. He said,

> Judges and Justices . . . are like umpires. Umpires don't make the rules, they apply them. The role of an umpire and a judge is critical. They make sure everybody plays by the rules, but it is a limited role. Nobody ever went to a ball game to see the umpire.[20]

Analogies are always dangerous; yet Roberts loved the comparison with baseball. In the Senate hearings, he went on to testify that he had no agenda:

> Mr. Chairman, I come before the Committee with no agenda. I have no platform. Judges are not politicians who can promise to do certain things in exchange for votes. I have no agenda, but I do have a commitment. If I am confirmed, I will confront every case with an open mind. I will fully and fairly analyze the legal arguments that are presented. I will be open to the considered views of my colleagues on the bench, and I will decide every case based on the record, according to the rule of law, without fear or favor, to the best of my ability, and I will remember that it's my job to call balls and strikes, and not to pitch or bat.[21]

Judges just call balls and strikes, and have no agenda? One of my British friends, herself an eminent jurist, found this a strange statement for a judge to make. In the near decade that he has been on the Court, Roberts has been hardly an umpire. Instead, he has vigorously pursued a conservative agenda. Although in his confirmation hearings, Roberts promised the Senate that he would be an objective umpire calling "balls and strikes," and not a pitcher or a batter, on the bench (with the possible exception of his Obamacare decisions) he has proved to be a partisan closer, voting most often with the conservative majority appointed like himself by Republican presidents. Critics say that he is a man in a hurry, a judicial Sammy Glick, running to get things done, without a full development of the law in the lower courts, before a conservative Justice has a heart attack and some liberal president appoints a liberal Justice to replace him.

When it comes to the cauldron of shifting doctrines governing constitutional and other policy-freighted issues, what Roberts told the Senate about umpiring or what Sotomayor told the Senate four years later about applying the law was sheer poppycock, or what Scalia derisively called "jiggery-pokery."[22] The Justices more often than not vote on social issues in tandem with the views of the president who appointed them; decide to take cases that will resolve political questions or issues of policy in accordance with partisan viewpoints; and make many of their decisions totally predictable before the case is even submitted.

The Constitution says that Supreme Court Judges shall be the subjects of political appointment. They do not take civil service examinations. Judges are of course human beings. They don't write on a blank slate. Beneath the robes, there is the database and vocabulary of lifetime experience. Writing about the ingredients that go into the total mix of judicial decision-making, Cardozo in *The Nature of the Judicial Process* stated it well:

> There is in each of us a stream of tendency, whether you choose to call it philosophy or not, which gives coherence and direction to thought and action. Judges cannot escape that current any more than other mortals. All their lives, forces which they do not recognize and cannot name, have been tugging at them—inherited instincts, traditional beliefs, acquired convictions; and the resultant is an outlook on life, a conception of social needs, a sense in [William] James's phrase of the "total push and pressure of the cosmos," which, when reasons are nicely balanced, must determine which choice shall fall.[23]

While labels can be grossly misleading, the Justices have been branded conveniently with the description "liberal" or "conservative." Such hashtags reflect, as Holmes put it, "prejudices which judges share with their fellow-men." How do we define a liberal as opposed to a conservative judge? Judge Richard Posner, a distinguished jurist, suggests an answer:

> Justices . . . appointed by Democratic Presidents are predicted to vote disproportionately for "liberal" outcomes, such as outcomes fa-

voring employees, consumers, small businessmen, criminal defendants (other than white-collar defendants), labor unions, and environmental tort, civil rights, and civil liberties plaintiffs. Judges appointed by Republican Presidents are predicted to vote disproportionately for the opposite outcomes.[24]

I would add to the mix issues of abortion, gay marriage, gun control, affirmative action, voting rights, and privacy, as well as limits on sectarian prayer in public school and capital punishment, with Justices appointed by Democrats predicted to vote disproportionately for those seeking to vindicate such rights, and Justices appointed by Republicans predicted to vote the opposite way.

Justices tend to vote the political views of the presidents who appoint them. When George W. Bush, a hardline conservative president, appointed Samuel Alito, a conservative Catholic, to replace Sandra Day O'Connor, a moderate conservative Protestant appointed by Reagan, the Court took a 180-degree lurch to the right on the abortion issue, and even on the issue of affirmative action.[25] When he appeared before the Senate, Alito was more guarded as to where he stood on the issue, but his mother gave the store away. She was quoted as saying, "Of course, he's against abortion." Undoubtedly, mother knows best.

This turnabout was astounding as it was remarkable. Professor Geoffrey Stone of the University of Chicago Law School has examined 18 of what he calls the "most important constitutional decisions" between 2000 and 2012, "ranging across a broad spectrum of issues." These included the "2000 presidential election, gun control, voter disenfranchisement, affirmative action, abortion, habeas corpus, due process for terrorist suspects, takings of private property, the death penalty, campaign finance reform, the freedom of religion, the rights of gays and lesbians, and the Commerce Clause." Stone notes that each ideological side won only half the cases. He then reasons that "given the current makeup of the Supreme Court, a change in the ideology of only one Justice will have a profound impact on the course of constitutional law." Had Kagan been on the Court in those years instead of Scalia, the liberals would have won 17 of the 18 cases instead of 9, and if Alito had been on the Court instead of Ginsburg, the conservatives would have won 16 of the 18 instead of 9.[26] Stone concludes, "This shows how polarized the Justices are." Judge Richard Posner has commented acutely that "if changing judges changes law, it is not even clear what law is."[27]

Posner, a distinguished jurist, rejects the notion that a Justice will ask himself how the president who appointed him would vote on a Constitutional question, and cast his vote accordingly. It may be far fetched to argue that Ruth Bader Ginsburg asks herself every time before she votes, "How would Bill Clinton come out on this one?" Or that Samuel Alito will ask himself how George W. Bush would have voted the question. But on the evidence, a Justice usually comes to a conclusion the appointing president might have most probably shared.

It is said that some successful lawyers know the law and that others, perhaps more successful, know the judge. The American people certainly do not know the Justices. Only one in three Americans can name a single Justice of the Supreme Court of the United States. Knowing the judge is important to our understanding the mentality of the judicial decision-maker, who he (or she) really is, how he got there, and what his biases and predilections are.

The all-white "nine" who gave us *Brown v. Board of Education* in 1954 consisted of seven Protestants, one Catholic, and one Jew.[28] The "straw that stirred the drink" in *Brown* was Chief Justice Earl Warren, a white Anglo-Saxon Protestant, who enunciated a rule for the ages:

> We conclude that, in the field of public education, the doctrine of "separate but equal" has no place. Separate educational facilities are inherently unequal. Therefore, we hold that the plaintiffs and others similarly situated for whom the actions have been brought are, by reason of the segregation complained of, deprived of the equal protection of the laws guaranteed by the Fourteenth Amendment.[29]

Although it is impossible to know with certainty, it is conventional wisdom that the Court would not have achieved unanimity in *Brown*, nor would it have gone as far as it did, without Warren's guiding hand.

Roberts is angered when the Court splits 5-4 or even 6-3 along ideological lines. He is concerned about the Court as an institution. As he said in the gay marriage case, "It may be tempting for judges to confuse our own preferences with the requirements of the law." Shortly after he took office, he suggested in a 2006 Georgetown Law School graduation address that he would prefer narrowly drawn decisions that would achieve "unanimity or near unanimity" rather than broad pronouncements for the future that would deeply divide the Court. "When in doubt," he said, "find a way to save the Court from partisan attack by voting to limit the reach of controversial decisions." "The more cautious approach," he said, "the approach that can get the most Justices to sign on to it, is the preferred approach."

He has largely failed to achieve this objective. The conservative majority splinters into Balkanized concurring opinions, differing as to the reasoning even when it agrees. The four liberals, who tend to vote in lockstep as a unified voting bloc, rarely issue separate opinions. "We [liberals] have made a concerted effort to speak with one voice in important cases," Ginsburg said in an interview last year.

Indeed, Court critics have said that even some of the "faux-unanimous" decisions lack clarity and are "flabby and flat," "fuzzy," and "unwieldy."[30] Scalia thundered against his colleagues for "issuing opaque opinions" that give little in the way of guidance to the lower courts. And as noted, while replacements in Court personnel over the next eight years will be affected by the 2016 presidential election, whatever the outcome, we can be confident that politics, and particularly identity politics, will dominate the appointing process. If it didn't, we could readily replace the nine Justices with nine mainframe computers woodenly spitting out answers based on black-letter precedent. What is self-evident is that unless we change our appointment process, the judiciary will become completely politicized, no matter who is the next president.

Constitutional interpretation of course begins with the language and plain meaning of the document. But it does not necessarily end there. Chief Justice Roberts told the Senate in his confirmation hearings that the role of the Justice in interpreting the Constitution is fairly a-personal:

> Senator Grassley: Well, is there any room in constitutional interpretation for the judge's own values or beliefs?
> Judge Roberts: No, I don't think there is. . . . [Y]ou don't look to your own values and beliefs. You look outside yourself to other sources. This is the basis for, you know, that judges wear black robes, because it doesn't matter who they are as individuals. That's not going to shape their decision. It's their understanding of the law that will shape their decision.[31]

Tell me another one!

The Justice may be an "originalist" and seek enlightenment in the original understanding of the Framers, insisting that the text of the Constitution trumps any common law precedents that depart from the original understanding of its meaning. The Justice may be a textualist and rely exclusively on the plain meaning of the words. He or she may be a pragmatist and rely on the intent of the Framers and the purpose they sought to accomplish. And what is the Justice to do if the language of the Constitution is ambiguous or overly broad and there is little illumination to be gained from the historical context? The document is brigaded with vague phrases like "due process of law," "establishment of a religion," "cruel and inhuman punishments," "equal protection of the laws," and "unreasonable searches and seizures" that are continually susceptible to new meanings and interpretations. But the bottom-line question is, What policy is the Justice advancing in his or her opinion? Is that policy more liberal or conservative? And then my question, Does the Justice's partisan take on life play a role in making policy? Of course, it does.

Kagan recently said that from her point of view, Justices do not view law through the Democratic or Republican lens as the public may believe. Rather, she said, differences in opinion arise from different methods of judicial analysis. She explained that her personal style of analysis when addressing big picture ideas that are not clearly defined, like due process or equal protection, focuses on precedent and its development over time. "I think really hard about the way interpretation of the law has developed over time and the principles that have emerged from all of those cases," she said. [32] But after thinking "hard" about the history and the precedents, where does she go from there? And to what extent do political or personal philosophical considerations influence her conclusions? How does she explain that her personal methodology lands her in exactly the same place as her liberal colleagues? The public (and in many cases the president) does not care so much as to how the Justices reach their conclusions, but what conclusions they reach.

And what happens if these methodological approaches do not end the inquiry? For example, in 1789 there was no wiretapping, and there were no smartphones. Al Gore had yet to invent the Internet (just kidding). Capital punishment was not considered either cruel or inhuman. Abortion was illegal. Same-sex marriage was unknown. The eminent English jurist William Blackstone, the great commentator on the laws of England, considered sodomy between consenting adults an "infamous crime against nature" and an offense of "deeper malignity" than rape. He deemed sodomy a heinous act "the very mention of which is a disgrace to human nature" and "a crime not fit to be named." How is the Justice to apply the values contained in an eighteenth-century document to the unforeseeable and rapidly changing twenty-first-century digital age? And how is the president to predict how a prospective nominee will tackle these problems?

Justice William Brennan put it this way:

> [W]e are an aspiring people, a people with faith in progress. Our amended Constitution is the lodestar for our aspirations. Like every text worth reading, it is not crystalline. The phrasing is broad and the limitations of its provisions are not clearly marked. Its majestic generalities and ennobling pronouncements are both luminous and obscure. The ambiguity, of course, calls for interpretation, the interaction of reader and text.

But not every prospective nominee to the Supreme Court will agree with Brennan's viewpoint as to how to come down on these weighty issues or even that there must necessarily be "an interaction of reader and text."

So what weight to give in this crucible of political disposition, as Roberts put it, to whom the Justices "are as individuals"? Does identity politics really matter once the appointee has cleared the Senate and has a lifetime appointment and ought to have total independence? I submit that it does, as it illuminates the partisan way that Justices go about doing what they do.

No matter who the president is after the 2016 election, the Supreme Court will continue to be a very political court where recent precedent is overruled or sterilized to accommodate an ideological agenda; nonjudicial and even foreign sources are used as intellectual tools of decision making; and the "moral values" of particular Justices flavor constitutional rights in a host of cases.

Assuming that Merrick Garland is not confirmed, and there is a Democrat in the White House, liberal Justices will surely fill the next four vacancies, and it will dramatically transform the conservative institution we have today. If, however, there is a Republican President, and conservatives fill the four seats, the majority right wing will have the votes, and own the Palace of Justice for decades. Waiting in the wings are the recurrent polarizing issues, which will be very much in play: reproductive rights, voting district apportionment, business and regulatory issues, fair-share fees payable to public-employees (where there was a four-four split, but the matter is sure to be revisited once there is a full bench), capital punishment, affirmative action, voting rights, and further defining the role of religion in public life.

Contemporary America has become increasingly multicultural. This often raises the question as to whether adjudication applying norms acceptable to all segments of society is even possible. To believe in the American experiment, we need to have faith that our people share with the Framers of the Constitution a moral judgment that certain things such as torture, discrimination, censorship, prolonged incarceration without a hearing, and a state-sponsored religion are wrong.

As Obama put it in his speech to the UN General Assembly on September 28, 2015,

> But some universal truths are self-evident. No person wants to be imprisoned for peaceful worship. No woman should ever be abused with impunity, or a girl barred from going to school. The freedom to peacefully petition those in power without fear of arbitrary laws— these are not ideas of one country or one culture. They are fundamental to human progress.

On other issues we are deeply divided. And when the Supreme Court divides 5-4, 4-4, or even 6-3 on polarizing issues, polls show that the American people lose confidence in the Court and its decisions. And, polls aside, the rule of law is seriously undermined.

Notes

1. I deal with the bench as a temporary Court of eight Justices on the premise that Garland has not been confirmed.

2. See e.g., Erwin Chemerinsky. *The Case against the Supreme Court*, New York: Viking (2014).

3. 410 U.S. 113 (1973).

4. *Richmond Med. Ctr. for Women v. Gilmore*, 219 F.3d 376, 376–77 (4th Cir. 2000). Notwithstanding, Senator Ted Cruz, who clerked for Luttig on the

Fourth Circuit before he clerked for Chief Justice Rehnquist, praised Luttig in the second Republican presidential debate as a "rock-ribbed conservative."

5. By Jeffrey Rosen, "Do You Believe in 'Super Precedents'?" *New York Times*, October 30, 2005. Available at http://www.nytimes.com/2005/10/30/weekinreview/so-do-you-believe-in-superprecedent.html.

6. 505 U.S 833 (1992).

7. 515 U.S. 70, 114 (1965).

8. 347 U.S. *supra*, 483 (1954).

9. A. E. Dick Howard, "The Changing Face of the Supreme Court," August 10, 2014. Virginia Law Rev. 231, 241 (2015).

10. *Grutter v. Bollinger*, 539 U.S. 306 (2003).

11. Steven Brill, *America's Bitter Pill—Money, Politics, Backroom Deals and the Fight to Fix Our Broken Healthcare System*, New York: Random House (2015) at 152.

12. "No person shall be held to answer for a *capital*, or otherwise infamous crime, unless on a presentment or indictment of a Grand Jury . . . nor be deprived of *life*, liberty, or property, without due process of law," U.S. Const., Amend. V.

13. Jennifer M. Lowe, *The Jewish Justices of the Supreme Court Revisited: Brandeis to Fortas*, Supreme Court Historical Society (1994), introduction by Ruth Bader Ginsburg.

14. 323 U.S. 214 (1944).

15. Franklin D. Roosevelt, 1932 radio address from Albany, NY.

16. *West Virginia State Board of Education v. Barnette*, 319 U.S. 624, 642 (1943).

17. *Metro Broadcasting, Inc. v. FCC*, 497 U.S. 547, 636 (1990) (Kennedy, J., dissenting) (rejecting the "demeaning notion that members of . . . defined racial groups ascribe to certain 'minority views' that must be different from those of other citizens").

18. *Schuette v. Coalition to Defend Affirmative Action*, 572 U.S. (2014). Slip op. at 12.

19. Marshall actually did not coin this oft-quoted phrase, although he wrote it in *Marbury v. Madison*, 5 U.S. 137, 163(1803) and added the word "emphatically." It comes from Part the First, Article XXX, of the Massachusetts Constitution of 1780, which reads in full, as follows: "In the government of this Commonwealth, the legislative department shall never exercise the executive and judicial powers, or either of them: The executive shall never exercise the legislative and judicial powers, or either of them: The judicial shall never exercise the legislative and executive powers, or either of them: to the end it may be a government of laws and not of men."

20. Transcript of Hearings of the U.S. Senate Committee on the Judiciary on nomination of John G. Roberts, Jr. to be Chief Justice of the United States at 55 (September 12, 2005).

21. *Id.* at 56.

22. Dissenting in *King v. Burwell*, U.S. (2015). Slip op. at 8.

23. Benjamin Cardozo, *The Nature of the Judicial Process*, New Haven, CT: Yale University Press (1921) at 12.

24. Richard A. Posner, *How Judges Think*, Cambridge, MA: Harvard University Press (2008) at 20.

25. When O'Connor retired, George W. Bush, obedient to the concept of a female seat, appointed another woman, Harriet Miers, to replace her. When Miers, an evangelical Christian who opposed abortion rights and faced bipartisan opposition in the Senate, withdrew her name from consideration, Bush appointed Alito, telling him, "You will owe your job to Harriet Miers."

26. By Geoffrey R. Stone, "The Supreme Court and the 2012 Election," Huffington Post, August 13, 2012. Available at http://www.huffingtonpost.com/geoffrey-r-stone/the-supreme-court-and-the_b_1773347.html.

27. Richard A. Posner, *How Judges Think*, Cambridge, MA: Harvard University Press (2008) at 1.

28. 347 U.S. 483 (1954). The minority Justices joining in the *Brown* decision were Frankfurter, a Jew, and Minton, a Catholic.

29. *Id.* at 495.

30. Adam Liptak, "Justices Are Long on Words but Short on Guidance," *New York Times*, November 18, 2010. Available at http://www.nytimes.com/2010/11/18/us/18rulings.html.

31. Transcript of Hearings of the U.S. Senate Committee on the Judiciary on Nomination of John G. Roberts, Jr. to be Chief Justice of the United States at 178 (September 13, 2005).

32. Statements made at Princeton University, November 20, 2014, reported by Jacqueline Gifford in the *Daily Princetonian*. Available at http://dailyprincetonian.com/news/2014/11/justice-kagan-81-discusses-legal-analysis-courts-perception/.

3

RELIGION AND THE PARTISAN COURT

Whatever issue may come before me as president—on birth control, divorce, censorship, gambling or any other subject—I will make my decision in accordance with . . . what my conscience tells me to be the national interest, and without regard to outside religious pressures or dictates.
—John F. Kennedy, Address to the Greater Houston Ministerial Association, September 12, 1960

There has always been a tradition of "ethnic politics" in America. By ethnic politics, I mean political selection based on gender, ancestry, or religious belief. In 1961 in New York City, Louis J. Lefkowitz, a Republican from the Lower East Side, who was the state attorney general, launched an unsuccessful effort to defeat Mayor Robert F. Wagner. His ticket included Representative Paul A. Fino of the Bronx, running for city council president, and John J. Gilhooley of Brooklyn, a former assistant secretary of labor, for city comptroller. Wagner's ticket included Mario Procaccino for city council president, and Abraham Beame for city comptroller. The ethnic calculus in the competing packages could not be clearer.

Nathan Glazer and Daniel P. Moynihan in *Beyond the Melting Pot: The Negroes, Puerto Ricans, Jews, Italians and Irish of New York City* (1970) cite the catchy jingle "How Can We Miss?" and the Lefkowitz slate as an example of New York City ticket-balancing "almost to the point, indeed, of caricature."

> How can you miss
> With a ticket like this
> Lefkowitz, Gilhooley and Fino
>
> . . . .
> That fine City Hall
> Will be open to all
> With Lefkowitz, Gilhooley and Fino

"Ethnic considerations have always been primary in New York City politics," Mr. Glazer and Mr. Moynihan wrote, referring to the practice of dividing candidacies for what were then the three major citywide offices—mayor, city council president, and comptroller—among a Jew, an Italian, and an Irishman (or an occasional white Protestant). As the man said, "In politics, you can't beat somebody with nobody."[1] And nothing seems to work like an ethnically balanced ticket.

Republican Emory Buckner, a gifted and distinguished Manhattan lawyer, became U.S. attorney for the Southern District of New York in 1925 and established a totally independent and nonpolitical office. He had learned, when Charles Whitman appointed him an assistant New York County district attorney in January, 1910, about the world of an ethnically "balanced" prosecutor's office. Felix Frankfurter facetiously wrote that Whitman had "every community represented on his staff—a Greek, a Pole, a Jew, of course; and he thought the bar should be represented too."[2]

When Coolidge appointed Buckner U.S. attorney some fifteen years later, he wrote Frankfurter that the staff he found was "terrible . . . appointments were made almost 100 per cent political. And when I say political, I mean political. . . . I found the Negroes had, and therefore were entitled to have in perpetuity, a representative. The same was true of the Italians, with their large voting strength."[3] Buckner proceeded to clean out the office and make appointments based solely on merit.

Add gender to the brew, and there is a sure-fire recipe for political success. There is also a history of ethnic politics in Supreme Court appointments. The American legal culture has been predominantly Protestant. Of the 112 Justices appointed since 1789, 89 have been WASP males. The rest have been something else (11 Catholic, 8 Jewish; 4 female; 3 African American or Latino). Presidents failed to appoint a minority Justice within the Court's first fifty years. In the last one hundred years, however, presidents have added "ethnic considerations," whatever their merit, to the process of judicial selection.

That there was historically a "Jewish seat" is well known. Beginning in 1916 with Brandeis, one Jew or another occupied the bench until 1969, an era spanning fifty-three years. Richard Nixon discontinued the practice, replacing Abe Fortas with Harry Blackmun, a Methodist and a conservative, who authored the 7-2 opinion in *Roe v. Wade.*[4] When asked by his attorney general when he was going to fill the Jewish seat, Nixon replied, "Well, how about after I die?"

Nixon did much to alter the Court's ideological balance. Between 1969 and 1971, he replaced four members of the Warren Court (Warren, Black, Harlan, and Fortas) with Justices of a more conservative stripe (Burger, Blackmun, Powell, and Rehnquist). In the forty-six years since Fortas left the Court, there has been a Republican-appointed conservative majority.

There was also a "Catholic seat." When in 1839 Andrew Jackson appointed Roger Taney Chief Justice, there were howls of protest in the Senate. Taney was the first Catholic to sit on the Supreme Court. The political opposition to a Catholic was so vehement that in the thirty years between Taney's death in 1864 and 1894 when Grover Cleveland appointed Edward Douglass White, there was a virtual sign outside the Supreme Court building: "Catholics need not apply." Since White, who later became Chief Justice, there has always been at least one reserved seat for a Catholic.

What is the political calculus that influences a president to make appointments to the Supreme Court as though he were in a Chinese restaurant choosing one from Group A and one from Group B on an ethnic bill of fare? Is there a need for "balance" on a constitutional court? Is it just a cynical gesture to minority voting blocs? Perhaps an ethnically balanced Court may seem desirable, but is it legitimate to weigh down the Court with Justices whose consciences may be committed for religious or ideological reasons to overruling such a pillar of reproductive freedom as *Roe v. Wade?*[5]

The demographics would hardly have justified the appointment of Brandeis just before the election of 1916. Although it is estimated that Woodrow Wilson captured 55 percent of the Jewish vote in 1916, Jews at that time represented only 3.2 percent of the U.S. population as opposed to roughly 2 percent at this writing (the cohort doesn't mean more Jews then, just fewer non-Jewish Americans). Today, the demographics wouldn't politically justify the appointment of the three Jews who presently sit on the Court. A better case could be made for the appointment of two African American Justices when blacks represent almost 13 percent of the U.S. population or three Latino Justices when Latinos represent over 16 percent of the U.S. population or four female Justices when women represent roughly 50 percent of the population. Nor do the demographics justify the appointment of six Catholics to a nine-person Court when Catholics represent roughly 24 percent of the U.S. population. The latest Pew studies report that the number of Americans identifying as "Christian" has declined from 78.4 percent to 70.6 percent over the last seven years with nearly 23 percent of all U.S. adults now saying they are religiously unaffiliated, up from about 16 percent in 2007.

Whatever the politics, the net result is six Catholics of varied ethnicity on a Court of nine. Indeed, since Rehnquist's elevation to Chief Justice in 1986, only one Protestant, David Souter, has been appointed. The Protestant majority ended in 1994 when Breyer assumed office. It is easy to see this composition as an expression of partisan politics. But is there the same political need for ethnic and gender "balance" on our precious constitutional court as might exist for a backroom Tammany Hall boss in New York City seeking to pander to various constituencies when he appoints a lowly alderman? Bring back the WASPs. They haven't done so badly for us.

There may be no surer way for presidents, wishing to appeal to an anti-abortion political base, to predict more or less reliably how a candidate for the Supreme Court will stand on overruling *Roe*, than to appoint a Catholic. As we have seen, presidents appointing candidates they thought were conservative or liberal have at times been unpleasantly surprised, as Eisenhower was with Warren and Brennan or George H. W. Bush was with David Souter.

Ethnic selection, including selection based on gender, has ramped up over the past three decades. Reagan made history in 1986 when he appointed Scalia as the first Italian American Justice and in 1981 when he appointed Sandra Day O'Connor as the first woman on the Court. She was the only woman on the Court bench until Ginsburg came along in 1993—a little over a decade later. Obama likewise made history when in 2009 he appointed Sotomayor, the first Latina, and gilded the lily with the 2010 appointment of an additional woman, Elena Kagan.

There has also been an "African American seat" with Clarence Thomas succeeding Thurgood Marshall in 1991.

Almost certainly there have been gay Justices, and at least four have been rumored; none have "come out," however, and their identities are beyond the scope of this book.[6] The issue of an "openly gay seat" hasn't come up. But you never know.

Judge Richard Posner has stressed the "innate personal characteristics" of judges, one of them being religion, as important factors in adjudication on all issues.[7] This is particularly true on the Supreme Court, which, face it, is ultra-partisan when it comes to controversial constitutional questions, such as abortion rights. As Posner puts it, "innate personal characteristics" would necessarily include "personal background characteristics such as race and sex."

In confronting the inevitable issue of same-sex marriage, the personal experiences of the Justices inevitably entered their thinking. It surely must have for Justice Lewis Powell, who voted with the five-Justice majority against gay rights in 1986.[8] Powell said once that he had never met a homosexual. It later came out that he had had several gay law clerks.[9] The present Court includes members whose personal lives include adoption, intermarriage, single parenting, divorce, widowhood, and never wed. Says Andrew Cherlin, a sociologist at Johns Hopkins University and an expert on marriage, their personal lives look "just like the rest of America."[10]

But abortion rights stand out as an inflexion point in judicial thinking. Posner writes, "Most judges who oppose abortion rights do so because of religious belief rather than because of a pragmatic assessment of such rights. (Many who support such rights are ideologically driven as well)."[11]

On the evidence, changing judges decidedly changes the law. The replacement of Justice O'Connor, a moderate conservative, with Justice Alito, an extreme conservative, marked the most tectonic change on the Court since President H. W. Bush appointed Thomas to replace Thurgood Marshall in 1991. No wonder, dissenting in the *Parents Involved* case, a 5-4 decision declaring a virtual end to affirmative action, with four separate concurring opinions, Justice John Paul Stevens said, "It is my firm conviction that no member of the Court that I joined in 1975 would have agreed with today's decision."

Franklin Roosevelt addressed this issue on March 19, 1937, in his ninth Fireside Chat when he showcased his "court-packing" plan, although his argument skirted policy and centered on age. Had he suggested enlarging the Court for every Justice who voted against New Deal legislation, rather than every Justice who was over the age of 70, the proposal would be clearly unconstitutional as undermining the independence of the judiciary. What he proposed was bad enough.

Holmes said that the law was "nothing more" than the "prophecies of what the courts will do."[12] It would seem self evident that a president interested in leaving a lasting ideological legacy long after he leaves office may use religion or gender or race as a yardstick in prophesying "what the courts will do" when, in any fair view of the world, such factors are significant, however hazardous, indicators for how a judicial candidate is likely to vote.

Does religion make a difference in decision making on the Court? In many respects it is the elephant in the room that no one wants to discuss. Jeff Shesol, author of the book *Supreme Power*, says that "religion is the third rail of Supreme Court politics. It's not something that's talked about in polite company." Nina Totenberg of NPR calls the subject "radioactive," a "topic with a hint of taboo."[13] Personal religious views are a private matter, and their privacy is to be respected. But Justices are public figures, and whether their public acts may (or may not) be influenced by religious doctrine is fair game for scrutiny.

When Chicago's Professor Stone, who has described Scalia as "one of the ablest, most interesting, most provocative, and most engaging justices ever to serve on the Supreme Court," had the cheek to suggest in 2007 that the abortion views of the five conservative Justices, as expressed in *Gonzales v. Carhart* (the partial-birth abortion case) mirrored Catholic doctrine, Scalia, who served on the Chicago faculty from 1977 to 1982, said he would boycott Chicago Law School until Stone left the faculty. Scalia did speak there in 2012, and Stone was still there. Kennedy, who wrote for the Court in *Carhart*, had declared, "Whether to have an abortion requires a difficult and painful moral decision. . . . While we find no reliable data to measure the phenomenon, it seems unexceptionable to conclude some women come to regret their choice to abort the infant life they once created and sustained . . . Severe depression and loss of esteem can follow."[14] In an angry dissent, Ginsburg dismissed Kennedy's wobbly notions of female hysteria as "an antiabortion shibboleth for which it concededly has no reliable evidence." She totally rejected Kennedy's unsupported assumption that women who have abortions suffer from "severe depression and loss of esteem." "This way of thinking," she wrote, "reflects ancient notions about women's place in the family and under the Constitution—ideas that have long since been discredited."[15] She told Jeffrey Toobin of the *New Yorker* in conversation that Kennedy's opinion in the case was "dreadful."[16]

Ethnic stereotypes and traits can be deceptive. Catholics are supposed to be more rigid and authoritarian, tilting toward order in the constitutional search for an ordered liberty, and callously indifferent to the "rights of man" as declared during the French Revolution. But this was not true of Justice Frank Murphy in the Roosevelt era or Brennan either, and it's certainly not true of what can be made of Sotomayor, although certainly it was more true of Scalia, and it's also more true of Thomas and Alito.

Breyer, known as a "raging pragmatist," views the Constitution as a "living text—subject to interpretation."[17] Yet he thinks the judiciary should avoid confrontation with the executive, and he suggests finding ways to "balance" interests, and compromise with discriminatory acts of the executive. By way of example, take Roosevelt's internment of Japanese Americans at a time of national emergency during World War II.

Breyer writes there was a pragmatic solution:

> Might the Court have found a workable way to hold the president accountable? Perhaps it could have developed a sliding scale in respect to the length of detention and the intensity of its examination of the circumstances. Perhaps it could have insisted that the government increase [loyalty] screening efforts the longer an individual is held in detention. Perhaps it could have required the government to have in place a plan for future screening. Perhaps it could have deemed critical the fact that the relocation was imposed within the United States itself during a period not of martial law but when ordinary civilian Courts were fully operative. Perhaps by focusing on these or similar possibilities, the Court might have written a legal rule that structured judicial review of military actions—ideally a rule

that steered between burdensome case-by-case judicial review and no review at all.[18]

Is Breyer a little too quick to compromise with evil here? The decision in *Korematsu*, as he later acknowledged, "counts for many as one of the three worst Court decisions in U.S. history, the other two being *Dred Scott* and *Plessy v. Ferguson.*"[19] Scalia might say that "balancing" interests and "sliding scales" are for wusses.

There are often no rules, and just as often many surprises, in these things. Brandeis and Cardozo, both Jews, voted with the majority in *Palko v. Connecticut*,[20] holding that double jeopardy did not apply to the states because the Fourteenth Amendment only "selectively incorporated" some elements of the Bill of Rights "essential to a fundamental scheme of ordered liberty" and double jeopardy wasn't one of them, failing to see that the Double Jeopardy Clause ought to apply to the states as well in virtue of the Due Process Clause of the Fourteenth Amendment. They thereupon dispatched Mr. Palko to the electric chair for a crime of which he had been previously acquitted. Brandeis quite astonishingly voted with Holmes to uphold the involuntary sterilization of a supposedly retarded young woman, Carrie Buck, on the basis that "three generations of idiots is enough." The decision in this eugenics case has been highly criticized.[21]

Jews are presumed to be Zionists, strong supporters of the State of Israel. Brandeis was an ardent Zionist who in the early years of the twentieth century advocated a Jewish state in Palestine at a time when most Jewish leaders were lukewarm or opposed to the idea. Yet the three Jewish Justices sided with the Obama administration and voted to reject Menachem Zivotofsky's suit to compel the State Department to record his place of birth in his passport as "Jerusalem, Israel," even though Congress expressly authorized such a designation.[22]

While religion is not supposed to matter in Court decisions, I have news for you. The evidence is that it is certainly part of the mix. Jews do not see eye to eye with Catholics on the important divide between church and state. This is doubtless born out of a five-millennia history of state-sponsored religious persecution. The First Amendment guarantees the free exercise of religion. It also provides in the Establishment Clause that "Congress shall make no law respecting an establishment of religion," declaring an ironclad division between church and state. Just how ironclad it is would appear to turn on the personal beliefs of the decider. Supreme Court cases interpreting the separation between church and state are myriad and often difficult to rationalize. Alito finds the Court's Establishment Clause jurisprudence "often puzzling." But one thing is clear under the Constitution: The government may not officially prefer "one religious denomination . . . over another."[23]

In 2014, five of the six Catholic Justices upheld the decade-old prayer practices of the town of Greece, a hamlet of about 94,000 outside Rochester in upstate New York.[24] It was an easy case for Clarence Thomas. He does not believe that the Establishment Clause applies to state and local governments. The ruling courted a bristling dissent from the Court's three Jewish Justices (Ginsburg, Breyer, and Kagan), who condemned the practice, with Sotomayor joining the dissenters. Sotomayor may have dissented to express solidarity with her Jewish colleagues or else with her former colleagues on the Second Circuit who in the ruling appealed from unanimously found an Establishment Clause violation.[25] Or perhaps this wise Latina woman related strongly to the sense of alienation and second-class citizenship felt by non-Christians having official business before the Greece town meetings.

Town meetings are where the governmental rubber meets the road in Greece. Such meetings are, on the town's own evidence, "the most important part of town government." It is an occasion when the citizenry of Greece petition their government on individualize matters. Stoplights at intersections, zoning variances, garbage collections, and the like are typical of the issues considered at town meetings.

Greece begins each monthly meeting with a prayerful invocation larded with Christian idiom, almost always delivered by a Protestant prelate. The minister faces the citizenry with his back to the town officials. The direction of prayer is toward the functionaries of Greece's government, who sit on a raised dais as though they were high priests on an altar speaking for the divinity.

Typical are prayers singing of the "beauties of spring . . . an expressive symbol of the new life of the risen Christ. The Holy Spirit sent to the apostles at Pentecost," adulating "in the name of our brother Jesus," acknowledging "the saving sacrifice of Jesus Christ on the cross," calling on those in attendance to rise or bow their heads in Christian prayer. The prayers of Greece are decidedly Christian, "specifying details upon which men and women who believe in a benevolent, omnipotent Creator and Ruler of the world are known to differ (for example, the divinity of Christ).[26] As the minister concludes, town officials make the sign of the cross, and there is a chorus of "Amens." The invocation ended, a citizen rises to complain about the town's contract with a cable company or a malfunctioning traffic light.

Greece is a predominantly Christian town, but with a Buddhist temple within its borders and several Jewish synagogues just outside. The town's practices in inviting unpaid voluntary prayer givers were anything but inclusive. Town clerks selected the prayer givers from a "list" of religious organizations within the town published by the chamber of commerce in a "community guide." There was apparently no intent to exclude these minority groups, but there was no demonstrated effort to include them either.

Jewish and Buddhist temples were conspicuously absent from the list. During one outlying year, after commencement of the lawsuit, the town elders invited a Jewish layman twice, as well as the chair of a Baha'i congregation, and even a Wiccan priestess. The Jews and the priestess had to shoot their way in and demand an invitation. The town invited the Baha'i representative on its own initiative. Then the town reverted to its past practice, which was to make no effort to include representatives of non-Christian religions. No wonder Judge Calabresi in the court of appeals found in Greece's invocation ceremony a decade-long "steady drumbeat of . . . sectarian Christian prayers."

The majority seemed to rest its case on the fact that the Christian prayers were not coercive and were neither proselytizing nor denigrative of any other religion. Anyone was free to leave for the prayer part. But symbols are important. Plaintiffs called the prayers "offensive," "intolerable," and an "affront to a diverse community."

Kagan took particular umbrage at the town's practices. Applauding the "breathtakingly generous constitutional idea that our public institutions belong no less to the Buddhist or Hindu than to the Methodist or Episcopalian," she dissented from the Court's 5-4 decision. The majority seems to be saying, she said, "What's the big deal, anyway?" The content of Greece's prayers, she found, is a big deal to "Christians and non-Christians alike."

Kagan was deft in taking Alito's accusation of "niggling" to task, even questioning whether the town of Greece made an honest mistake:

The Town's clerks, [Alito] writes, merely "did a bad job in compiling
the list of chaplains . . ." Now I suppose one question that account
raises is why in over a decade, no member of the Board noticed that
the clerk's list was producing prayers of only one kind. But put that
aside. Honest oversight or not, the problem remains: Every month
for more than a decade, the Board aligned itself, through its prayer
practices, with a single religion. That the concurring opinion thinks
my objection to that is "really quite niggling" . . . says all there is to
say about the difference between our respective views.

In Kagan's view, it is not who was aimed at in Greece's practice, it is
who was hit. And who was hit were non-Christians seeking a forum in
which to petition their government, confronted at the outset of the
proceeding with a sectarian prayer as part of the price of admission.
The prayers in Greece, she argued, are clueless in "understanding that
the American community is today, as it long has been, a rich mosaic of
religious faiths."[27]

Does the Court's religious composition really matter? John F. Kennedy in his September 1960 Houston speech reminded the nation of
the "no political test for office" clause in the Constitution[28] and visualized a country where "no one is denied public office because his religion differs from the president who might appoint him." And that should
be good enough for anyone.

But where does a Catholic Justice stand on overruling *Roe v. Wade*,
in which the Supreme Court held that laws prohibiting abortion in the
first 24 weeks of pregnancy are unconstitutional? *Roe* was a 7-2 decision
in which three of Nixon's four "conservative" nominees to the Court
voted with the majority.

Roe held women had a fundamental right to get abortion on demand
under certain circumstances. At the time *Roe* was decided, most
Americans agreed that abortion was a matter exclusively for a woman
and her physician. Even 56 percent of Catholics agreed. There was, as
Brandeis put it, "a right to be let alone" by the state. When John Paul
Stevens was nominated in 1975, two years after *Roe*, not one senator
asked him about the decision.

But Republican strategists, noting that there was political conflict
over abortion rights that preceded and followed *Roe*; that the Catholic
church opposed abortion on moral grounds and decriminalization as
well; and that most Catholics traditionally voted Democratic, sought to

unearth Catholic voters from their political roots. Accordingly, they cobbled together a divisive political agenda that would appeal to Catholics, evangelicals, and religious fundamentalists. The new social platform was anti-gay, anti-evolution, anti-women's rights, and anti-abortion. Number one on the hit parade was overruling *Roe v. Wade*. The result was the political polarization of America, which I would argue contributes to the dysfunctional government we have today with Gallup polls showing that only 8 percent of the American people respect Congress as an institution.

The *Roe* honeymoon did not last long. Conservative Republican presidents appointed three Catholic Justices in quick succession: Scalia in 1986, Kennedy in 1988, and Thomas in 1991. They were later joined by two more: Roberts in 2005 and Alito in 2006. With the Court already having a Catholic majority, it was coals to Newcastle when Obama appointed Sotomayor in 2009.

The Republican expectation was that all or most of their appointees would vote to overrule or limit *Roe*, but thus far that expectation has been unfulfilled. The Supreme Court has not decided a major abortion case since 2007, when in *Gonzales v. Carhart* it upheld 5-4 the federal Partial-Birth Abortion Ban Act that prohibited late-term partial birth abortion even when necessary to safeguard a woman's health.[29] In that case the Court sustained against constitutional attack a federal statute criminalizing post-viability abortion at about twelve weeks utilizing a procedure known as "intact dilation and extraction." While the Catholic majority declined to overrule *Roe*, it was clearly tottering on the brink.

Did Catholic abortion doctrine influence the views of Justices Roberts, Scalia, Thomas, Kennedy, and Alito? Professor Stone submits that it did.

> What, then, explains this decision? Here is a painfully awkward observation: All five justices in the majority in *Gonzales* are Catholic. The four justices who are either Protestant or Jewish all voted in accord with settled precedent. It is mortifying to have to point this out. But it is too obvious, and too telling, to ignore. Ultimately, the five justices in the majority all fell back on a common argument to justify their position. There is, they say, a compelling moral reason for the result in *Gonzales*. Because the intact D & E seems to resemble infanticide it is "immoral" and may be prohibited even without a clear statutory exception to protect the health of the woman.[30]

The voting patterns of the Justices indicating a faith-based interpretation of the Constitution on this issue are overwhelmingly conclusive. Scalia repeatedly stated he wanted to overrule *Roe*,[31] and Thomas concurred in the *Carhart* case when he said that *Roe* had "no basis in the Constitution."[32] Alito, voting with the majority in *Carhart*, declined to say he would vote to overrule *Roe*. But in voting to sustain a procedure—with no exception to safeguard a woman's health—that his predecessor Sandra Day O'Connor had said was constitutionally defective, he took the Court on a 180-degree course change to the right. Although he hasn't yet drunk the Kool-Aid, Alito will at the first opportunity most certainly vote with Thomas to overrule *Roe*. Alito has won the adulation of conservative Professor Michael Stokes Paulsen, who describes him as "the most consistent, solid, successful conservative on the Court." Paulsen adds, "There are louder talkers, flashier stylists, wittier wits, more poisonous pens, but no one with a more level and solid swing than Justice Samuel Alito."[33] Paulsen is the author of an article for the *Right to Life News* titled "The Unbearable Wrongness of *Roe*."

Justice Kennedy, who wrote the opinion of the Court in *Carhart*, sustained the act as expressing respect for the "dignity of human life." He found the act to implicate "ethical and moral concerns that justify a special prohibition." In his confirmation hearings, senators had asked Kennedy about a conversation he had had with Senator Jesse Helms in which Kennedy had expressed admiration for Helms's pro-life views on abortion, saying, "I am a practicing Catholic." Kennedy reassured the senators that he would deem it "highly improper for a judge to allow his or her personal or religious views to enter into a decision respecting a constitutional matter." You would not know this from reading his opinion for the majority in *Carhart*.

A traditional tool of constitutional interpretation is that courts generally should stand by their decisions and not overrule them. Lawyers call this the principle of *stare decisis*. But there is no magic to *stare decisis*. As already noted, in striking down school desegregation, *Brown v. Board of Education*[34] overruled *Plessy v. Ferguson*,[35] which had been settled law for almost sixty years. Chief Justice Roberts, cautious about overruling prior decisions, has pointed out, "There is a difference between judicial restraint and judicial abdication." Had the Court never gone against *stare decisis*, he reminds us, "segregation would be legal, minimum wage laws would be unconstitutional, and the Government could wiretap ordinary criminal suspects without first obtaining warrants."

There is conflict among legal scholars as to whether *Roe* can be legitimately overruled. At his confirmation hearings, Roberts, who said he believes there is a right of privacy, declined to say whether *Roe* was a "super-duper precedent" that could not be disturbed. Would Roberts, who attended parochial elementary and high schools in Indiana before going on to Harvard, jump at the chance to overrule *Roe* if the occasion arose, especially when he may harbor a personal belief that abortion is immoral? What is a "super-duper precedent"? It is what the Court says it is. Conservatives like Scalia and Thomas insist that any precedent should be overturned if it is inconsistent with the original understanding of the Constitution.

Roe has not aged well in the four decades of its existence. Even Ginsburg, who wasn't on the Court when *Roe* was decided, evidently fearful of a polarized *Roe* backlash that might erode respect for the Court, stated last year at the University of Chicago Law School that *Roe* went "too far too fast" and that regulation of abortion rights should have been left to the states.

The "religious test for office" clause of the Constitution is most often cited to refer to the *exclusion* of a candidate for public office on the basis of religion.[36] In his September 1960 Houston speech to the Protestant ministers, John F. Kennedy invoked the "religious test" clause of the Constitution in an eloquent plea for a fair assessment of his candidacy, stating, "And neither do I look with favor upon those who would work to subvert Article VI of the Constitution by requiring a religious test—even by indirection."

But the clause may also be interpreted to apply to religion as a *qualification* for office as seen from a strange episode in our history involving George W. Bush's nomination of Harriet Miers to the Supreme Court of the United States.

What is the meaning of a "religious test for office"? Does it mean that the Constitution would prevent a president from choosing a candidate because he admires his or her religious conviction? Does it mean that a president may not constitutionally consider a candidate's religion as a factor bearing on the approval of his political base? Does it mean that it would be unconstitutional for the Senate to inquire into the personal views of a Supreme Court nominee who holds a religious belief that abortion or capital punishment or homosexuality or teaching evolution is immoral and to wonder whether such a religious belief might conflict with his or her constitutional oath of office? It would appear not.

The "religious test" clause probably has no independent significance. It means no more than what the Framers of the Constitution understood it to mean in 1789, namely, a distinctly confined set of situations where the government requires a candidate to take an oath avowing allegiance to a particular religious faith or else an oath forswearing such allegiance. Originalists like Scalia would look to the original meaning, which was just that.

Thus, a president or a senator, considering the religion of a Jew, a Catholic, or an evangelical Christian or the race of an African American as the basis for appointment, might be politically savvy or just obtuse in this attitude, but his or her religious or race conscious approach would not be unconstitutional.

The delight of social conservatives over the appointment of Harriet Miers occurred only weeks after voices from the same band of the political spectrum declared that any discussion of the religion of John Roberts should be off limits in his confirmation process and that questions about his views amounted to an unconstitutional "religious test" of his faith as a Roman Catholic. "We have no religious tests for public office in this country," bellowed Senator John Cornyn (R-TX), insisting that any inquiry into a nominee's religious views was "offensive." *Fidelis*, a conservative Catholic group, declared, "Roberts's religious faith and how he lives that faith as an individual has no bearing and no place in the confirmation process."[37]

Not everyone agreed. Some Senate Democrats on the judiciary committee said that they would not ask Roberts about his religious beliefs, although they said they might go into his "personal beliefs" on certain issues or his overarching judicial philosophy, a euphemism for personal beliefs about abortion rights. Senator Richard Durbin (D-IL) told John King of CNN in connection with the Roberts nomination that asking a nominee about his or her religion "is a legitimate inquiry as long as it doesn't go too far and too deep. Each of us respect[s] a person for their religious beliefs and [it] should never be a disqualification from office."[38] Durbin had asked Roberts in an informal session what he would do if the law required a ruling that the Church considered immoral.

Roberts reportedly answered that he would probably have to recuse himself.[39] Conservatives savaged Durbin for probing Roberts's religious beliefs when he came before the Senate, although it was the Republican committee chairman, Arlen Specter, who questioned Roberts as to whether his religion would cause a problem to him as a Supreme Court Justice in deciding whether or not to overrule certain highly charged cases like *Roe v. Wade* as reaffirmed in *Casey v. Planned Parenthood.* Roberts gave these answers:

> Chairman Specter: There had been a question raised about your personal views, and let me digress from *Roe* for just a moment because I think this touches on an issue which ought to be settled. When you talk about your personal views, and as they may relate to your own faith, would you say that your views are the same as those expressed by John Kennedy when he was a candidate and he spoke to the Greater Houston Ministerial Association in September of 1960, "I do not speak for my church on public matters, and the church does not speak for me"?
> Judge Roberts: I agree with that, Senator, yes.
> Chairman Specter: And did you have that in mind when you said, "There is nothing in my personal views that would prevent me from fully and faithfully applying the precedent as well as *Casey*"?
> Judge Roberts: Well, I think people's personal views on this issue derive from a number of sources, and there's nothing in my personal views based on faith or other sources that would prevent me from applying the precedents of the Court faithfully under principles of *stare decisis.*[40]

Of course, Roberts's final answer was pure doubletalk. Principles of *stare decisis*, as interpreted by Roberts, might lead him to overrule *Roe v. Wade* if he thought it was wrongly decided. The answer gave little comfort to either side of the issue. The Roberts nomination sailed through the Senate.

The late Christopher Hitchens wrote for *Slate* magazine in August 2005 that although "[t]he Constitution rightly forbids any religious test for public office . . . what happens when a religious affiliation conflicts with the judge's oath to uphold the Constitution?" Hitchens goes on, "[W]e have increasingly firm dogmas on two issues that come before the court; abortion and the teaching of Darwin in schools. So please do not accuse me of suggesting a 'dual loyalty' among American Catholics.

It is their own church and its conduct and its teachings that raise the question."[41] Of course, the Catholic Church by October 2014 had given up its opposition to Darwin when Pope Francis, in dedicating a bust of his predecessor, conservative Pope Benedict XVI, said that theories of evolution and the Big Bang are "not opposed to the notion of creation because evolution presupposes the creation of human beings that evolve." The issue of abortion persists, and the issue of evolution may still exist with regard to any evangelical nominees to the Court.

When Sandra Day O'Connor, a moderate conservative, retired from the Court in 2005, George W. Bush initially desired a woman to fill the female seat. Hopefully, this would be the last time that a president would ever consider there to be an "ethnic seat" on the Court. A woman who was an evangelical Christian and who opposed abortion rights would make two warm colors for Bush's conservative palette. His own White House Counsel, Harriet Miers, appeared to fit the bill very nicely. The only problem was that the Miers nomination sparked immediate criticism, largely from Bush's own party, who saw the nomination as an act of political cronyism. Robert Bork, himself a rejected nominee for the Supreme Court, saw the Miers nomination as a "disaster," and "a slap in the face to the conservatives who've been building up a conservative legal movement for the last 20 years." Miers actually had thin credentials for the Supreme Court as she had no prior judicial experience and no track record of knowledge of constitutional law.

The evidence of the gender- and faith-based nature of the Miers appointment was overwhelming. James Dobson, a Miers supporter, was chairman of a pro-life, anti–gay rights organization called Focus on the Family. He told of a conversation he had with Bush political guru Karl Rove. Rove, the political architect of Bush's two election victories, told Dobson that Bush "was looking for a certain kind of candidate, namely a woman to replace Justice O'Connor." In addition, Miers would be a faith-based nomination. "Miers is an evangelical Christian," Rove told Dobson, "she is from a very conservative church, which is almost universally pro-life, that she had taken on the American Bar Association on the issue of abortion . . . that she had been a member of the Texas Right to Life."[42]

Marvin Olasky, a conservative Christian writer, said he supported Miers because she had an "internal compass that includes a needle pointed toward Christ," and that there were "judicial implications of her evangelical faith unseen on the Court in recent decades."[43] Jay Sekulow, counsel for the American Center for Law and Justice, said on Pat Robertson's television show that the Miers nomination was "a big opportunity for those of us who have a conviction, that share an evangelical faith in Christianity, to see someone with our positions put on the court."[44]

Bush himself admitted that the Miers nomination had been an "outreach effort" to conservatives, telling journalists in a dead give-away that the nomination was faith-based: "People ask me why I picked Harriet Miers . . . They want to know . . . as much as they possibly can before they form opinions. And part of Harriet Miers's life is her religion."[45]

Anticipating a tough confirmation fight in the Senate, Miers eventually withdrew her name from nomination. She lacked the robust intellectual credentials that Court watchers were used to seeing on the High Court bench. When Bush then appointed Alito as a fifth Catholic Justice, he told Alito that he owed his nomination to Harriet Miers. But there was a hardly a peep about the new nominee's religious beliefs.[46] "This would give a whole new meaning to the Catholic rite of confirmation," said Barbara A. Perry, a former professor at Sweet Briar College who writes about Catholics and the Supreme Court. "This would mean that the religion factor no longer matters."[47] The issue had been talked into the ground.

Ethnic judges do not forget their origins, any more than Catholic or Jewish justices forget their religious beliefs. Few people do. Justice Sonia Sotomayor famously observed prior to her appointment, "I would hope that a wise Latina woman would more often than not reach a better conclusion than a white male." Scalia, the first Italian American to be appointed to the Court, was asked by a reporter from the *Boston Herald* in 2006 how he would respond to critics who say his religion impairs his fairness in rulings. "To my critics, I say, 'Vaffanculo,'" Scalia reportedly said, flicking his right hand from under his chin. In Italian, this not-so-subtle phrase means "Fuck off," and in Sicily the accompanying hand flick is regarded as equally crude.

A newly appointed Justice Kagan didn't forget who she was either. In her confirmation hearings, Senator Lindsey Graham (R-SC) asked her how she had spent the previous Christmas Day, a Sunday. The nominee's response: "You know, like all Jews, I was probably at a Chinese restaurant." Kagan's ethnicity has carried over into her judicial opinions. In addition to Chinese food, Kagan evidently relishes words found in *The Joys of Yiddish*.[48] Dissenting in a case that invalidated an Arizona law authorizing state funded campaign financing that would level the playing field between moneyed and non-moneyed candidates, Kagan lashed out at the suggestion of Chief Justice Roberts that Arizona's statute burdened the First Amendment rights of candidates who preferred private to public financing by disbursing funds to their opponents. She used a word not in the lexicon of Oliver Wendell Holmes. "Some people might call that *chutzpah*." That's Yiddish for "real nerve."[49]

Preserving a minority "seat" on the Court may be a lesser consideration nowadays. The next vacancy after Scalia will probably be caused by the retirement of the oldest Justice, Ruth Bader Ginsburg. It is possible that her successor will be a white Anglo-Saxon Protestant male, and unlikely that a Jewish female will replace her. If a Democrat is the president, and the nominee passes the Senate, the Ginsburg replacement will probably vote to reaffirm *Roe v. Wade*. But you never know.

As Machiavelli said, "Politics is the art of the possible."

Notes

1. Attributed to Benjamin B. Odell, New York representative and governor, around 1900. Also attributed to Abraham Lincoln, responding to the suggestion that he fire General McClellan and replace him with "anybody." Lincoln said, "I can't fight a war with anybody. I must have somebody."

2. Martin Mayer, *Emory Buckner: A Biography*, New York: Harper & Row (1968) at 35.

3. *Id.* at 177.

4. Nixon found Blackmun after the Senate rejected his first two choices, Clement Haynsworth and G. Harrold Carswell, as unqualified. Senators viewed Haynsworth's rulings as a judge in civil rights and labor cases to be unacceptable, and the Senate rejected Carswell as unqualified because of a "white supremacist" background, as well as on similar grounds.

5. In Chief Justice Roberts's confirmation hearing, Senators repeatedly asked him whether he would vote to overrule *Roe*. His answer was noncommittal.

6. One almost made it. As noted above, Nixon appointed G. Harrold Carswell in 1970. Carswell failed to receive Senate confirmation. In 1976, six years

after his nomination, Carswell was convicted of battery for making sexual advances to a male undercover officer in a Tallahassee men's room.

7. Richard A. Posner, *How Judges Think*, Cambridge, MA: Harvard University Press (2008) at 10.

8. *Bowers v. Hardwick*, 478 U.S. 186 (1986).

9. *Bowers* was overturned in 2003 when there were more openly gay law clerks on the Court.

10. By Robert Barnes, "High Court Reflects Diversity of Modern Marriage," *Washington Post*, http://www.washingtonpost.com/politics/high-court-reflects-diversity-of-modern-marriage/2013/03/17/123cbaec-8b2c-11e2-b63f-f53fb9f2fcb4_story.html.

11. *Id.* at 13.

12. Holmes, "The Path of the Law," note 4, *supra*.

13. http://www.npr.org/templates/story/story.php?storyId=125641988.

14. 550 U.S. 124 (2007).

15. 550 U.S. 124.

16. Available at http://www.newyorker.com/magazine/2013/03/11/heavyweight-ruth-bader-ginsburg.

17. Stephen Breyer, "On Reading Proust," interview by Ioanna Kohler, *New York Review of Books*, November 7, 2013.

18. Stephen Breyer, *Making Our Democracy Work—A Judge's View*, New York: Vintage (2010) at 191–92.

19. Stephen Breyer, *The Court and the World: American Law and the New Global Realities*, New York: Knopf (2015).

20. 302 U.S. 319 (1937). The Court later overruled *Palko* in *Benton v. Maryland* 395 U.S. 784 (1969).

21. *Buck v. Bell*, 274 U.S. 200 (1927); Erwin Chemerinsky, *The Case against the Supreme Court*, New York: Viking (2014).

22. *Zivotofsky v. Kerry*, 576 U.S. (2015).

23. *Larson v. Valente*, 456 U.S. 228, 224 (1982).

24. *Town of Greece v. Galloway*, 572 U.S. (2014).

25. *Galloway v. Town of Greece*, 681 F.3d 20 (2d Cir. 2012).

26. *Lee v. Weisman*, 505 U.S. 577, 641 (1992) (Scalia, J. dissenting). The record showed that about two-thirds of Greece's prayers over a decade invoked "Jesus," "Christ," "Your Son," or "the Holy Spirit," and 85 percent in the 18 months before start of the lawsuit.

27. 134 S. Ct. 1811, 1849.

28. U.S. Constitution, VI, 3.

29. 550 U.S. 124 (2007). It is notable that a Republican Congress termed the law the "Partial Birth Abortion Ban Act." "Partial birth abortion" is a term unknown to the medical lexicon.

30. http://www.huffingtonpost.com/geoffrey-r-stone/our-faithbased-justices_b_46398.html.

31. *Webster v. Reproductive Health Services*, 492 U.S. 490, 532 (1989); *Planned Parenthood of Southeastern Pa. v. Casey*, 505 U.S. 833, 944 (1992) (concurring in part and dissenting in part), reaffirming *Roe v. Wade*.

32. *Id.*

33. By Linda Greenhouse, "It's All Right with Sam," *New York Times*, January 7, 2015. Available at http://www.nytimes.com/2015/01/08/opinion/its-all-right-with-samuel-alito.html.

34. 347 U.S. 483 (1954).

35. 163 U.S. 537 (1896).

36. [N]o religious Test shall ever be required as Qualification to any Office or public Trust under the United States.—U.S. Constitution, VI, 3

37. "Conservatives Complain of Stealth Religious Test." Available at http://www.crosswalk.com/1342318.

38. "The Situation Room: Harriet Miers Nomination," CNN, October 5, 2005. Available at http://transcripts.cnn.com/TRANSCRIPTS/0510/05/sitroom.02.html.

39. By Jonathan Turley, "The Faith of John Roberts," *Los Angeles Times*, July 25, 2005. Durbin subsequently challenged the accuracy of this account, but Turley said he had notes of the interviews and stood by what he wrote, saying he had obtained the information from Durbin himself and had confirmed the story with another person who attended the meeting.

40. Transcript of Hearings of the U.S. Senate Committee on the Judiciary on Nomination of John G. Roberts, Jr., to be Chief Justice of the United States (September 13, 2005) at 146.

41. By Christopher Hitchens, "Quit Tiptoeing Around John Roberts's Faith," August 1, 2005. Available at http://www.slate.com/articles/news_and_politics/fighting_words/2005/08/catholic_justice.html.

42. "Another Look at the Nomination," October 12, 2005. Available at http://www.thedenverchannel.com/news/dr-james-dobson-focus-on-the-family-10_12_05-transcript-1.

43. By E. J. Dionne, Jr., "Faith-Based Hypocrisy," *Washington Post*, October 7, 2005.

44. *Id.*

45. By Elisabeth Bumiller, "Bush Criticized Over Emphasis on Religion of Nominee," *New York Times*, October 13, 2005.

46. By Lynette Clemetson, "Alito Could Be 5th Catholic on Current Supreme Court," *New York Times*, November 1, 2005.

47. *Id.*

48. Leo Rosten, *The Joys of Yiddish*, New York: W.H. Allen (1970). Roberts denied that the argument was chutzpah.

49. *Arizona Free Enterprise Club v. Bennett*, 564 U.S. (2011; italics hers).

4

TWO OF THE EIGHTY-NINE WASP MALE JUSTICES

Marshall and Holmes

[W]e must never forget that it is a Constitution we are expounding.
—John Marshall

The Supreme Court is now 100 percent minority, but it was white Anglo-Saxon male Justices who dominated most of its history. It was eighty-nine white Anglo-Saxon male Justices who largely voted to vindicate the basic rights of excluded minorities to live free of racial, religious, and gender discrimination. Seven white Anglo-Saxon Protestant male Justices were part of the unanimous Court that decided *Brown v. Board of Education*. It was white Anglo-Saxon male Justices who vindicated free speech rights, rights to strike, and rights to decent working conditions. In this chapter, we profile two such Justices, Marshall and Holmes, examine their lives, and see how they molded and shaped the law as it stands today.

JOHN MARSHALL—ELABORATING THE RULE OF LAW

No discussion of the Supreme Court as the guardian of the Constitution can take place without reference to the wisest of its Justices, the fourth

Chief Justice of the United States, John Marshall, who established the seminal doctrine of judicial review in 1803.[1]

Marshall grew up in a log cabin in rural Virginia. The oldest son of an affluent land surveyor, he was home schooled by his parents who gave him a thorough grounding in English literature, poetry, and history. Since his parents had decided that he would become a lawyer, he was also made to study Blackstone's *Commentaries on the Laws of England*, a seminal text in the field of English common law.

He had a stint in the Continental Army under the command of George Washington where he endured the brutal winter at Valley Forge. He became a Federalist through and through. Upon his discharge, he read law at William & Mary, graduated Phi Beta Kappa, and was admitted to the Virginia Bar in 1780.

Marshall began to practice law. A political animal, he nurtured his fledgling law practice with the contacts that came from a political career, having won a seat in the Virginia House of Delegates. After holding a number of other politically appointed posts in the administration of John Adams, he became the fourth Chief Justice of the United States in 1801 at the age of 46.

Anything but a legal scholar, Marshall's genius was that of a consensus builder who arrived at thoughtful, thorough conclusions. He relied on a colleague, Justice Joseph Story, as his legal brain trust to find the precedents supporting his positions.

The principle of judicial review did not originate with Marshall. In *The Federalist Papers*, the principal source for the Framers' intent, Alexander Hamilton wrote that the boundaries of the Constitution "can be preserved in practice . . . through the medium of courts of justice, whose duty it must be to declare all acts contrary to the manifest tenor of the Constitution void."[2] As Justice Stephen Breyer elaborates in his fine book *Making Our Democracy Work: A Judge's View*, the "Constitutional Convention and ratification process resounded with similar language."[3] Hamilton in *The Federalist Papers*[4] asserted that the Constitution must trump any federal law. As Breyer states, "[t]he Constitution is fundamental, it represents the will of the people, and it is the source of lawmaking authority. A statute, by contrast, represents the exercise of constitutionally delegated authority and reflects the will of the people *only indirectly* through their legislators."[5] Declared Hamilton, the "interpretation of the laws is the proper and peculiar province of the courts."

But the judiciary, although said to be a coequal branch of government, is the weakest of the three as it lacks both the sword entrusted to the president and the purse entrusted to Congress. And what is the judiciary to do with its power of review if a broad spectrum of the public disagrees with its decisions?

At the time of ratification of the Constitution, the Hamiltonian/Federalist concept of judicial review remained an unsettled question. Jefferson and the Republicans believed that each of the three departments had the right to decide for itself what its duty was under the Constitution "without any regard to what others may have decided for themselves under a similar question." It didn't turn out that way.

Nowhere in the Constitution itself does it provide that the federal courts have the power to hold an act of Congress or of the president unconstitutional. How did they get this awesome power? The answer is that John Marshall with a deft political hand just seized it.

Marshall, probably with Story's help, wrote the landmark opinion in *Marbury v. Madison* that established judicial review as the foundation of the Supreme Court's constitutional jurisprudence. The facts in the case are an example of baroque politics. On his last day in office in March, President John Adams had named forty-two justices of the peace and sixteen new circuit court judges for the District of Columbia. These were known as the "midnight appointments." Adams signed the commissions; they were sealed by his secretary of state, who just happened to be at the time John Marshall on his way to becoming Chief Justice; but someone didn't get the memo and failed to deliver them to certain of the judges Adams had appointed.

One of the unfortunate men so appointed as a justice of the peace for the District of Columbia was William Marbury, who brought the case. The "midnight appointments" were designed by the Federalists to take control of the judiciary before Thomas Jefferson took office. When Jefferson refused to honor Marbury's appointment, Marbury petitioned the Supreme Court *in the first instance* of a *writ of mandamus*, a court order to compel Jefferson's secretary of state, James Madison, to deliver his commission. You couldn't ask for a better cast of characters.

Marbury invoked the Judiciary Act of 1789, which granted the Supreme Court original jurisdiction to issue writs of mandamus "to any . . .

persons holding office, under the authority of the United States." The problem was that the Judiciary Act, in purporting to confer original jurisdiction on the Supreme Court, flat out contradicted Article III, Section 2 of the Constitution, which said nothing about holding office under the authority of the United States. The Constitution provided that "[i]n all cases affecting ambassadors, other public ministers and consuls, and those in which a state shall be party, the Supreme Court shall have original jurisdiction. In all the other cases before mentioned, the Supreme Court shall have appellate jurisdiction." Marbury's case did not invoke the appellate jurisdiction of the Court, nor was it a case "affecting ambassadors, other public ministers and consuls and those in which a state shall be a party." Accordingly, since the Court lacked jurisdiction to hear Marbury's case, Marbury lost even though he had a right to the commission, and Madison and Jefferson won. But there was more to it than that.

It is trite law that if a court lacks jurisdiction, it has no power to act, so once Marshall determined there was no jurisdiction, the case should have been closed. Courts should not give advisory opinions, or "neighborly advice." Marshall, however, found that Marbury was entitled to his commission since delivery was a ministerial act of the executive branch. The right, having been established, the remedy of mandamus, a legal remedy seeking to require public officials to do what they are supposed to do, would lie, and he could order the new president, Thomas Jefferson, to deliver the commission. But Marbury had invoked a statute that was trumped by the Constitution. So in what lawyers call *dicta*—judicial musings not necessary to a decision in which judges try to show how smart they are—Marshall elaborated a hierarchy of law declaring the Hamiltonian/Federalist view that a statute of Congress that conflicted with the Constitution was invalid.

The rule he enunciated was that of judicial review—that "[i]t is emphatically the province and duty of the judicial department to say what the law is;" that the Supreme Court had the power to hold acts of Congress, of the president, and of the states, unconstitutional; that we were a government of law, not men; and that all law and all public acts, including those of the president, must pass Constitutional muster to be valid. It was not only, as Breyer puts it, a "judicial tour de force," it was a coup d'état. Marshall assumed for the Supreme Court powers that the Constitution did not expressly delegate to the judiciary. The article of faith that it is "the province and duty of the judicial department to say what the law is" has left an indelible impression on the law for over two centuries.

The judiciary was now established as a coequal branch of government, serving as a "check and balance" on and to the executive and the legislative branches of government. The Constitution was to become a living document with the Court the guardian of the Constitution. As Marshall observed in 1819, "we must not forget, it is a Constitution we are expounding."[6] The Court would use this newly acquired power sparingly. Following *Marbury*, it would not declare another act of Congress unconstitutional for fifty-four years until it decided *Dred Scott v. Sandford*.[7] State enactments were another matter.

There was one other battle to be fought in Marshall's power grab: how to make the executive branch of government implement the Court's decisions. This would take patience. *Marbury* was easy. Marshall dismissed Marbury's case for lack of jurisdiction even though he held that Marbury was right. Thus he decided in Jefferson's favor so he did not have to face the problem of taking on the president. Jefferson was happy to relegate Marbury's commission to the dustbin of history. Had Marshall ordered Jefferson to give Marbury his judicial commission, and had Jefferson refused, he would have provoked a constitutional crisis. But he didn't. Still, the camel's nose was in the tent. It was a *constitution* Marshall was expounding. Other cases that took on the executive branch would present a more complex, difficult and different sort of problem.

Neither the Constitution nor Marshall's decision in *Marbury* deals with how the decisions of the Court are to be implemented. This is left to the executive branch of government, and to the great respect that the public must have for the Court's interpretations if they are to have any meaning. The Court's legitimacy must come from popular acceptance of its decisions, and from their implementation by the executive. If the Court's decisions stray too far off the spectrum, the citizenry will reject them, and possibly elect to disobey them. They can also elect presidents and senators who will appoint Justices to eventual vacancies who are more correct thinkers.

In the early 1800s, Georgia had been having some problems with its Cherokee neighbors. The Cherokees occupied some lands in the north Georgia mountains where gold had been discovered in 1828 near Dahlonega, the subsequent location of a U.S. mint. There was a gold rush on, and the Georgians wanted to exploit the real estate. The Cherokees had challenged the constitutionality of removal laws. These were laws enacted by Congress and by Georgia that established a purported basis for seizing Cherokee lands and distributing the acreage to the state's white citizens. The Cherokee Nation asked the Supreme Court for an injunction, claiming that Georgia's state legislature had created laws that "go directly to annihilate the Cherokees as a political society, and to seize, for the use of Georgia, the lands of the nation which have been assured to them by the United States in solemn treaties repeatedly made and still in force."[8]

Marshall's reaction was extraordinary. He said, "If courts were permitted to indulge their sympathies, a case better calculated to excite them can scarcely be imagined."[9] But not wishing to embroil itself in such a politically charged dispute, the Supreme Court did what it often does when perplexed about the policy implications of its decisions: it ducked and threw out the case on dubious technical grounds. Marshall did find, however, that the Cherokee Indians were a "domestic, dependent nation." In words defining Indian law, Marshall famously said that the relationship of the tribes "to the United States resembles that of a ward to his guardian."[10] So they had no right to independent nationhood under the Constitution. Naturally, the Cherokees resisted Georgia's efforts to remove them, and the issue lived on to be resolved another day.

Samuel Worcester, a Vermonter, was a sort of "outside agitator." A missionary engaged in preaching the Gospel to the Cherokees, he also advised them on their legal and political rights with regard to the removal laws. The Cherokee's appeal to Andrew Jackson, Congress, and the Georgia legislature largely fell on deaf ears. So Worcester and others counseled them to seek relief in the U.S. Supreme Court. Worcester's stirring of the soup made him a marked man. He had been "residing" on Cherokee land without a license in violation of a Georgia law that required "all white persons residing within the limits of the Cherokee Nation" to take an oath to support the laws of Georgia, which would include laws providing for Cherokee removal. Worcester declined to take the loyalty oath. Three times arrested for violating the law, Worcester stood trial, was convicted, and sentenced to four years of hard labor. Worcester appealed to the Supreme Court.[11]

Worcester's supporters hoped that his vindication would establish the Cherokee's rights to their lands. As it unfolded, no such luck. Georgia sadly evicted the Cherokee from their ancestral lands in a forced migration known as the "Trail of Tears." The Cherokee encountered exposure, disease, and starvation while en route to their destinations. Many died, including 2,000–6,000 of the 16,542 relocated Cherokee. Some of them moved out West with the gold miners, hence, Cherokee, California.

Back to Worcester. Marshall held that the Georgia statute criminalizing the presence of non–Native Americans on an Indian reservation was unconstitutional as the federal government has the exclusive authority to deal with Indian nations. The Constitution provides that "[t]he Congress shall have the Power . . . To regulate Commerce with foreign Nations, and among the several States, and with the Indian Tribes."[12] Accordingly, Marshall set aside the conviction and ordered Georgia to release Worcester. He had flung the gauntlet.

Subservience of the executive branch to Court rulings was essential if the rule of law was to be "faithfully executed." As shrewd as Marshall was in not taking on Jefferson in the *Marbury* case, he almost tore apart the Union in the *Worcester* case. The story may be apocryphal, but Andrew Jackson's indignant response to the *Worcester* decision ordering the release of Worcester was "John Marshall has made his decision: now let him enforce it." This comment probably came from a letter Jackson wrote in connection with the *Worcester* case when he wrote, "[T]he decision of the Supreme Court has fell still born, and they find they cannot coerce Georgia to yield to its mandate."[13] The "mandate" was that Worcester be freed.

Georgia was not so quick to release Worcester, and Andrew Jackson was not about to send troops to Atlanta to enforce the Court's mandate as Eisenhower a century later did in Little Rock. Nor was he to send 127 U.S. marshals to Georgia as John Kennedy did in Mississippi in 1962. Jackson's obduracy might have created an unfortunate confrontation between the Court and the president, except that Georgia freed Worcester after several months.

Why is this tale of a nineteenth-century gold-rush flap involving an itinerant preacher and community activist, jailed for political agitation on an Indian reservation in northwest Georgia, relevant to a partisan Supreme Court? The point is that Marshall kicked it all off in the early days of our country with the sine qua non for establishing judicial power for centuries to come, and the Court has to this day exercised this power by making policy choices that are more politically than legally informed. It was here that the Court asserted its jurisdiction to curtail the excesses of the other two branches of government and to order compliance with its mandates. If the Court was ever to protect and define the basic constitutional rights of unpopular minorities, it required this appropriation of an awesome judicial power to interpret and define the law. And the indispensable feature was the power to make all of the people, including the executive branch of the government, submit to its mandates. Thus began the rule of law in the United States of America.

In a bloodless revolution through the power of words and ideas, Marshall had established the principle of judicial review (it is "the province and duty of the judicial department to say what the law is"), and the executive branches of the state and federal government, as well as everyone else, had to comply with the Court's decrees.

OLIVER WENDELL HOLMES—ELABORATING THE RULES FOR FREE SPEECH

Oliver Wendell Holmes, Jr., became a member of the Massachusetts Bar on March 4, 1867. He was almost 26 years old, having lost three years while he fought in the Civil War. Before he could be admitted, Holmes was to be examined on the law by a crusty old Boston lawyer called Asaph Churchill. "Good morning, Holmes," Churchill said. "How is your father? We were at college together. Afterward, I believe he was not so successful at law as at writing verse. . . . Now, Holmes, who owns the land between high and low water mark?" "The owner of the adjoining land," Holmes answered. Let off thus rather easily, he passed.[14] Things were quite clubby in those days.

Holmes came from an intellectually rich background, which he could trace back to the American Revolutionary War. His great-grandfather Wendell on his mother's side was a judge. His grandfather Reverend Abiel Holmes was an author and Calvinist minister given to things of the mind. His father, Oliver Wendell Holmes, Sr., had abandoned legal studies to become a highly respected doctor, a famed poet, and the renowned author of a collection of essays titled *The Autocrat of the Breakfast Table*. His mother, Amelia Lee Jackson, was the granddaughter of a Cabot, the daughter of an esteemed Massachusetts Supreme Judicial Court justice. No wonder Holmes expressed his ambition in this fashion: "Life is action and passion. I think it is required of a man that he should share the action and passion of his time at peril of being judged not to have lived." Service to the nation was embedded in his DNA.

Holmes Sr. achieved particular fame in 1830 with the poem "Old Ironsides," in which he protested the proposed scrapping of the frigate U.S.S. *Constitution*, victor in a naval battle in the War of 1812 with H.M.S. *Guerrière*. The *Constitution*, a 44-gunner, was one of the original six frigates of the U.S. Navy:

> Her deck, once red with heroes' blood,
> Where knelt the vanquished foe,
> When winds were hurrying o'er the flood,
> And waves were white below,
> No more shall feel the victor's tread,
> Or know the conquered knee;—
> The harpies of the shore shall pluck
> The eagle of the sea!

The "harpies of the shore" relented, and "Old Ironsides" remains the oldest commissioned ship in the world still afloat.

As a lawyer, and as a law professor at Harvard, Holmes was said to know more law than anyone. In November 1880, he gave the first of twelve Lowell lectures, a historical analysis of the common law, to a general audience of Boston culture vultures. His father had been the Lowell lecturer some twenty-seven years before when he had spoken about the English poets and ended his talk with a recitation of some verses of his own. In the audience in 1880 were members of Holmes's family: Dr. and Mrs. Holmes; the lecturer's wife, Fanny, and his sister; members of the legal community, including the young Louis Brandeis, the cream of Harvard Law's professoriate; and Boston Brahmins from the world of banking. Many were friends of the lecturer's parents. After famously stating to the chagrin of some of his colleagues that the "life of the law has not been logic; it has been experience," he declared his overarching judicial philosophy: "The very considerations which judges most rarely mention, and always with an apology, are the secret root from which the law draws all the juices of life. I mean of course considerations of what is expedient for the community concerned."

The bankers in attendance looked at one another in abject disbelief. Surely the "community" referred to was the Brahmins, the only community they knew. Surely, "community" did not refer to the most recently arrived American citizens, such as the Jews, the Irish, and the Italians. If it did, Holmes was advocating judicial legislation, governmental regulation, "an assault on liberty to whom a measles sign on the front door would have been an affront to the castle which was a man's home."[15]

Despite Holmes's heretical thinking, the governor of Massachusetts appointed him to the Supreme Judicial Court, the state's highest, in 1882. He became the chief justice in 1899. Although largely aloof from partisan politics, Holmes was a Republican in the tradition of his family. President Theodore Roosevelt was looking for a "party man" to appoint to the Supreme Court. As TR wrote to Senator Henry Cabot Lodge on July 10, 1902,

> [A man] is not in my judgment fitted for the position unless he is a party man . . . Marshall rendered such invaluable service because he was a statesman of the national type, like Adams who appointed him, like Washington whose mantle fell on him. Taney was a curse on our national life because he belonged to the wrong party and faithfully carried out the criminal and foolish views of the party which stood for such a construction of the Constitution as would have rendered it impossible to preserve the national life [referring, of course, to the *Dred Scott* decision].

Roosevelt appointed Holmes to the Court December 4, 1902. Holmes was 61 years old.

Although Holmes hated to dissent, he was known as the "great dissenter." Actually, this may refer to the quality rather than the quantity of his dissenting opinions. In his twenty-nine years on the Court, out of 5,950 cases on which he sat in which decisions were rendered, Holmes dissented only 173 times, as compared with 1,633 dissents by other Justices. Dividing the total dissents, 1,806, by the number of Justices, it appears that proportionately, Holmes dissented less than his brethren.

One of Holmes's biographers, Catherine Drinker Bowen, argues,[16]

Time, events, history itself, would prove his dissents. One by one they became law. . . . Child labor can be regulated by Congress.[17] . . . The liberty of the citizen to do what he pleases does not mean he can force other men to work twelve hours a day.[18] . . . [As he said,] "I think the strike a lawful instrument in the universal struggle for life."[19]

Holmes is best remembered for his opinions elaborating the First Amendment's guaranty of free speech. Freedom of speech, he said in a series of monumental dissents, even in wartime, may not be constitutionally abridged unless there is a "clear and present danger" that it will bring about some evil that Congress may lawfully proscribe.[20] He thought,

[T]he best test of truth is the power of the thought to get itself accepted in the competition of the market. . . . That, at any rate, is the theory of our Constitution. It is an experiment, as all life is an experiment. Every year, if not every day, we have to wager our salvation upon some prophecy based upon imperfect knowledge. While that experiment is part of our system, I think that we should be eternally vigilant against attempts to check *the expression of opinions that we loathe* and believe to be fraught with death, unless they so imminently threaten immediate interference with the lawful and pressing purposes of the law that an immediate check is required to save the country.[21]

Holmes epitomized his conception of the First Amendment in perhaps his most memorable statement: "Free thought—not free thought for those who agree with us but *freedom for the thought we hate.*"[22] This observation would become his most lasting legacy.

The free speech protections of the First Amendment are not absolute. No one has the right to speak whenever or however he or she pleases, or to use any form of speech he or she chooses. The expression of speech must be "reasonable in time, place and manner." It must be on a matter of public concern. The criminalization of obscenity, for example, is constitutionally permissible. What precisely constitutes obscenity has yet to be determined. Justice Stewart famously said, "I know it when I see it."[23]

The states are free reasonably to regulate the time or place of speech to protect the privacy of the home or the solemnity of a religious service, provided that such regulation is not based as well on the content of the speech. So is the interdiction of "fighting words," personally abusive words likely to insult the listener and provoke violent action, also provided that such restriction is not content based. Similarly, an ordinance prohibiting noisy trucks in residential areas at hours of repose might be OK, but not OK if the ordinance prohibits only speech criticizing elected officials. But free speech does protect from censorship unpopular speech; hate speech; offensive speech; unwanted speech in a public place; particular forms of speech, however immoderate or intemperate; and speech that the state deems to be an unsuitable level of discourse.

The Supreme Court applied this principle in 1971 to reverse the defendant's conviction in the landmark "fuck the draft" case.[24] Cohen, a Vietnam War protester, had worn a jacket festooned with this once unprintable epithet inside a corridor of the Los Angeles Municipal Courthouse. He testified that he wore the jacket knowing that the words were on the jacket as a means of informing the public of the depth of his feelings against the Vietnam War and the draft. The California court convicted Cohen of disturbing the peace and sentenced him to 30 days' imprisonment. As for the public utterance of the f-word, the Supreme Court said, "[W]e cannot indulge the facile assumption that one can forbid particular words without also running a substantial risk of suppressing ideas in the process."[25]

Holmes's principle was put on further trial in a case involving 30 neo-Nazis who, brandishing swastikas, announced plans to parade in Nazi-style uniforms through Skokie, Illinois, a predominantly Jewish community of about 70,000, which included in its population 5,000 Holocaust survivors.[26] The case captured international attention. There was testimony in the record that the demonstration might lead to violence. The City of Skokie subsequently enacted three ordinances designed to prevent the march. One required applicants for parades and public assemblies to post a bond to cover public liability and property damage. The second prohibited the dissemination of material inciting religious or racial hatred. The third prohibited public demonstrations by members of political parties wearing military-style uniforms. When the city refused to issue a permit for the march, the Nazis, represented by the American Civil Liberties Union, sued in federal and state court. The lower federal courts declared the ordinances unconstitutional as violating the free speech rights of the Nazis. The Supreme Court, with

Blackmun and White dissenting, let stand the decisions of the lower courts. The Nazis were free to march in Skokie. Later, they called off the plan and marched instead in Chicago.

Blackmun dissenting wrote that the Skokie case "affords the Court the opportunity to consider whether . . . there is no limit whatsoever to the exercise of free speech. There indeed may be no such limit, but when citizens assert . . . that the proposed demonstration is . . . taunting and overwhelmingly offensive . . . that assertion . . . deserves to be examined." He then fell back on Holmes. "It just might fall into the same category as one's right to cry 'fire' in a crowded theater, for 'the character of every act depends upon the circumstances in which it is done.'"[27]

Building on the *Skokie* jurisprudence, the Court considered a situation that arose in St. Paul, Minnesota. In the pre-dawn hours of June 21, 1990, a group of teenagers, including the petitioner, assembled a wooden cross crudely made from broken chair legs, and burned it inside the fenced yard of a black family. While the conduct could have been punished under a number of stern and familiar laws proscribing criminal behavior, St. Paul elected to proceed under its Bias-Motivated Crime Ordinance, which provided that anyone placing "on public or private property" an object "including . . . a burning cross or Nazi swastika" that arouses "anger, alarm or resentment" in others "on the basis of race, color, creed, religion or gender" is guilty of a misdemeanor. Petitioner moved to dismiss on the ground that the ordinance was unconstitutional under the First Amendment. The Supreme Court unanimously reversed the lower courts, which had denied the motion. In writing for the Court, which struck down the St. Paul ordinance, Scalia channeled Holmes in vindicating freedom for the thought we hate: "Let there be no mistake about our belief that burning a cross in someone's front yard is reprehensible. But St. Paul has sufficient means at its disposal to prevent such behavior without adding the First Amendment to the fire."[28] St. Paul lost; hate speech won.

The Court's most recent hate speech case was *Snyder v. Phelps*.[29] On March 3, 2006, Marine Lance Corporal Matthew Snyder was killed accidentally while in the line of duty in Iraq. His father selected the Catholic church in his hometown of Westminster, Maryland, as the place for the funeral service. Fred Phelps founded the Westboro Baptist Church in Topeka, Kansas, in 1955. One of Westboro's central tenets is that God hates and punishes the United States for its tolerance of homosexuality in the military. It often expresses its views by picketing military funerals, and it has picketed nearly six hundred funerals in twenty years. Phelps and members of his family decided to travel to Maryland to picket. They selected as picketing sites public streets near the Maryland State House, the Naval Academy at Annapolis, and Matthew Snyder's funeral. The picketers selected a site on public land roughly one thousand feet—and separated by several buildings—from the church where the funeral service occurred. The group sang hymns, recited Bible verses, and displayed their signs for about thirty minutes before the funeral. The signs stated, among other things, "America Is Doomed," "Thank God for Dead Soldiers," "Priests Rape Boys," and "God Hates Fags."

Snyder's father, who said that his son was a "hero" and the "love of my life," sued Westboro and the Phelpses for intentional infliction of emotional distress. Snyder admitted that he could see only the tops of the picket signs as he drove to the funeral and that he did not see what was written on the signs until later that night when he watched news broadcasts on television. After a jury trial, the trial court awarded Snyder $5 million in compensatory and punitive damages. The Phelpses appealed on grounds that the First Amendment guaranteed their right of expression; the Supreme Court agreed, and reversed the money judgment. Writing for the eight-Justice majority, Chief Justice Roberts reaffirmed the principle that the First Amendment reflects "a profound national commitment to the principle that debate on public issues should be uninhibited, robust and wide-open." He said, "The arguably inappropriate or controversial character of a statement is irrelevant to the question of whether it deals with a matter of public concern."[30] Roberts found it irrelevant that the expression of Westboro's views may have been "particularly hurtful" to Matthew Snyder because "Westboro's choice added to [Snyder's] incalculable grief."[31] It is hard to conceive of a more sorry result coming from the application of a lofty principle.

Summarizing his argument, Roberts wrote in terms that Holmes would have relished. "Speech is powerful! It can stir people to action, move them to tears of both joy and sorrow, and—as it did here—inflict great pain. . . . As a Nation we have chosen a different course—to protect even hurtful speech on public issues to ensure that we don't stifle public debate."[32] Hate speech had won another victory in the Supreme Court.

Unlike Germany, France, and Canada, America has no laws forbidding hate speech. When such laws have been enacted or civilly punished as happened in the *Snyder* case, they have been uniformly struck down as unconstitutional. In America, we "have chosen a different course." In Germany, Nazi music and iconography are banned. In France, the satirical French weekly magazine *Charlie Hébdo* has been the object of innumerable lawsuits for its satires of political figures and of Islam. The Canadian constitution grants everyone freedom of thought, belief, opinion, and expression, subject to "such reasonable limits prescribed by law as can be demonstrably justified in a free and democratic society." The Canadian Criminal Code forbids "hate propaganda," meaning "any writing, sign or visible representation that advocates or promotes genocide." "Genocide" is defined as the destruction of "any section of the public distinguished by colour, race, religion, ethnic origin or sexual orientation."[33] The Canadian Supreme Court, in banning hate speech, said quite tellingly that the "[t]he Holocaust did not begin in the gas chambers. It began with words." But as Roberts said in *Snyder*, "speech concerning public affairs is more than self-expression; it is the essence of self-government."[34]

The debate over hate speech has intensified with the rise of Islamic terror. On January 7, 2015, there was the horrific massacre at the Paris offices of *Charlie Hébdo*, whose editor Stéphane Charbonnier, known as "Charb," was gunned down in cold blood along with eleven others. Two days later, another terrorist murdered four Jews in a Kosher supermarket near Vincennes. Three police officers also died at the hands of the terrorists. Over a million people took to the streets to voice their conviction that civilization will not bow to nihilistic terror in any form, and that freedom of speech is an everlasting value of free peoples everywhere.

Elements of the liberal community argued for governmental censorship of cartoons and articles that might offend Islamists or, in the alternative, that media organizations should self-regulate and refrain from publishing cartoons and commentaries satirizing Islam, the prophet Mohammed, or other marginalized communities. On the other side of the debate were Holmesian free speech advocates such as Ayaan Hirsi Ali who contended that we must not allow terrorists to define the permissible scope of free expression. She wrote for the *Daily Beast*, "We need to stand up for free speech. This is who we are, these are our values. And yes, our values include tolerance of those who wish to make fun of religion. In the press, in the universities, in the schools, we have to make sure that Muslim immigrants who come to the West understand that our rules protect satirists from jihadists, and not the other way round."[35]

Mathias Dopfner, chef executive officer of the giant media conglomerate Axel Springer, which includes *Die Welt*, announced he would republish the front cover of *Charlie Hébdo* the day after the massacre in solidarity with the murdered journalists. Holmes's "freedom for the thought we hate" is alive and well in the world—even in countries such as Germany that punish hate speech as a crime.

The Court's attitude toward free speech is somewhat more partisan when it comes to speech about abortion. The hostility of the Court's conservative majority to abortion rights could not be clearer. The conservative Justices are just salivating for a case where they can overrule or further chip away at *Roe v. Wade*. An easy, fact-specific, free speech case unanimously struck down a Massachusetts law creating an overly broad thirty-five-foot buffer zone around abortion clinics within which protesters and counselors could not attempt to talk women out of exercising their reproductive rights.[36] There is something ugly and offensive about a perfect stranger approaching a woman contemplating an abortion and asking her whether she has thought about her decision enough and explored all the alternatives. And there is an element of, as Professor Chafee put it, "Your right to swing your arms ends just where the other man's nose begins."[37] One might ask, where does the nose begin when the issue is abortion?

To fairly compete in the marketplace of ideas, and be truly free, speech must be robust and provocative and even disagreeable. The First Amendment protects annoying and disturbing and salacious speech as well as a "motherhood" flag-waving speech on the Fourth of July. "Freedom for the thought we hate." The scorned and rejected of all stripes, expressing bad ideas and distributing revolutionary pamphlets, have exercised their free speech rights on public streets since the dawn of the republic.

The Court held the Massachusetts statute unconstitutional since the buffer zone could have been more narrowly drawn. Fifteen feet might have been buffer zone enough. In an unprecedented move, the Court even "suggested" that Massachusetts could consider an ordinance such as that adopted in New York City, that not only prohibits obstructing access to a clinic, but also criminalizes following and harassing "another person within 15 feet of the premises of a reproductive facility."[38]

Not much news there. But Justices Alito, Thomas, Kennedy, and Scalia took occasion in separate concurring opinions to blast what they saw as favored treatment for abortion rights activists. They thought the whole set-up abridged free speech, and was flat out unconstitutional. "Today's opinion carries forward this court's practice of giving abortion rights activists a pass when it comes to suppressing the free-speech rights of their opponents," Scalia thundered in his inimitably mordant style. "There is an entirely separate, abridged edition of the First Amendment applicable to speech against abortion."[39] In so writing, he expressed a pronounced bias in favor of "freedom for the thoughts we love," not only within earshot but even in your face.

CAMPAIGN FINANCE AND DEREGULATION—SPEECH UNKNOWN TO MARSHALL AND HOLMES

Once upon a time, political liberals were all for Holmesian concepts of free speech since free discussion, as they saw it, acted as a change agent in society. The doctrine reached its apex in the 1964 decision *New York Times v. Sullivan*[40] (a decision which Donald Trump says he wants to overturn so he can more readily sue media organizations he doesn't like), where the Court ruled that First Amendment values precluded a public official from suing for libel unless he could establish by "clear and convincing evidence" actual knowledge of the falsity of the publication or reckless disregard for the truth. "The Constitution accords citizens and press an unconditional freedom to criticize official conduct," said Justice Goldberg in his concurring opinion.[41] Obama has invoked American freedom of speech as a model for other liberal democracies such as France and Germany, where its value is controversial. But how can America hold itself out as a model for other countries when under our Constitution political influence is built on money?

There then is the issue of what constitutes speech. In recent years, conservative Justices have turned First Amendment doctrine on its

head. Speech has become an elastic concept. It is not necessarily limited to standing on a soapbox in Union Square. Forms of speech may
extend to the offensive conduct of topless female panhandlers in Times
Square, a few blocks uptown. As we have seen, it may extend to flag
burning or burning a fiery cross as a form of symbolic expression. Con-
ceptions of free speech can be used to protect entrenched political and
economic interests as well. Commercial free speech permits tobacco
growers, airlines, big pharma, and oil interests to saturate the marketplace with information designed not to expand knowledge, but to max-
imize profits. Lincoln Caplan, a senior research scholar at Yale Law
School, in a brilliant article in the *American Scholar*, observes, "However sacred the idea of free speech remains for us today, we should recognize that its most fervent champions are not standing up for mistrusted
outliers, such as Holmes had in mind, or for the dispossessed and pow-
erless. Today's advocates do the bidding of insiders—the super-rich and
the ultra-powerful, the airline, drug, petroleum, and tobacco industries,
all the winners in America's winner-take-all society."[42]

The Court held that free speech includes the expenditure of money
to finance political campaigns. The last straw is the Court's opinion in
Citizens United v. Federal Election Commission,[43] a 5-4 decision upholding corporate free speech, and validating the heavy reliance of politics on money as the source of influence and power. *Citizens United* was
a constitutional attack, launched by a politically conservative organization, on Section 203 of the McCain-Feingold campaign finance law,
which limited "independent" corporate spending in elections and made
it illegal for a corporation (or a union, for that matter) to disseminate
political messages within sixty days of a primary or thirty days of a
general election. At issue was the exhibition of a corporation-financed
film called *Hillary* within the proscribed period. The film was critical of
Hillary Clinton.[44] The Court struck down the McCain-Feingold ban
under the Free Speech Clause of the First Amendment. Public-interest
organizations reported five years after the decision that, as a result of
Citizens United, corporations and other associations had expended
more than a billion dollars on political campaigns, and the Center for
Responsive Politics estimated that business had outspent labor by about
fifteen to one.

Scalia's *Citizens United* concurrence argued that the First Amendment protected corporations as well as individuals. "Free speech pro-

tects speech, not speakers," he stated. There, Scalia took on the dissent for daring to encroach on his originalist preserve by venturing to discuss the "original understandings of the Constitution." The dissent, he said, "never shows why 'the freedom of speech that was the right of Englishmen' did not include the freedom to speak in association with other individuals, including association in the corporate form. To be sure, in 1791 (as now) corporations could pursue only the objectives set forth in their charters; but the dissent provides no evidence that their speech in the pursuit of those objectives could be censored."[45]

Citizens United was the most partisan decision since *Bush v. Gore*, one that Ginsburg called the "most disappointing" Supreme Court decision in her twenty-two-year tenure "because of what has happened to elections in the United States and the huge amount of money it takes to run for office."[46]

The partisan divide in the Court over free speech shakes out between the liberal Justices who favor governmental regulation of certain kinds of corruption-tainted speech and conservative Justices who want to expand free speech protections dramatically in a way that would go so far as to weaken or curtail many forms of economic regulation.[47] In *Reed v. Town of Gilbert* this past Term, the Court considered an Arizona town ordinance regulating various categories of public signage.[48] The ordinance, while imposing no regulation on what a sign might say, prescribed differing restrictions as to size, number, and time of permitted display, depending on whether the sign's content was "ideological," "political," or that of "temporary directional signs relating to a qualifying event." A "qualifying event" the Town of Gilbert defined as a meeting sponsored by a religious or charitable organization. The code treated ideological signs most favorably; next, political signage; and least favorably, temporary directional signs such as "This Way to the Church Fair." Gilbert did not discriminate against the content of the signage, but most certainly its subject matter. Thomas wrote the opinion for a unanimous Court, striking down Gilbert's ordinance under a strict scrutiny standard. "Strict scrutiny" is a red light in Supreme Court jurisprudence—a strong presumption against "constitutionality," the term the Court uses when it wants to strike down a statute as an automatic violation of the First Amendment. To survive strict scrutiny, a government must show that the law under attack is "narrowly tailored to serve compelling state interests," an almost impossible feat. "Intermediate scrutiny" is a yellow light that might call for more of a rule-of-reason analysis where a law reasonably regulates the "time, place or manner" of speech.

Kagan, in a concurring opinion, expressed herself with the unmistakable bluntness of her native West Side of Manhattan. The Town of Gilbert's rationalization for its discriminatory ordinance, she wrote, didn't "pass strict scrutiny, intermediate scrutiny or *even the laugh test*."[49]

What is especially interesting about the *Town of Gilbert* case, once you penetrate its almost unfathomable doctrinal verbiage, is that Thomas and his four conservative colleagues probably agreed with the Town of Gilbert, as well as the lower courts, that the ordinance at issue was not content based. "Content based" is an analytical tool the Court has used in First Amendment cases to mean instances of blatant censorship. That is where the government passes a law calculated to promote or suppress an idea, usually to avoid criticism directed at, you guessed it, the government. Instead, the Court struck down the Town of Gilbert's ordinance, holding that even in the absence of content-based regulation, "content discrimination" targeting the topic or *subject matter* of the speech will not pass constitutional muster. Under this analysis, the Town of Gilbert ordinance was automatically subject to strict scrutiny and therefore unconstitutional.

The Court said flatly that the content discrimination approach is "an essential means of protecting freedom of speech even if laws that might seem 'entirely reasonable' will sometimes be 'struck down because of their content-based nature.'" In a concurring opinion, Alito explained the conservatives' expansion of First Amendment doctrine that "[l]imiting speech based on its 'topic' or 'subject' favors those who do not want to disturb the status quo. Such regulations may interfere with democratic self-government and the search for truth."[50] Pure applesauce.

The Court's reasoning would place in jeopardy, among others, laws regulating the sale of securities, providing for consumer protection, drug labeling, outlawing misleading advertising, and restricting telemarketing. No wonder three of the Court's four liberal Justices shuddered. While concurring in the result, the liberals put down a cautionary marker that there must be sensible limits to free speech expansion. Breyer warned that content discrimination targeting the subject matter "cannot and should not *always* trigger strict scrutiny. . . . Regulatory programs almost always require content discrimination. And to hold that content discrimination triggers strict scrutiny is to write a recipe for judicial management of ordinary government regulatory authority."[51] Said Kagan, "Because I see no reason why such an easy case calls for us to cast a constitutional pall on reasonable regulations quite unlike the law before us, I concur only in the judgment."[52]

Town of Gilbert, which Kagan called "such an easy case," has already excited a firestorm of controversy. Robert Post, dean of the Yale Law School, said the decision was "so bold and so sweeping" that the Court "could not have thought through its consequences." Floyd Abrams, dean of constitutional lawyers, called the decision a "blockbuster" and predicted a "second look" at the constitutionality of federal and state securities laws and other regulatory statutes.[53]

Some lower courts have already interpreted the case to invalidate such measures as anti-panhandling laws in Illinois, laws in New Hampshire making it illegal to photograph a completed election ballot and show it to others, and laws in South Carolina that banned robocalls speaking on commercial and political topics, but not on other topics. No guarantees, but we may be in for a time of judicially imposed deregulation.

We've come a long way in free speech from Oliver Wendell Holmes. Watch that space!

As for Holmes, he might have wanted to become Chief Justice, but he was a little old for the job—80 years old when Chief Justice White died in 1921. He continued to serve on the Court until his ninetieth year when health forced his retirement.

Holmes continued his life of the mind until his death at age 93. Reflecting on his need to continue his work until he could no longer do so, he poignantly said,

> The riders in a race do not stop short when they reach the goal. There is a little finishing canter before coming to a standstill. There is a time to hear the kind voices of friends and to say to one's self: "The work is done." But just as one says that, the answer comes: "The race is over but the work never is done while the power to work remains." The canter that brings you to a standstill need not be

coming to rest. It cannot be while you still live. For to live is to function. That is all there is in living.

Many believe Holmes was our greatest justice. He loved liberty and the values that enshrine it. He believed in a living Constitution. A man could not have asked for a more worthwhile life.

Notes

1. *Marbury v. Madison*, 5 U.S. 137 (1803).
2. Federalist 78 (Alexander Hamilton).
3. Note 37, *supra*.
4. *Id.* at 78, 81.
5. Breyer at 7.
6. *McCulloch v. Maryland*, 17 U.S. 316, 407 (1819).
7. 60 U.S. 393 (1857).
8. *Cherokee Nation v. Georgia*, 31 U.S. 1, 15 (1832).
9. 31 U.S., *supra*, at 15.
10. 31 U.S., *supra*, at 17.
11. *Worcester v. Georgia*, 31 U.S. 515 (1832).
12. Constitution, Art. I, Sec. 8.
13. David Loth, *Chief Justice John Marshall and The Growth of the American Republic*, New York: W.W. Norton & Company (1949) at 365.
14. Note 54, *supra*, at 236.
15. *Id.* at 282.
16. Note 54, *supra*, at 418.
17. *Hammer v. Dagenhart*, 247 U.S. 251 (1918).
18. *Lochner v. New York*, 195 U.S. 45 (1905).
19. *Coppage v. Kansas*, 236 U.S. 1 (1915); *Truax v. Corrigan*, 257 U.S. 312 (1921), reaffirming the statement he had made in *Plant v. Woods*, 176 Mass 492 (1900).
20. *Gitlow v. New York*, 268 U.S. 652, 673 (1925).
21. *Abrams v. United States*, 250 U.S. 616, 630 (1919).
22. *United States v. Schwimmer*, 279 U.S. 644, 655 (1929); Anthony Lewis, *Freedom for the Thought We Hate—A Biography of the First Amendment*, New York: Basic Books (2007).
23. *Jacobellis v. Ohio*, 378 U.S. 184, 197 (1964).
24. *Cohen v. California*, 403 U.S. 15 (1971).
25. *Id.* at 26.
26. *Smith v. Collin*, 439 U.S. 916 (1978).

27. Citing Holmes's opinion in *Schenck v. United States*, 249 U.S. 47, 52 (1910).

28. *R.A. v. City of St. Paul*, 505 U.S. 377 (1992).

29. 562 U.S. (2011).

30. Internal quotation marks omitted.

31. 562 U.S. Slip op. at 10.

32. *Id*. at 15.

33. Criminal Code of Canada §§ 318–20.

34. 562 U.S. Slip op. at 6. Internal quotation marks omitted.

35. Available at http://www.thedailybeast.com/articles/2015/01/08/ayaan-hirsi-ali-our-duty-is-to-keep-charlie-hebdo-alive.html.

36. *McCullen v. Coakley* (2014).

37. Zechariah Chafee, "Freedom of Speech in War Time," 32 Harvard Law Rev. 932, 957 (1919).

38. N.Y.C. Admin Code §8-803(a)(3) (2014).

39. *Id*. Slip op. at 1.

40. 376 U.S. 254 (1964).

41. *Id*. at 305.

42. By Lincoln Caplan, "The Embattled First Amendment," *American Scholar* (March 4, 2015). Available at https://theamericanscholar.org/the-embattled-first-amendment/-.Vb4aPoukJpw.

43. 558 U.S. 310 (2010).

44. Ironically, Clinton, if elected president, may get to appoint the successor of one of the Justices in the *Citizens United* majority, Kennedy.

45. 558 U.S. Slip op. at 1.

46. Remarks at an evening sponsored by Duke University Law School, July 29, 2015. Reported by the *New York Times* on "FirstDraft. Jul.30." Available at http://www.nytimes.com/politics/first-draft/2015/07/30/today-in-politics-polls-keep-bolstering-a-trump-seemingly-impervious-to-scrubbing/#post-mb-9.

47. By Adam Liptak, "Court's Free-Speech Expansion Has Far-Reaching Consequences," *New York Times*, August 17, 2015. Available at http://www.nytimes.com/2015/08/18/us/politics/courts-free-speech-expansion-has-far-reaching-consequences.html.

48. *Reed v. Town of Gilbert*, 576 U.S. (2015).

49. *Id*. Slip op. at 6.

50. *Id*. Slip op. at 1.

51. *Id*. Slip op. at 2 (emphasis in original).

52. *Id*. Slip op. at 7.

53. By Adam Liptak, "Court's Free-Speech Expansion Has Far-Reaching Consequences," note 47, *supra*.

5

THE CATHOLIC SEAT

[I]n the course of 170 years of Catholics on the Supreme Court, it does not appear that the identification of a Justice as a Catholic carries with it predictive value as to his vote.
—Judge John T. Noonan, Jr.[1]

Since there is no longer one Catholic seat on the Court but five, it may be important to see the turns and twists in the road to how we got here. It has become a cliché that a Justice's identification as a Catholic is a strong predictor as to how he or she will vote. This is particularly true on social issues involving faith or morals, such as abortion, separation of church and state, gay rights, family values, and similar issues arising under states' morals legislation.

History has shown us that this has not always been the case.

The first Catholic to fill a seat on the Supreme Court was Roger B. Taney, who served as Chief Justice for 28 years from 1836 to 1864. Taney was the third longest serving Chief Justice behind Marshall (34 years), and Rehnquist (33 years). Andrew Jackson did not appoint Taney to get electoral votes. There was a strong anti-Catholic feeling in the country at the time. The nomination faced vicious criticism on the basis that as a Catholic, Taney was "subservient to a foreign potentate."[2] It was only Taney's extraordinarily close relationship with the president that vouchsafed his appointment.

Taney, the fifth Chief Justice, authored the 1857 decision in *Dred Scott v. Sandford,* holding that slaves were property and could not be freed of their subjugated status by moving from a slave state to a free state.[3] Therefore, they could not sue under the law that allowed a citizen of one state to sue a citizen of another state. The Court's reasoning was grounded in originalism, but it was a partisan decision. The majority of the Justices had been slave owners, and several still owned slaves. Taney elaborated that when the Constitution was ratified, slaves were "a subordinate and inferior class of beings, who had been subjugated to the dominant race." The Court went on to declare the Missouri Compromise of 1820 unconstitutional. It held that

> the right of property in a slave is distinctly and expressly affirmed in the Constitution. . . . [I]t is the opinion of the court that the act of Congress which prohibited a citizen from holding and owning property of this kind in the territory of the United States north of the line therein mentioned, is not warranted by the Constitution, and is therefore void.[4]

The compromise, engineered by the "Great Compromiser" of the Senate, Henry Clay, admitted Missouri to the Union as a slave state, but it prohibited slavery in the former Louisiana Territory north of the parallel 36° 30'. Many historians say that the *Dred Scott* decision was a principal *casus belli* of the Civil War.

Commenting on the decision, Justice Breyer in his book *Making Democracy Work: A Judge's View*[5] says that the Court misunderstood "the law, its own authority and the likely public reaction, [and] refused justice to an individual because of his race."

In 1868, following the Civil War, the Fourteenth Amendment was ratified to counteract the pernicious effect of the *Dred Scott* decision. It granted, among other things, citizenship to "all persons born or naturalized in the United States," which included former slaves recently freed. In addition, it prohibited states from denying any person "life, liberty or property, without due process of law" or to "deny to any person within its jurisdiction the equal protection of the laws." In litigation before the Supreme Court, the Fourteenth Amendment has been cited more than any other provision of the Constitution. It is the first mention in the Constitution of equality before the law.

Taney was born to a slaveholding family of tobacco planters in Calvert County, Maryland. He believed that African Americans were not citizens of the United States entitled to the equal protection of the laws or the privileges and immunities of national citizenship and that they were born of an "inferior order."[6] If Taney's Catholicism didn't spur his decision, it certainly didn't preclude it. The Jesuits owned slaves in Maryland until 1838. Taney lived long enough to swear in Abraham Lincoln as sixteenth president.

The next Catholic was Edward Douglass White, appointed by Grover Cleveland in 1894. White served as an associate Justice until 1910. White's Mass-going on Sundays supposedly impressed Cleveland. Republican William Howard Taft elevated White to the Chief Justice spot in 1910, and White remained in that august capacity until 1921.

In 1898, William McKinley appointed one of his congressional cronies, Joseph McKenna, who served on the Court until 1925. McKenna was hardly notable as a Justice, but he did write one great dissenting opinion, joined in by Holmes, holding that whether a punishment is "cruel and unusual" was not to be determined by eighteenth-century practice but by evolving societal standards.[7]

Despite the fact that there had been three Catholics sprinkled on the Court over the prior eighty-six years, the "Catholic seat" idea emerged when Justice William R. Day retired in 1922. Martin Manton, chief judge of the U.S. Court of Appeals for the Second Circuit, angled for the position, and President Harding was all set to appoint him. Manton was a Catholic, and his supporters convinced Harding of a need for a Catholic seat.

Religious appointments, just to get a representative of one group or another on the Court, can get a president into trouble, and Manton is a shining example. Manton had come to the federal bench after a stellar career as a criminal defense lawyer. He had represented Charles Becker, a corrupt New York City police lieutenant who, in 1912, orchestrated the Times Square execution of Herman Rosenthal, a small-time bookmaker. Rosenthal decided to cooperate with the authorities and testify about Becker's extorting money for police protection, so Becker ordered the hit. Rosenthal's executioners were members of the Lenox Hill gang: Harry Horowitz, alias "Gyp the Blood,"[8] "Lefty" Louis Rosenberg, "Dago Frank" Cirofici, and "Whitey" Louis. All, including Becker, were convicted of murder and died in the electric chair, which made Becker the first American police officer ever to receive the death penalty.

For his role in representing Becker in a highly profiled case, or perhaps for political reasons,[9] Woodrow Wilson appointed Manton to the Southern District in 1916. At age 36, Manton was the youngest federal judge in the country, and he served on the district court for two years before his elevation to the court of appeals.

Chief Justice William Howard Taft, who knew a "hawk from a hand-saw," blocked Manton's proposed Supreme Court appointment. There was something about Manton that didn't add up.

Manton served on the court of appeals for a little more than two decades from 1918 to 1939, where he sat on panels with Augustus Hand, Learned Hand, and Thomas Swan, the greatest appellate judges of their era. Manton eventually became chief judge of the Second Circuit, and as such, he was in charge of assigning pending cases to particular colleagues on the court for disposition. Frequently he assigned cases in which he had a personal interest to none other than himself. Unfortunately, Manton became, as his prosecutor John P. Cahill, U.S. attorney for the Southern District, painted him at trial, a "merchant of justice."

As a successful lawyer, Manton was rumored to be worth over one million dollars before taking the bench. He had suffered, however, major financial reverses after the great crash of 1929. He had a bagman named Fallon with whom he enjoyed an extraordinarily close relationship. The *New York Times* called Fallon a "salesman of judicial favoritism." The evidence showed that Manton owned stock in companies that were litigants before him and in whose favor he decided. It also showed that at least six litigants paid Fallon more than $175,000, exclusive of purported loans, with the understanding that the funds would be paid or loaned to Manton to procure Manton's judicial favor.

There was no showing that any of the decisions Manton made favoring his financial benefactors were other than correct, but the court held this was beside the point.[10] The conspiracy contemplated the payment of money to a judge to exercise judicial power in favor of the bribe givers without regard to the merits. As the appellate court put it,

> Judicial action, whether just or unjust, right or wrong is not for sale; and if the rule shall ever be accepted that the correctness of judicial action taken for a price removes the stain of corruption and exonerated the judge, the event will mark the first step toward the abandonment of that imperative requisite of even-handed justice.[11]

The *Manton* case of course created a sensation.

Having resigned from the bench, Manton stood convicted of conspiracy to obstruct justice and to defraud the United States. The trial judge sentenced Manton to two years in a federal penitentiary, a remarkably lenient sentence by today's standards, particularly in light of the seriousness of the offense. The federal court had risen to the challenge and purged itself of "corruption in the palace of justice."

Harding was determined to appoint another Catholic to the Catholic seat. Manton's appointment having been torpedoed by Chief Justice Taft, who sensed Manton was corrupt even before his resignation, Harding appointed Justice Pierce Butler, who served from 1923 until his death in 1939.

A former corporate lawyer, Butler was a staunch conservative, and his critics blamed this disposition on his devoutly Catholic beliefs. He was one of the original "Four Horsemen" on the Court, who repeatedly voted in the 1930s to invalidate New Deal legislation.[12] He wrote the opinion upholding the denial of citizenship to a Hungarian immigrant pacifist who refused to swear she would "take up arms" for the United States.[13] He voted to invalidate an Oregon law prohibiting parents from sending children to religious schools.[14]

There were, however, two notable exceptions to Butler's conservative bent, but these were also consistent with Catholic "pro-life" dogma. Because he dissented without opinion in both cases, we have little insight into what influenced his views, but the suspicion that his religion influenced his vote is there.

One was the case of *Buck v. Bell*.[15] Carrie Buck was born in Charlottesville, Virginia, in 1906. Abandoned by her parents, she was raised in foster care by the Dobbs family, whose nephew raped and impregnated her at age 17. Shamed by the incident, the Dobbses committed her to the Virginia State Colony for Epileptics and Feebleminded where she gave birth to a daughter, whom officials took away. Virginia then sought to have Carrie sterilized under a statute permitting involuntary sterilization of those of low intelligence. At the sterilization hearing, one of the authors of the state's eugenics law testified that Carrie and her daughter were congenitally "feeble minded" and that Carrie was of a mental age of nine years.

Butler filed the sole dissent in *Buck v. Bell*, an 8-1 decision where Holmes, incidentally joined by Brandeis, famously wrote the questionable opinion of the Court upholding the forced eugenic sterilization.

"Three generations of imbeciles are enough," Holmes declared.[16] The country can't be "swamped with incompetence." Not everything Holmes did was wonderful; it turned out that neither Buck nor her daughter was in fact mentally retarded.

Referring to Butler's dissent in *Buck v. Bell*, Holmes later wrote his friend the English socialist Harold Laski that the "religious are astir." Holmes believed that Butler's vote was dictated by his religion. Before Buck was decided, Holmes remarked, "Butler knows this is good law, I wonder whether he will have the courage to vote with us in spite of his religion."

Butler also dissented without opinion in *Palko v. Connecticut*,[17] a capital case, in which the Court held 8-1 that the Fifth Amendment's Double Jeopardy Clause was not binding on the states. Was it that Butler didn't like capital punishment because his Catholicism informed him to take a pro-life stance? Or did he think double jeopardy was binding on the states? We will never know. The Warren court later overruled *Palko* in the late 1960s.[18]

On Butler's death in 1939, Franklin D. Roosevelt appointed Frank Murphy to succeed him. Murphy's Irish-Catholic rearing was a profound influence on Roosevelt in making the appointment. Supreme Court expert Professor Barbara A. Perry writes that Murphy's Catholic faith "must be considered one of the two or three leading factors in making Murphy the choice to fill [Pierce] Butler's so-called 'Catholic seat.'"[19] Another consideration may have been the events of 1937 when Roosevelt's court-packing plan saw a deserved demise.

Murphy came from a background that in the Gilded Age of the late 1800s might have been called "rum, Romanism and rebellion."[20] The British had hanged Murphy's great-grandfather in Ireland for "insurrection." His paternal grandparents were "Forty-Eighters" from County Mayo, and his father, a lawyer, was jailed in Canada for participating in the Fenian disturbances of 1866. Murphy's mother's devout Roman Catholicism informed him that "the most precious virtue of all is the desire to serve mankind" and instilled in him an egalitarian philosophy that one must never forget the "obligation of the strong toward the weak."[21]

Murphy had come to the bench from a political background. He had served as mayor of Detroit. His political deftness won the attention of Franklin Roosevelt, who appointed him governor general of the Philippines in 1933. In 1936 Roosevelt urged Murphy to run for governor of Michigan, and he was elected. Subsequently, in 1939 Roosevelt appointed Murphy attorney general of the United States, a position from which he was elevated to the Court.

Everything in Murphy's experience indicated that he would be the strong liberal Justice on the Court that he was. As mayor of Detroit, he had become a champion of federal aid to the cities during the Depression and formed a "Colored Advisory Committee" to ensure that relief was distributed without regard for race, creed, or color.

Indeed, as Detroit's mayor, Murphy appeared to have the greatest feeling for African Americans because they "get the worst of every deal."[22] This feeling was reciprocated. As then NAACP Special Counsel Thurgood Marshall put it,

> [I]n the field of civil rights, Mr. Justice Murphy was a zealot. To him, the primacy of civil rights and human equality in our law and their entitlement to every possible protection in each case, regardless of competing considerations, was a fighting faith. . . . But Mr. Justice Murphy's orientation in matters of civil liberties was fixed. *His sense of values was unchanging.* He followed wherever his abiding primacy of civil rights might lead.[23]

In the Philippines, Murphy acquired a healthy respect for Asian peoples, encouraged the Filipino movement for independence, and developed an empathy for Japanese people shared by few Westerners. Murphy "thought that Americans were extraordinarily naïve about the Far East. . . . He was impressed with the 'energy of character, the discipline, capacity to sacrifice, [the] enterprise and above all the simplicity of life among the Japanese.'"[24]

As governor of Michigan, Murphy included in his administration several African Americans who held the highest-ranked posts in Michigan history. Murphy later became a board member of the NAACP.

As attorney general, Murphy founded the Civil Rights Division of the Justice Department. Even as the country moved toward war, Murphy tried to balance simultaneously the demands of national security and protecting the country against sabotage and subversion with the need to guard against encroachment upon individual civil liberties.[25] That particular balancing act took some doing then, as it does today.

Both Butler and Murphy, sons of Irish Catholic immigrants, reflected their backgrounds as minorities in America. Their judicial phi-
losophies, however, were widely disparate. As a Justice, Murphy more
than fulfilled Roosevelt's expectations. He was totally result-oriented,
and that result nearly always came down on the side of civil liberties. As
his biographer punned of Murphy's later Supreme Court service, he
"tempered justice with Murphy."[26]

While it is an axiom of Supreme Court jurisprudence that the Justices will not reach a constitutional issue to decide a case unless they
have to, Murphy was quick to use the Constitution as a standard whenever he saw a breach of civil liberties. As he told his brother George,
"the Court is ticklish about involving the Constitution if the case can be
decided on any other grounds. For my part, I want to utilize the great
charter whenever it is necessary to sustain the rights of man."[27] The
Catholic Church, as expressed in the Declaration of the French Revolution, did not always support the "rights of man" in the years prior to
Vatican II, but they were certainly part of the ethos of liberal Catholics
of Murphy's time.

Murphy expressed the centrality of the "rights of man" in his thinking in his brief concurrence in *Adamson v. California*.[28] Though the
case is best known for a duel between Frankfurter and Black over
selective incorporation of the Bill of Rights to the states through the
Fourteenth Amendment's Due Process Clause, Murphy's dissenting
opinion visualized the possibility of "new rights," unenumerated but
imbedded in the Constitution—namely a substantive due process. He
thus elaborates what must surely be a religiously based political philosophy:

> I agree that the specific guarantees of the Bill of Rights should be
> carried over intact into the first section of the Fourteenth Amend-
> ment. But I am not prepared to say that the latter is entirely and
> necessarily limited by the Bill of Rights. Occasions may arise where a
> proceeding falls so far short of conforming to fundamental standards
> of procedure as to warrant constitutional condemnation in terms of a
> lack of due process *despite the absence of a specific provision of the
> Bill of Rights*.[29]

Murphy's Irish Republican Catholic heritage would not allow him to
be passive when it came to protecting the rights of the downtrodden in

society. Judge Noonan has stated, "[I]t is tempting to ascribe this conscientious position to a religious conscience but the evidence is lacking."[30] It is? In Murphy's case, there is plenty of historical evidence to the contrary, your Honor, both direct and circumstantial. If a Catholic Celtic conscience didn't inform Murphy's jurisprudence, where else did it come from?

Though reasonable minds may differ as to what conclusion may be indicated by a Catholic theology, all the evidence suggests that Murphy's result-oriented judicial philosophy was plainly influenced by his conscience, and not by legal sources, which I argue was informed by his liberal Irish-Catholic view of the world. In one case, in a concurring opinion, he even referred to deportation as "being excommunicated."[31]

Murphy in his time was regarded as a legal lightweight who at best somehow stumbled onto correct outcomes and who was at worst "a New Deal political hack."[32] This rap is surprising and decidedly unfair in light of his profound contribution to civil liberties jurisprudence.[33]

Felix Frankfurter, the quintessential legal scholar, was particularly steamed up about Murphy's result-oriented conclusions. Although Frankfurter considered Murphy to be a man of principle, he did not see him as qualified to sit on the high court. A bulwark of "judicial restraint," Frankfurter, a former Harvard Law professor, constantly attacked Murphy's desire to write his personal compassion into the law. He compared this result-oriented philosophy to what had happened in Germany, and charged Murphy with being "too subservient" to his "notions of doing 'the right thing.'"

Frankfurter sometimes addressed Murphy as "Dear god," and in a note regarding a Federal Power Commission case, he said that "even a god" ought to read the record before deciding. In another note he passed to Murphy during the 1944 Term, in which he could not conceivably have been serious, he playfully listed as among Murphy's "Clients: Reds, Whores, Crooks, Indians and all other colored people, Longshoremen, M'tgors [debtors with a mortgage] and other Debtors, R.R. Employees, Pacifists, Traitors, Japs, Women, Children and Most Men." He wrote further to Murphy (one would hope with tongue in cheek), "Must I become a Negro rapist before you give me due process?"[34]

Scholars have universally praised Murphy's stance against the racism inherent in the government order interning Japanese Americans during

World War II. In a January 1945 letter to Murphy, Norman Thomas, the only national leader to denounce the incarceration in 1942 when it happened, hailed Murphy's dissenting opinion from the court's ruling in *Korematsu v. United States*[35] as "one of democracy's great documents."[36]

In the ringing dissent, which Thomas admired, Murphy wrote,

> I dissent, therefore, from this legalization of racism. Racial discrimination in any form and in any degree has no justifiable part whatever in our democratic way of life. It is unattractive in any setting, but it is utterly revolting among a free people who have embraced the principles set forth in the Constitution of the United States. All residents of this nation are kin in some way by blood or culture to a foreign land. Yet they are primarily and necessarily a part of the new and distinct civilization of the United States. They must, accordingly, be treated at all times as the heirs of the American experiment, and as entitled to all the rights and freedoms guaranteed by the Constitution.[37]

This was among the first times the word "racism" found its way into a Supreme Court opinion (Murphy had previously used the term twice in a concurring opinion in *Steele v. Louisville and Nashville R. Co.*,[38] issued the same day as *Korematsu*). He would use that word again in five separate opinions before the word "racism" disappeared from Murphy's and the High Court's vocabulary for almost two decades.

Korematsu was a dark day in Supreme Court history. The Justices, by a 6-3 vote, upheld the constitutionality of the government's 1942 decision to remove 110,000 Japanese Americans, 62 percent of whom were American born, from their homes on the West coast to "relocation camps" in eastern California and the Rocky Mountains. American citizens were given 48 hours to dispose of their homes, businesses, and furniture. The relocation camps were a euphemism for concentration camps. There they lived behind barbed wire and under armed guard. The guards were under orders to shoot to kill. According to William Manchester, during the period of resettlement they lost an estimated "$70 million in farm acreage and equipment, $35 million in fruits and vegetables, and nearly a half billion in annual income, and savings, stocks and bonds beyond reckoning."[39]

The opinion of the Court was authored by liberal Justice Hugo Black, and other liberal stalwarts such as Chief Justice Harlan Fiske Stone, William O. Douglas, and Wiley Rutledge joined Black's decision. Felix Frankfurter wrote a separate concurrence in which he argued that the appropriate standard was that of "reasonably expedient military precautions in time of war" and that the internment orders passed muster under that essential legal test.[40]

The internment order, endorsed by Assistant Secretary of War John McCloy, flew in the face of the epic warning of Brandeis in dissent in *Olmstead*, "The greatest dangers to liberty lurk in insidious encroachment by men of zeal, well-meaning but without understanding."[41] A "man of zeal" of a different stripe in the internment cases was the racist Army general John Lesesne DeWitt. From 1939 to 1943, DeWitt was in charge of the Western Defense Command headquartered at the Presidio of San Francisco. He once said that there "isn't such a thing as a loyal Japanese." DeWitt knowingly presented false data to the Justice Department to be submitted to the Supreme Court in connection with the Japanese internment cases.

An interesting footnote to history is that Earl Warren, who as Chief Justice wrote the unanimous decision in *Brown v. Board of Education*, when he served as attorney general of California in 1942, supported the internment. He told a group of state law-enforcement officers that the fact "we have no fifth column activities" or "sabotage" shows a conspiracy by Japanese Americans not to strike "until the zero hour arrives."[42] He later apologized.

Frank Murphy was the most consistent champion of civil liberties among the Justices of his time. In the *Japanese-American Cases*,[43] he became the first Justice to suggest and apply an equal protection guarantee through the Due Process Clause of the Fifth Amendment to action by the federal government that denied civil rights and liberties— an insight that did not become trite Supreme Court law until 1954 when the Court decided *Bolling v. Sharpe*.[44] In *Bolling*, the Warren Court unanimously channeled Murphy, holding that the Fourteenth Amendment's Equal Protection Clause, which forbids the states to discriminate on the basis of race, applies, through the Fifth Amendment Due Process Clause, to the federal government. *Bolling*, decided the same day as *Brown v. Board of Education*, involved segregation in the DC public school system. Chief Justice Warren, who wrote for the

Court in *Bolling*, never mentioned Murphy's opinions in the *Japanese-American Cases*, probably because, as attorney general of California, he had been responsible for the very mistreatment of Japanese Americans during the war that Murphy had condemned. It is a certainty, however, that Murphy made an unheralded contribution to the later exposition of equal protection doctrine.During his last three years on the Court, Murphy voted for claimants in civil liberties cases 53 out of 56 times as contrasted with Justice Douglas who voted for the claimed right 47 out of 56 times, and with Justice Black who voted for 39 out of 56 times.

In dissent after dissent, Murphy was a voice in the wilderness on behalf of the "clear constitutional rights of the inarticulate and the friendless."[45] He wrote for the Court that the act of picketing was protected speech under the First Amendment. He stood for using a rigorous interpretation of Holmes's "clear and present danger" test for constitutionally protected political action, indicating that he probably would have joined the dissenters in *Dennis v. United States*,[46] a case which criminalized the activities of Communist leaders in the 1940s for advocating the overthrow of the government by force and violence. He certainly would have joined the majority in *Brandenburg v. Ohio*,[47] which overruled *Dennis* and required the government to provide incitement to "imminent lawless action." Murphy served until his death on July 19, 1949. Though Tom Clark, a Protestant, technically succeeded Murphy, President Truman was quick to appoint another Catholic, Sherman Minton, to fill the vacant Catholic seat. Minton took office October 12, 1949. When Minton, in failing health retired in 1956, Eisenhower appointed Brennan only after his aides went to Brennan's priest and inquired, "Is he a good Catholic?"

Religion was a factor in Brennan's 1956 confirmation hearings. The National Liberty League, a group seldom heard from since, which claimed it was dedicated to the separation of church and state, argued that no Catholics should sit on the Court given the country's "predominantly Protestant" status. Senator Joseph C. O'Mahoney (D-WY), himself a Catholic, asked the nominee the following question that the league's president Charles Smith had put forward as calculated to compel the nominee to "reveal" whether as a Roman Catholic "bound by . . . [his] religion to follow the pronouncements of the Pope on all matters of faith and morals . . . [he] would . . . be able to follow the requirements of [his] oath or would . . . be bound by [his] religious obligations."

Brennan's answer was emphatic,

> [C]ategorically . . . in everything I have ever done, in every office I have held in my life or that I shall ever do in the future, what shall control me is the oath that I took to support the Constitution and laws of the United States and so . . . upon cases that come before me for decision that it is that oath which governs.

Four years later John F. Kennedy took a leaf from Brennan's book in his September 12, 1960, speech to the Protestant ministers when he said,

> But if the time should ever come—and I do not concede any conflict to be even remotely possible—when my office would require me to either violate my conscience or violate the national interest, then I would resign the office; and I hope any conscientious public servant would do the same.

In modern times, three Catholic Justices were appointed in quick succession: Scalia in 1986, Kennedy in 1988, and Thomas in 1991. There then followed Roberts in 2005, Alito in 2006, and Sotomayor in 2009. Prior to Scalia's death, the Court had six Catholic Justices sitting in the majority.

Resignation may be the only option for the Catholic Justice who feels conflicted between the dictates of conscience and his or her oath of office. At a University of Chicago/Pew Forum on Religion and Public Life on January 25, 2002, Scalia said that "the choice for the judge who believes the death penalty to be immoral is resignation rather than simply ignoring duly enacted constitutional laws and sabotaging the death penalty. He has, after all, taken an oath to apply those laws, and has been given no power to supplant them with rules of his own."[48] It is highly questionable whether he would ever have felt the same way about *Roe v. Wade*.

Notes

1. John T. Noonan, Jr., "The Religion of the Justice: Does It Affect Constitutional Decision Making?" 42 Tulsa Law Rev. 761 (2007). Noonan is a senior judge of the U.S. Court of Appeals for the Ninth Circuit.

2. Carl Swisher, *Roger B. Taney*, New York: Macmillan (1935) at 317.

3. 60 U.S. 393 (1857).

4. *Dred Scott v. Sandford*, 60 U.S. 452.

5. Note 20, *supra*.

6. *Dred Scott v. Sandford*, 60 U.S. 407.

7. *Weems v. United States*, 217 U.S. 349, 380-81 (1910; originalists, like Antonin Scalia, deprecate such liberal interpretations as the Constitution means what I would like it to mean).

8. Gyp the Blood was a vicious Manhattan gangster of the period. Standing just under 5 feet 5 inches and weighing 140 pounds, he would on a small bet from one of his colleagues grab passers-by and break their backs over his knee.

9. Manton's law partner was one W. Bourke Cockran, a power in Democratic politics.

10. Manton famously dissented in one case that had not been fixed, *United States v. One Book Entitled Ulysses*, 72 F. 2d 705 (2d Cir. 1934).

11. *United States v. Manton*, 107 F2d 834, 846 (2d Cir 1938).

12. As noted earlier, these were, in addition to Butler, McReynolds, Sutherland, and Van Devanter.

13. *United States v. Schwimmer*, 279 U.S. 644 (1929).

14. *Pierce v. Society of Sisters*, 268 U.S. 510 (1925).

15. 274 U.S. 200 (1927).

16. 274 U.S. 200 (1927).

17. 302 U.S., *supra*, 39 (1937).

18. *Benton v. Maryland*, 395 U.S. 784 (1969).

19. Barbara A. Perry, "The Life and Death of the 'Catholic Seat' on the United States Supreme Court," 6 J. Law & Pol. 55, 80 (1989).

20. A phrase borrowed from the 1884 presidential election where at a Republican meeting a group of New York preachers made the statement "We are Republicans, and don't propose to leave our party and identify ourselves with the party whose antecedents have been rum, Romanism and rebellion." The slur energized the Irish and Catholic vote in New York City heavily against James Blaine, costing him New York State, and insuring the election of Grover Cleveland by the narrowest of margins.

21. Howard, *supra*, note 21 at 5–6.

22. Sidney Fine, *Frank Murphy: The Detroit Years*, Ann Arbor: University of Michigan Press (1975), at 179.

23. "Mr. Justice Murphy and Civil Rights," 48 Mich. Law Rev. 739 (1950).

24. Sidney Fine, *Frank Murphy: The New Deal Years*, Chicago: University of Chicago Press (1979), at 104.

25. Sidney Fine, *Frank Murphy: The Washington Years*, Ann Arbor: University of Michigan Press (1984), at 111.

26. *Ibid.*

27. J. Woodford Howard, Jr., *Mr. Justice Murphy: A Political Biography*, at 353.

28. 332 U.S. 46 (1947).

29. *Id.* at 124.

30. See Noonan, *supra*, note 28 at 763.

31. *Bridges v. Wixson*, 326 U.S. 135, 159 (1945).

32. John P. Roche, "The Utopian Pilgrimage of Mr. Justice Murphy," 10 Van. Law Rev. 369 (1957).

33. See the superb comment of Matthew J. Perry, "Justice Murphy and the Fifth Amendment Doctrine: A Contribution Unrecognized," 27 Hast. Const. Law Qtrly, 242 (2000).

34. Sidney Fine, *Frank Murphy: The Washington Years*, at 258–59.

35. 323 U.S. 214 (1944).

36. Letter of Norman Thomas to Frank Murphy (January 6, 1945), reprinted in Sidney Fine, *Frank Murphy: The Washington Years*, at 450; and J. Woodford Howard, Jr., *Mr. Justice Murphy: A Political Biography* (1968) at 337.

37. 332 U.S. at 242.

38. 323 U.S. 192 (1944).

39. William Manchester, *The Glory and the Dream*, New York: Little Brown, Boston (1974) at 299.

40. *Korematsu*, 323 U.S., *supra*, at 225. (To recognize that military orders are "reasonably expedient military precautions" in time of war and yet to deny them constitutional legitimacy makes of the Constitution an instrument for dialectic subtleties not reasonably to be attributed to the Framers, of whom a majority had had actual participation in war.)

41. 277 U.S. 438, 471 (1928).

42. Testimony given before Tolan Committee, February 2, 1942. Referred to at https://books.google.com/books?id=QZg6Ft_jvJ0C&pg=PA349&lpg= PA349&dq=warren+japanese+zero+hour&source=bl&ots=XlUZ5GIPq5& sig=zoS6RWACDXwwS0YEKEgZOzqqYYw&hl=en&sa=X&ved= 0CB4Q6AEwAGoVChMIoJjRlNTExwIVCMuACh2yjwKP -v=onepage&q= warren japanese zero hour&f=.

43. This term has been used collectively to refer to the trilogy of *Hirabayashi v. United States*, 320 U.S. 81 (1943), *Korematsu* and *Ex Parte Endo*, 323 U.S. 283 (1944), in which Murphy concurred, dissented, and concurred respectively.

44. 347 U.S. 497 (1954), unanimously holding that the Fourteenth Amendment's Equal Protection Clause, which forbids the states to discriminate on the basis of race, applies, through the Fifth Amendment Due Process Clause to

the federal government. *Bolling*, decided the same day as *Brown v. Board of Education*, involved segregation in the Washington, DC, public school system. It is a certainty that Murphy made an unheralded contribution to the later exposition of equal protection doctrine.

45. *Screws v. United States*, 325 U.S. 91, 138 (1945).

46. 341 U.S. 494 (1951) (upholding prosecution of Communist leaders who advocated violent overthrow of government).

47. 395 U.S. 444 (1969) (holding an Ohio statute prohibiting advocacy of violent overthrow violated First and Fourteenth Amendments).

48. http://features.pewforum.org/death-penalty/resources/transcript3.html.

6

THE JEWISH SEAT

Tradition, Tradition!

The undersigned feel under the painful duty to say to you that taking into view the reputation, character and professional career of Mr. Louis D. Brandeis he is not a fit person to be a member of the Supreme Court of the United States.
—Letter, dated March 14, 1916, to the Chairman of the Senate Judiciary Committee signed by seven former presidents of the American Bar Association.

It may surprise some to know that the first Jew to be offered appointment to the Supreme Court was not Louis D. Brandeis in 1916 but Judah P. Benjamin in 1853. Benjamin, a wealthy slave owner from Louisiana and a highly respected Louisiana lawyer, was the author of a seminal treatise on sales law, read by practitioners to this day. President Millard Fillmore offered Benjamin a Supreme Court appointment, but Benjamin turned it down as he had just been elected a U.S. Senator. Benjamin went on to become secretary of state of the Confederacy. He would have been better advised to accept the Supreme Court appointment.

The story of Brandeis is fascinating. The child of Jewish immigrants from Prague who had come to the United States after the failure of the revolutionary movement of 1848 to create an independent Bohemia, he was born in Louisville on November 13, 1856, the youngest of four children. His father was a prosperous grain and produce merchant who later lost his money. Educated in private and public schools in Louisville, Brandeis studied in Europe for several years, but he did not attend college, although he was a precocious student. At age 18, he entered Harvard Law School to follow in the footsteps of his maternal uncle, Lewis Dembitz, a leading Louisville lawyer. He achieved one of the best records in the law school's history.

By the time he was 21 years of age, Brandeis had earned fame for a brilliant legal mind. Writing his mother from Harvard in March 1878, William E. Cushing described his classmate, as follows:

> My friend Brandeis is a character in his way—one of the most brilliant legal minds they have ever had here. . . . [H]as a rather foreign look and is currently believed to have some Jew blood in him, though you would not suppose it from his appearance—tall, well-made, dark, beardless, and with the brightest eyes I ever saw.

Upon graduation from Harvard, Brandeis enjoyed a distinguished career at the Bar. Secure in his practice, he cast himself as the "people's lawyer," and espoused the cause of the "little man" against the rich, the privileged, the money trusts, and the vested interests. He helped save the Boston subway system; he opposed the monopolistic attempt of the New Haven Railroad to remain the sole provider of public transport in New England; he worked to change the Massachusetts liquor laws to prevent dealers from bribing public officials; he recommended to the state legislature a savings bank life-insurance program, which became law.

His seminal article, published in the *Harvard Law Review*, titled "The Right to Privacy," in the words of Dean Roscoe Pound, "added "a chapter to our law."[1] In the article, he argued that the Framers of the Constitution valued "the right to be let alone . . . the right most valued by civilized men." Brandeis's recognition of a right to privacy is the bedrock of the Supreme Court's reproductive rights jurisprudence developed in *Griswold v. Connecticut* and *Roe v. Wade*. Chief Justice Roberts served as a law clerk to Judge Henry Friendly on the Second Circuit. Friendly had been a Brandeis clerk. In the course of his own confirmation hearings, Roberts acknowledged that the Constitution guaranteed a "right of privacy" even though the word "privacy" appears nowhere in the text.

When Oregon retained him to defend its ten-hour law for working women before the Supreme Court, Brandeis devoted only a few pages of his brief to legal argument. The rest would be a presentation of social and economic data showing the evil of long hours, and the benefits of legislative limitation. His "Brandeis brief," unconventional at the time, citing sociological and economic data to show a reasonable relationship between the legislation and public health, remains an innovation followed by lawyers and judges to this day. A judge is presumed to know the law, he wrote, "but there is no presumption that he knows the facts." The argument carried the day, and the Court, citing Brandeis by name, upheld the Oregon statute.[2]

President Woodrow Wilson was in a rough presidential race in 1912, with all shades of the political spectrum getting into the act. The election was a rare four-way contest. The Republican Party, with the support of its conservative wing, renominated incumbent president William Howard Taft. The Socialists nominated Eugene V. Debs. When former president Theodore Roosevelt failed to receive the Republican nomination, he called his own convention and created the "Bull Moose Party."

Wilson, who wasn't nominated until the forty-sixth ballot of the Democratic convention, had made the issue of economic regulation central to his campaign. Brandeis, although nominally a Republican, was quick to hop on Wilson's bandwagon. The two met privately in New Jersey in August and discussed economic issues. What emerged was the program of "regulated competition" that Brandeis had elaborated. The plank carried over into policy in the Wilson administration. It is the basis for the regulatory framework we have today.

Wilson became a minority president with only 42 percent of the vote. But he carried 40 states in the Electoral College; Roosevelt carried 6; and Taft carried but 2.

A committed Zionist by 1912, Brandeis was a controversial figure. When Wilson was elected in November, he considered nominating Brandeis for a cabinet post but changed his mind in the face of a hue and cry from corporate executives whom Brandeis had bested in court. Without official position, Brandeis emerged as chief domestic adviser during Wilson's first term. He played a pivotal role in the Federal Reserve Act of 1913, the development of the antitrust division of the

Justice Department charged with enforcing the Sherman Antitrust Act, as well as the Federal Trade Commission Act of 1914.

On January 28, 1916, the progressive President Woodrow Wilson, son of an elder in the Presbyterian Church, dropped a political bombshell on a placid Washington. Without consulting a single senator, he appointed Brandeis to the Supreme Court. Brandeis was 59 at the time of his nomination.[3]

The nation was quick to take sides. Brandeis was well known as a progressive reformer with his monographs attacking big business (*The Curse of Bigness*) and the money trust (*Other People's Money*), and his appointment rocked the business community. Organized businessmen protested, calling Brandeis a socialist, a union sympathizer—the next best thing to an anarchist. One reporter wrote that the financial districts were "stunned as if a bomb had exploded from an unseen Zeppelin." Another said that Wall Street's groan was "like the echo of a national disaster."

Over his forty-year career at the Bar, Brandeis had managed to make a fair number of powerful enemies. The nation's press was sharply divided over the appointment. In New York, the *Sun*, the *Press* and the *Times* were against; only the *World* was in support. In Brandeis's hometown of Boston, the *Transcript* deplored the nomination; the *Post*, however, praised Brandeis as "a great force for progressive thought and action in the field of political and economic reform."

On January 31, the *Boston Globe* epitomized the case of the anti-Brandeis:

> That Mr. Brandeis is a radical, a theorist, impractical, with strong socialistic tendencies.
>
> That he is given to extravagance in utterance, inspired by prejudice and intolerance.
>
> That he is a "self-advertiser," reckless in his methods of seeking personal exploitation.
>
> That he does not possess the "judicial temperament" that would fit him for the duties of the Supreme Court judge, in that he would be influenced by personal considerations rather than the merits of the cases submitted for impartial analysis and exact judgment.

Although his opponents had not publicly referred to the fact that Brandeis was a Jew, there was little doubt that ancestry and anti-

Semitism were factors in the thinking of the opposition.

Justice William O. Douglas said of the Brandeis appointment,

> Brandeis was a militant crusader for social justice whoever his oppo-
> nent might be. He was dangerous not only because of his brilliance,
> his arithmetic, his courage. He was dangerous because he was incor-
> ruptible . . . [and] the fears of the Establishment were greater be-
> cause Brandeis was the first Jew to be named to the Court.

U.S. District Judge Charles Amidon of Fargo, North Dakota, wrote
Brandeis on February 1 of what was in store:

> By your zeal for the common good, you have created powerful ene-
> mies. They will do their utmost to defeat your confirmation in the
> Senate. . . . You will be accused of everything, from grand larceny to
> a non-judicial temperament. Fake telegrams will be sent to Washing-
> ton in the name of persons who never sent them or signed them.
> Forged signatures will be entered on petitions of protest. . . . Please
> do not allow the reluctance which every man of honor feels against
> defending his own life to prevent meeting the issue. You owe it to
> your country.

Then came five months of brutal confirmation hearings in the U.S.
Senate in which there was relentless probing of his conduct as a Boston
lawyer, his alleged lack of judicial temperament, his allegedly bad reputation at the Boston Bar, and certain alleged acts of unprofessional
conduct. One witness even referred to him as a "second Daniel." It was
a theater of the absurd. The Senate heard forty-three witnesses, and the
transcript consumed 1,300 pages of testimony. Brandeis did not attend
the hearings.

The course of the confirmation hearings may be culled from a marvelous biography of Brandeis by Alpheus Thomas Mason.[4]

Chairman of the Iowa Railroad Commission (ICC) Clifford Thorne
had had it in for Brandeis since 1913 when the railroads made a bid
before the ICC for an across-the-board 5 percent rate increase. ICC
Commissioner James Harlan had retained Brandeis as special counsel
to represent the public interest in connection with the proposed rate
hike. When Brandeis was appointed, Thorne, representing the shippers, wrote him on October 27, 1913: "I think this method of procedure

is wise. There should be a head to the *public's* presentation." Talk about a prior inconsistent statement!

While Brandeis was perceived to be on the side of the shippers, and against the railroads, he was really engaged to represent the public interest, sorting out the competing claims and making a fair and impartial recommendation to the commission.

Both Thorne and Brandeis wound up opposing the hike, but Brandeis in closing argument contended that the railroads should cut costs and create surplus, giving railroads that are "managed well," "with integrity and skill," "an opportunity to earn." Thorne opposed a surplus or else suggested a small surplus, which Brandeis dismissed as "niggardly." This sent Thorne into orbit.

Accusing Brandeis of a pro-railroad stance and going over to the enemy, Thorne launched a vicious attack, referring to Brandeis's Jewish heritage:

> What a most delightful and pretty bit of argument from the railroad standpoint. A second Daniel, indeed a second Daniel, well worthy that distinguished ancestor of our modern advocate for the people's side in the greatest controversy of the present generation.[5]

No wonder then that Thorne's animus toward Brandeis impelled him to wire Republican members of the Judiciary Committee about the putative betrayal in the rate case two years before:

> I was an admirer of Mr. Brandeis up until the closing argument in the eastern advanced rate case. His act on that occasion . . . in my judgment had all the essential elements of the act of a traitor. The gentleman whom you have under consideration was guilty of infidelity, breach of faith, and unprofessional conduct.

Again a biased attack, verbose in conclusion and sparse in fact! Other witnesses in a position to know, who understood Brandeis's true role before the commission, seriously undermined Thorne's testimony.

A supporter of Brandeis was Joseph N. Teal, counsel for the shippers. Teal testified that Brandeis "was employed by the Commission to see that all interests were properly represented. He was not retained for the purpose of developing the railroad side . . . nor any particular side." ICC Commissioner Harlan testified that he had retained Brandeis to undertake the task of seeing that all sides and angles of the case are presented of record, without advocating any particular theory for its disposition. Of course, there were two sides to the case. There was the railroad side and there was the shippers' side, and both sides were very ably represented. *But I do not understand that Mr. Brandeis was on either side. He was there in the public interest.*

Sidney Winslow of the United Shoe Machinery Company, a former Brandeis client, accused Brandeis of "unprofessional conduct and conduct not becoming an honorable man." The why and wherefore of this accusation was that "Mr. Brandeis has, at the instance of new clients, attacked as illegal and criminal the very acts and system of business . . . which he assisted to create, and which he advised were legal, and he has persistently sought to injure our business."

One of Brandeis's ardent supporters was George W. Anderson, U.S. attorney for Massachusetts, who acted as Brandeis's advocate before the Senate committee. He questioned Winslow sharply as to the basis of his attack on the candidate, and totally demolished his testimony:

Q: I ask you to state specifically what facts he learned, as counsel or director that he subsequently used in criticism of, or attack upon, your company?
A: I suppose that is a broad question.
Q: No, it is not a broad question. It is a very narrow question.
A: It is? I do not criticize Mr. Brandeis acting for anyone, if he had at all times scrupulously or, I might say, fairly, confined himself to statements that were correct and true. . . . I want the committee to understand distinctly that I am not here by any malice toward Mr. Brandeis. I would lean over backward rather than urge anything against him.

A Brandeis character witness, Boston lawyer Arthur D. Hill, wrote to Anderson. His letter became a part of the record before the Senate:

He is a radical and has spent a large part, not only of his public, but of his professional career, in attacking established institutions, and this alone would in my judgment, account for a large part of his unpopularity. . . . The fact too, that Mr. Brandeis has been the object of constant attack, and in particular of a very skillful and long continued press campaign engineered on behalf of the New Haven [Railroad] . . . has probably increased the feeling against him. . . . When you add to this that Mr. Brandeis is an outsider, successful, and a Jew, you have, I think sufficiently explained most of the feeling against him. . . . Once on the bench, his strong qualities, his great ability, his knowledge not only of law but of economics and social conditions, and his capacity for taking a broad judicial view of any question to which he applies his mind, will be of inestimable value.

Another witness against Brandeis was Dr. James Cannon, bishop of the Methodist Church in Massachusetts. He testified that for all he knew Brandeis "may be of the highest character and doubtless possesses unusual mentality and legal ability." But the good bishop was a "dry," and Brandeis had represented the Massachusetts Liquor Dealers' Association before the state legislature more than two decades earlier. The bishop found this representation to be disqualifying.

When a senator on the committee suggested the possibility that a judge might have personal views about whether a law was good, but that despite this he could fairly construe the law as written, the Bishop answered,

Yes, I think that is true, yet I think it is difficult for men to divest themselves in interpretation of what they think is a sound public policy and for the moral and material welfare of the state, to be entirely unbiased when it comes to a decision. *Judges are men, like everybody else.*

A petition signed by fifty-five proper Bostonians, including Harvard president Abbott Lawrence Lowell, Charles Francis Adams, and C. Minot Weld, accused Brandeis of lacking judicial temperament and capacity. Lowell, a Boston Brahmin, has been described as a "dangerous bigot—a man of virulent prejudices who systematically used his position of power to exclude and oppress those whom he hated."[6] He had sought to introduce a quota system for Jews at Harvard, had excluded African Americans from residing in the freshman dormitories, and had conducted a purge of gays on campus. One of his gay targets thereafter committed suicide. The petition of these honorable men stated, "We do not believe that Mr. Brandeis has the judicial temperament and capacity which should be required in a judge of the Supreme Court." Brandeis was able to "connect the dots," and relate every one of the fifty-five protestants to a controversy where every one of them had opposed Brandeis, and Brandeis had emerged the victor. In addition, there were strong economic and social ties between and among the fifty-five petitioners.

Walter Lippmann commented on the fifty-five protestants in the *New Republic* of March 11, 1916, writing,

> It was a special community that had found Mr. Brandeis untrust-worthy . . . the powerful but limited community which dominated the business and social life of Boston. He was untrustworthy because he was troublesome. He was disloyal, if at all, to a group. All the smoke of ill-repute which had been gathered around Mr. Brandeis originated in the group psychology of these gentlemen and because they are men of influence it seemed ominous. But it is smoke with-out any fire except that of personal or group antagonism. . . . They come of a proud line and are jealous of a noble tradition.

Reverend A. A. Berle, seeing things a little differently, had written to Senator Chilton on February 18, 1916, as follows:

> It would be fair to say that if any man *bearing an old New England name* and practicing at the Bar in Boston had everything which is alleged against Mr. Brandeis alleged against him, and were nominat-ed for the Supreme Court, no one would dream of raising these questions.

William Howard Taft, who would become Brandeis's colleague on the Court when Taft was appointed Chief Justice in 1921, found the nomination "laughable," "when you consider Brandeis's appointment, and think of the men who were pressing me for the place." Taft was one of seven signers of a letter opposing confirmation, stating that Brandeis was not "a fit person" to be on the Supreme Court. The letter, dated March 14, 1916, was signed by seven past presidents of the American Bar Association, and addressed to the chairman of the Senate Judiciary Committee. The signers included, in addition to Taft, such legal lumi-naries as Joseph Choate and Elihu Root. By "gentlemen's agreement," they did not overtly press the point that Brandeis was a Jew.

Another of the seven signers of the ABA letter was Moorefield Sto-rey, a Boston lawyer.[7] Storey was a patrician reformer and champion of civil rights, the first president of the NAACP. He was the ideal figure to give the anti-Semitic opposition some cover. He harbored a long-standing grudge against Brandeis, who had beaten his pants off eighteen years before in at least two cases. In his summation in the *New England Mortgage Securities* case, Brandeis, who had no illusions about Storey, had compared Storey's conduct to that of the French army in the Dreyfus case, and he quoted a passage from *The Merchant of Venice* that Storey sought "to do a great right" by doing "a little wrong."[8]

Exemplifying the jaundiced, conclusory, and groundless nature of the opposition to the nomination, Storey testified before the Senate, as follows:

> Storey: I think his reputation is that of a man who is an able lawyer, very energetic, ruthless in the attainment of his objects, not scrupulous in the methods he adopts, and not to be trusted. . . .
>
> Senator Fletcher: Have you been engaged on opposite sides of different cases?
>
> Storey: I have been engaged against Mr. Brandeis in three or four matters. I do not remember ever trying any question of facts against him. I have been employed against him in cases where a question of law was presented to the court and arguments made on either side. I have never had any personal quarrel with Mr. Brandeis at all or any difficulty at all. Our public activities and interests have been on different lines. . . . I have been interested in various . . . matters where I have never met him. He, on the other hand, has been interested in a different class of questions where I have never read much of anything he said. If you were to ask me what is his attitude on any of these public questions, I do not think I should be able to tell you. I remember his saying the railroads would save so much a day, and that is the only statement of his which is crystallized in my mind. Even that I could not quote accurately.
>
> Senator Fletcher: You say he is not to be trusted. What do you mean by that—as to his personal obligations?
>
> Storey: If you mean whether he pays his debts, certainly he will. I mean to say there is a radical lack of confidence in him among a representative class of men in the community in which I live, and which has existed for a good while.

In short, Storey had no facts on which to base his conclusion that Brandeis was untrustworthy.

While the anti-Semitism that motivated the attacks on Brandeis was thinly veiled, its immutable presence was not lost on the candidate. As Brandeis wrote to his brother on March 2,

> It is not as unpleasant to us as would seem to the outside. This attack continued throughout nine years has quite accustomed us to it and we are glad to have it out. At all events the country including Boston will know what I have been "up against." I suppose eighteen centuries of Jewish persecution must have inured me to such hardships and developed the like of a duck's back.

When the Senate confirmed Brandeis by a vote of 47 to 22 on June 1, 1916, twenty-one Republican Senators and one Democratic Senator voted against his nomination. After he was seated, one of his new colleagues, Justice James McReynolds, rose and left the room whenever Brandeis spoke at a conference of the Justices. Brandeis was undeterred. Frequently joining with Holmes in memorable dissent, he became one of the most famous and influential figures ever to serve on the high court, and he is generally acknowledged to be one of our greatest Justices. His dissenting opinions are, according to legal scholars, some of the "greatest defenses" of freedom of speech and the right to privacy ever written. Many of them have become the law.

Brandeis saw law not as a system of artificial reason, but as a logical extension of ethical ideals with freedom at its core. In *Olmstead v. United States*,[9] he bristled at the willingness of his colleagues to endorse the government's use of wiretap technology to gather evidence and argued passionately for an individual's "right to be let alone." His ringing dissent is still one of the most quoted opinions in the Court's history. "Men born to freedom are naturally alert to repel invasion of their liberty by evil-minded rulers," he wrote. "The greatest dangers to liberty lurk in insidious encroachment by men of zeal well-meaning but without understanding." He might have been writing about the domestic surveillance activities of the NSA today.

Was Brandeis a legalistic jurist who woodenly applied the text of the Constitution to the case before him or was he the judge Bishop Cannon predicted who would find it "difficult," when it was a conflict between the law and a "sound public policy and for the moral and material welfare of the state, to be entirely unbiased when it comes to a decision"? Given Brandeis's progressive record on so many issues, it is difficult to say that Cannon was wrong when he testified that "[j]udges are men like everybody else." Brandeis was a partisan, but above all else, he was a free man.

Following the appointment of Brandeis as the first Jewish justice, there arose in the minds of presidents a Jewish "seat" on the Supreme Court, which attitude lasted for fifty-three years. When Oliver Wendell Holmes retired in 1932 at age 90, Herbert Hoover hesitated to appoint the iconic jurist Benjamin Cardozo, chief judge of the New York Court of Appeals, as the second Jewish justice because there would then be two Jewish justices on the Court at the same time. He eventually bowed to overwhelming pressure from law school deans, judges, and lawyers throughout the nation. When Cardozo died in 1938, Franklin D. Roosevelt appointed Harvard professor Felix Frankfurter to succeed him, but only after he knew that Brandeis would resign from the Court the next month. The Senate confirmed the occupant of the next "Jewish seat," Felix Frankfurter, without a dissenting vote.

Irving Kaufman, the feisty judge who condemned Ethel and Julius Rosenberg to death in the electric chair, coveted the Jewish seat on the Supreme Court occupied by Felix Frankfurter. Frankfurter, who had filed a dissenting opinion in the Rosenberg case, was annoyed that Kaufman had said he went to the synagogue for divine guidance before imposing the death sentence.

Frankfurter wrote to Learned Hand that Kaufman's odd comment about going to the synagogue was "unjudicial" and a blatant effort to fuel enthusiasm for his drive to win a "Jewish seat" on the Court. "I despise a judge who feels God told him to impose a death sentence," Frankfurter wrote to Learned Hand in 1958. "I am mean enough to try to stay here long enough so that K[aufman] will be too old to succeed me." Frankfurter got his wish.

If you want to talk with your maker, sometimes it's better to make the conversation a private affair.

Notes

1. 4 Harvard Law Rev. 193 (1890).
2. *Muller v. Oregon*, 208 U.S. 412 (1907).

3. As governor of New Jersey, Wilson had in 1911 appointed Samuel Kalisch as the first Jewish justice of the New Jersey Supreme Court. As president of Princeton, he appointed the first Jewish professor.

4. Alpheus Thomas Mason, *Brandeis, A Free Man's Life*, New York: Viking Press (1946).

5. Mason, *supra*, at 345; quoted in the *New York Sun*, May 7, 1914.

6. By Simon W. Vozick-Levinson, "Writing the Wrong: A. Lawrence Lowell," *Harvard Crimson* (November 3, 2005). Available at http://www.thecrimson.com/article/2005/11/3/writing-the-wrong-a-lawrence-lowell/.

7. Storey did not sign as one of the fifty-five protestants, but his son, Richard C. Storey, did. Richard apparently signed in his father's law office.

8. *The Merchant of Venice* 4.1.

9. 277 U.S. 438, note 58 at 471 (1928).

7

AND GOLDBERG BEGAT FORTAS

End of the Jewish Seat

And God blessed them, and God said unto them, Be fruitful, and
multiply.
—Genesis 1:28

The tradition of the "Jewish seat" on the Supreme Court continued for
53 years, resembling the begats in the book of Genesis. The end of the
affair actually had more elements of a Greek tragedy (hubris, catharsis,
reversal of fortune, and catastrophe) than it did of biblical implications.

After John F. Kennedy convinced the Houston ministers and, for
that matter, the rest of the country that there should be no religious test
for office, it was not surprising that he appointed two Jews to his cabinet: Abraham Ribicoff and Arthur Goldberg. Arthur Goldberg was a
member of Kennedy's inner circle whom JFK made secretary of labor.
Goldberg was a Chicago labor lawyer, the child of immigrants from
Eastern Europe. In September 1962, just shy of two years after Goldberg's appointment as secretary of labor, Kennedy named him to the
Supreme Court to fill the Jewish seat vacated by Felix Frankfurter.

Goldberg, the youngest of eight children, had come up the hard way
on Chicago's West Side. His father, a produce peddler, had died when
he was eight years old, and Goldberg's siblings worked to support the
family. Goldberg as the youngest was allowed to finish his education,
and he graduated from high school at age 16. He was bright, he was
compassionate, he was liberal, and he was immensely egotistical. The

Leopold and Loeb murder case in 1923, which occurred when Goldberg was 15, apparently sparked Goldberg's interest in the law and his aversion to capital punishment. Leopold and Loeb, wealthy and overly privileged students at the University of Chicago, had sought to commit the perfect crime. Their prey was Loeb's second cousin, Bobby Franks, who was the same age as Goldberg at the time. The pair murdered Franks in cold blood. The crime, however, was imperfect. Police found Leopold's glasses at the crime scene, the pair got caught, and they confessed. Clarence Darrow waived a jury and delivered a magnificent summation for the defense. He succeeded in sparing his clients the death penalty. The failed "perfect crime" captured the imagination of the times.

Goldberg served just short of three years on the Court, where his career was quite promising. A liberal Justice, he favored a broad construction of the Constitution. His opinion in *Griswold v. Connecticut*[1] was a landmark, holding that the Constitution protected a right to privacy. The case involved a Connecticut statute that prohibited someone from using "any drug, medicinal article or instrument for the purpose of preventing conception." Goldberg and six other Justices, struck down the law on the grounds that it violated the "right to marital privacy." The case was the legal rock on which *Roe v. Wade* was built.

By 1965 Kennedy was dead, and Lyndon Johnson was the president. Goldberg yearned for higher office, and Johnson wanted to appoint his close political crony Abe Fortas to the Supreme Court.

The only problem was that Fortas was Jewish, and Goldberg occupied the Jewish seat. To put Fortas on, Johnson knew he had to get Goldberg off, which was difficult as Goldberg had a lifetime appointment. So Johnson did what he was best at—discerning every man's price. Johnson knew that Goldberg itched for higher office. His first pass at Goldberg was to make him secretary of health, education and welfare, but the Justice declined. Then came an offer that the arrogant Goldberg couldn't refuse, U.S. ambassador to the UN. That wasn't enough. So Johnson promised Goldberg that he would have full discretion in negotiating an end to the war in Vietnam. He told him that if he were successful in doing this, he would support Goldberg in becoming the first Jewish president of the United States. Perhaps there was also an understanding that once Goldberg had finished the job at the UN,

Johnson would re-appoint him to the Court. In any event, the stratagem worked, and Goldberg resigned from the Court.

Goldberg's ethnicity was central to Johnson's thinking. In his later released audio tapes, Johnson said,

> Goldberg would be able to answer the Russians . . . very effective-ly . . . He's got a bulldog face on him, and I think this Jew thing would take the *New York Times*—all this crowd that gives me hell all the time—and disarm them. And still have a Johnson man. I've al-ways thought that Goldberg was the ablest man in Kennedy's Cabi-net, and he was the best man to us. . . . Goldberg sold bananas, you know. . . . He's kind of like I am . . . He's shined some shoes in his day and he's sold newspapers, and he's had to slug it out.

The resignation and the promises were all part of a political double-cross. Goldberg resigned. Johnson appointed Fortas. When Goldberg was done at the UN, Johnson failed to appoint him to anything. Gold-berg returned to private practice. It was a long way down.

The relationship between Fortas and Lyndon Johnson had been closer than an undershirt for many years. Fortas had plotted the legal strategy that assured Johnson's 1948 Senate election by eight-seven votes. It doesn't get much closer than that.

It should not be surprising that the relationship between Fortas and Johnson continued even after Fortas went on the Court. Johnson re-garded Fortas as the "best lawyer I know," and he repeatedly sought his advice on major issues. Sometimes their communications bordered on the unethical. In one instance, they talked about a major litigation pending before the Court.

In his marvelous tell-all book *The Triumph & Tragedy of Lyndon Johnson*, a 1991 work that has just been republished, Johnson's top domestic adviser, Joseph A. Califano, Jr., makes the shocking revelation that Johnson and Supreme Court Justice Abe Fortas not only had *ex parte* conversations about a case pending before the Supreme Court, but that Fortas suggested language to the White House that he wanted to see in the government's brief, and then quoted that language in his opinion, no less!

In April 1966, the Interstate Commerce Commission (ICC) ap-proved the proposed merger of the Pennsylvania and New York Central Railroads over the objections of the Justice Department, which had big antitrust concerns about the combination. Stuart Saunders, chairman of the Pennsylvania Railroad, was a seasoned businessman who had supported Johnson politically, and he was a big Democratic contributor, which in those days meant cash money. Saunders had a track record in big railroad mergers. He was eager to consummate this one as it would be a mega-merger, the largest in history, the resulting entity to be the Penn Central Railroad.

Competing railroads opposed the merger, and they sought to overturn the determination of the ICC. They took their case to the federal courts, where a three-judge court heard the matter and refused to block the merger. The aggrieved railroads went to the Supreme Court. Johnson's Justice Department under Bobby Kennedy, and later Nicholas Katzenbach, had decided not to oppose the merger. Katzenbach's successor as attorney general, Ramsay Clark, sensing corruption in the political deal that had been made, took a different view of the matter and determined that Justice would join the other railroads in opposing the merger under the antitrust laws. Solicitor General Thurgood Marshall was poised to file a brief in the Supreme Court advocating Justice's position. After all, the solicitor general is under the attorney general and is supposed to do his master's bidding.

This angered Saunders, who thought he had a commitment from Kennedy and LBJ that if the ICC approved the merger, the Justice Department would not oppose. So Saunders began to pressure the White House to make Clark's Justice Department reverse its position.

Meanwhile, Johnson called a Thanksgiving Day cabinet meeting at the White House of relevant department heads to consider the matter. Transportation Secretary Alan Boyd, sharply differing with Clark, favored the merger. Johnson wanted the government to submit either no brief or one favoring the merger. When there was an impasse at the cabinet level, Johnson phoned Fortas, a close confidant who was angling to become Chief Justice of the United States. The tape recording of the conversation was destroyed at Johnson's direction. Johnson, however, told Califano that Fortas had said there was no need for the Supreme Court to send the case back to the ICC, and the government's brief should indicate that all the agencies responsible for transportation policy, notably Boyd's Transportation Department, believed the merger should go forward. From his conversation with Fortas, Johnson concluded that the government should file no brief at all. Fortas later called

Califano at home and repeated the advice Johnson said he had given. Califano, a Harvard-trained lawyer, remembered being astounded that he was talking to a Supreme Court Justice, without any of the other parties being present, about what should go into a government brief before the Court.

Johnson directed Califano to call Marshall about the brief, and also to have Gardner Ackley, chairman of the Council of Economic Advisers, visit with Marshall, and present him with a memorandum on the point. Ackley reported back to the White House that "Marshall is obviously unhappy with the situation . . . and would like to find a way out."

Marshall agreed to file a new brief. Califano advised Saunders, who had camped out at the Hay-Adams Hotel across the street from the White House, that the new brief was one he would be happy with.

In a 5-4 decision the Court sent the case back to the ICC for further proceedings. Fortas was one of the dissenting Justices who wanted the merger to go forward. In his dissenting opinion, he quoted from the portion of Marshall's brief that made the very point he had suggested to Johnson. "The United States does . . . not challenge the merger itself. Indeed, the Solicitor General has represented to the Court that 'the agencies of the Executive Branch that have substantive responsibilities for the formulation of economic and transportation policy believe that the merger is in the public interest and that its consummation should be promptly effected.'" On January 15, 1968, the Supreme Court finally approved the merger.

As is self-evident, you can't have a fair and impartial justice system if one side can talk to the judge about the merits of the controversy without the other side being present. It makes the judge a partisan before there is even a hearing. It is an article of faith among lawyers and judges in this country that such contacts, known as *ex parte communications*, are impermissible on the part of the lawyer, and also impermissible on the part of the judge.

This important principle is enshrined in Disciplinary Rule 7-110(B) of the Model Code of Professional Responsibility of the American Bar Association binding on all lawyers. DR 7-110(B) provides that "[i]n an adversary proceeding, a lawyer shall not communicate, or cause another to communicate, as to the merits of the cause with a judge . . . before whom the proceeding is pending [in the absence of the lawyer on the other side of the controversy]." There are exceptions, but they are not relevant to the present discussion.

Similarly, Canon 3(A)(4) of the Code of Conduct for United States Judges provides that "a judge should not initiate, permit, or consider ex parte communications or consider other communications concerning a pending or impending matter that are made outside the presence of the parties or their lawyers."

Oddly, the Code of Conduct for United States Judges does not apply to Justices of the Supreme Court as it does to all other federal judges. In this sense, the Justices are above the law. Still, Chief Justice Roberts said in his 2011 report on the judiciary that the Justices will "consider" the code of conduct, whatever that means, even though not strictly bound by its terms.

The entire episode, ignored by the media in 1991 when Califano first published his book, is shocking. The conduct of Johnson and Fortas in discussing a case before the Court offends the Code of Conduct for United States Judges. Even if the code is not binding on Supreme Court Justices, what happened seriously undermined the independence of the judiciary.

On March 31, 1968, in a televised address to the nation largely about his domestic agenda, a tired Lyndon Johnson rocked the country with twenty words tacked on to the end of his speech: "Accordingly, I shall not seek—and will not accept—the nomination of my party for another term as your President." Only a small group of associates other than his family knew of the decision. One of them was Abe Fortas.

In mid-June, Chief Justice Warren resigned from the Court, effective with the qualification of his successor. Obsessed with his legacy, and fearing a Nixon victory in the November elections, Johnson on June 26, 1968, nominated Fortas to be the first Jewish Chief Justice of the United States. Johnson knew that his "Great Society" and racial justice legacy would play out in the Court in the years to come, and he wanted to be sure that his man in the Marble Palace was there to protect his political accomplishments. Johnson reasoned that if he could not get Fortas confirmed, at least Warren would be there to hold down the liberal fort.

Johnson paired the Fortas nomination with that of another long-time political crony, Homer Thornberry of Texas, a capable court of appeals judge, who had succeeded in 1948 to Johnson's congressional seat when

Johnson went to the Senate. Johnson nominated Thornberry to fill the seat that Fortas would vacate should he be confirmed as Chief Justice. The political musical chairs, as it turned out, smacked of the re-arrangement of deckchairs on the *Titanic.*

While Johnson early on had obtained the support of key southern Senator Richard Russell of Georgia and also Republican Minority Leader Everett Dirksen, he knew he had to move quickly if his nominees were to be confirmed.

Fortas became the target of conservative opposition. They knew of his liberal predispositions. He had represented Owen Lattimore, the old China hand whom Joe McCarthy had accused of being a "top Russian espionage agent." He had also represented the petitioner in *Gideon v. Wainwright,*[2] a landmark case in which a unanimous Supreme Court upheld an indigent's constitutional right to have a lawyer appointed at government expense to defend him in a criminal case.

Robert P. Griffin, a Michigan Republican serving his first term in the Senate, spearheaded the opposition to Fortas. He announced that he opposed any appointment made by a possibly lame-duck president. Right-wing Senators John Tower of Texas and Strom Thurmond of South Carolina were quick to join Griffin's camp. The day before Johnson announced his picks for the Court, Judiciary Committee Chairman James Eastland of Mississippi told the White House, "Abe Fortas cannot be confirmed as Chief Justice." Arkansas Dixiecrat Senator John McClellan spoiled to have "that S.O.B Fortas" before the Senate "so that [I can] fight his nomination." The first day after the names of Fortas and Thornberry went to the Senate, Griffin had eighteen Republican senators pledged to oppose. Griffin was on an attack-and-kill campaign that was prepared to filibuster to block the nominations.

There were the inevitable charges of anti-Semitism, which Johnson encouraged. Griffin countered with a statement, intended to establish his pro-Jew street cred, that he would support Goldberg's return to the Court, indicating that he would back a Jewish nominee even if put forward by a lame-duck president. Griffin's response was that "Goldberg was on leave of absence and had originally been nominated by Kennedy."[3]

Convinced that the opposition to Fortas was rooted in bigotry and opposition to his civil rights program, Johnson, the "master of the Senate," assumed command of the confirmation fight. He told Joe Califano to tell Henry Ford, an important Griffin constituent, that "it wouldn't be a good thing for the country for the first Jewish Chief Justice to be turned down."[4] He thought Jewish businessmen should be concerned that Griffin's campaign to turn down the first Jewish Chief Justice would arouse anti-Semitic feeling. He told a White House aide to "get every Jew out there in Illinois to go up to Dirksen and thank him for his support." He wanted someone to contact Albert Jenner, chairman of the American Bar Association Committee on the Judiciary, and voice his concern that the Senate "might turn down Fortas because he was a Jew." He wanted Califano to enlist the aid of Jewish organizations. When staff member Harry McPherson showed Johnson a photograph of Fortas wearing a yarmulke as he played a violin duet at a benefit with a prominent Jewish philanthropist, suggesting that they circulate the photo to some Jewish groups, Johnson said, "This doesn't mean a damn thing. I've had on more of those than Abe has."

Fortas testified before the Senate Judiciary Committee for four days in July 1968. He managed to deflect questioning about his liberal voting record on the Court, citing the independence of the judiciary. On his relationship with Johnson, he lied and said he had not advised Johnson on any cases pending before the Court. Califano and other Johnson aides who knew the truth "winced" at Fortas's testimony because they knew how "misleading and deceptive" it was.[5] The Penn Central merger affair was probably only one ugly example of the improper *ex parte* communications between Fortas and Johnson. After four days, Fortas refused to reappear for further questioning before the committee.

As the hearings ensued, Griffin dropped a bombshell. Fortas had received $15,000 as an honorarium for nine speaking engagements at American University Law School. The money represented more than 40 percent of a Supreme Court Justice's salary, and it was seven times what any other American University seminar leader had ever been paid. The funding came not from American University, but from a number of clients and partners of Fortas's former law firm, many of whom might reasonably expect to have business before the Court.

There was also a letter addressed to a number of prominent businessmen soliciting contributions for the honorarium. This was the turning point. After B. J. Tennery, dean of American University Law School, his testimony prepared by Fortas himself, testified on September 13, Everett Dirksen switched positions and joined the opposition.

The Griffin filibuster began, and the vote on the motion to close debate was 45 for and 43 against, 14 short of the required two-thirds majority, but the bare majority that both Fortas and Johnson needed to save face. Fortas immediately wrote to Johnson withdrawing his nomination. Fortas returned to the Supreme Court as an associate Justice. The Thornberry nomination became moot since there was no vacant seat to fill. David Leonhardt of the *New York Times* recently called the Fortas nomination "one of the most consequential blunders in modern American politics."[6] Nixon would appoint Warren Burger as Chief Justice in 1969, and the top seat on the Court has been occupied by a conservative ever since.

In 1969 there was a new scandal. Fortas had accepted a $20,000 retainer from the family foundation of financier Louis Wolfson, a friend and former client, in January 1966. Fortas had signed a contract with Wolfson's foundation. In return for unspecified advice, the foundation was to pay Fortas $20,000 a year for the rest of Fortas's life (and then pay his widow for the rest of her life). Wolfson was under investigation for securities violations at the time, and it was alleged that he expected that this arrangement with Fortas would help him avoid criminal charges or else secure a presidential pardon. Wolfson did ask Fortas to help him secure a pardon from Johnson, which Fortas claimed that he did not do. The evidence, however, is murky on this point. Fortas recused himself from Wolfson's case when it came before the Court and had earlier returned the retainer, but not until Wolfson had been twice indicted. Subsequently, Wolfson was convicted, and served time in jail. Fortas resigned in disgrace May 14, 1969.

Neither Goldberg nor Fortas did quite so well as did their co-religionists. Fortas was the last to hold the Jewish seat. Nixon appointed Harry Blackmun, a Methodist, to fill the seat Fortas vacated. From then on there were no Jews on the Court until the appointment of Ruth Bader Ginsburg in 1993.

There are now three Jews serving on the Supreme Court. If the Senate confirms Merrick Garland as Scalia's replacement, there will be a fourth. Happily, the era of the Jewish "seat," like the era of the Catholic "seat," has come to an end.

Does a Justice's religion really matter? In his tough *Washington Post* piece titled "The Supreme Court Is a Political Court: Republicans' Actions Are Proof," Judge Richard Posner argues that Catholicism influenced and has influenced conservatives Scalia, Roberts, and Thomas, but Kennedy and Sotomayor less so. The three Jewish Justices, Ginsburg, Breyer, and Kagan, he contends, have not been "influenced by Judaism in their judicial work."[7]

Notes

1. 381 U.S. 479 (1965).
2. 372 U.S. 335 (1963).
3. Joseph A. Califano, *The Triumph and Tragedy of Lyndon Johnson*, New York: Random House (1991) at 310.
4. *Id.*
5. *Id.* at 314.
6. http://www.nytimes.com/2014/06/03/upshot/the-supreme-court-blunder-that-liberals-tend-to-make.html.
7. By Richard A. Posner, "The Supreme Court Is a Political Court: Republicans' Actions Are Proof," *Washington Post*, March 9, 2016. Available at https://www.washingtonpost.com/opinions/the-supreme-court-is-a-political-court-republicans-actions-are-proof/2016/03/09/4c851860-e142-11e5-8d98-4b3d9215ade1_story.html?hpid=hp_no-name_opinion-card-a%3Ahomepage%2Fstory.

8

THE SUPREME COURT TACKLES
THE MIDDLE EAST

Is Jerusalem Part of Israel?

You ought to let the Jews have Jerusalem: it was they who made it
famous.
—Winston Churchill 1955[1]

In 2002, Menachem B. Zivotofsky was born in Jerusalem of American
parents. His parents wished to record his American citizenship and
obtain for him a U.S. passport.[2] An American passport contains a field
for place of birth. Typically this is the city and country where it happened. The significance of reciting the place of birth is not to accord
recognition to the state where birth occurred. The State Department
itself has explained that "identification"—not recognition—"is the principal reason that U.S. passports require 'place of birth.'"[3]

Zivotofsky's parents, perhaps for symbolic reasons, wanted Menachem's place of birth to read "Jerusalem, Israel" as Jews think of Jerusalem as the unified capital of the State of Israel and the capital of the
Jewish people. The State Department refused, finding the request inconsistent with the government's foreign policy of "neutrality" with respect to sovereignty over Jerusalem. Other Americans born in Jerusalem do not necessarily share Zivotofsky's desire for passport identification. Noah Goldberg, an American born in Jerusalem in 1995 to two
distinguished journalists then stationed in Israel, Amy Wilentz and Nick

Goldberg, writes, "I am infinitely willing to sacrifice one line on a passport in recognition of . . . the rich, complex, painful, and constant history of Jerusalem."[4]

In 2002 the Democratic-controlled Congress enacted a law, the Foreign Relations Authorization Act. Section 214 of the Act is titled "United States Policy with Respect to Jerusalem as the Capital of Israel." At the heart of the dispute was Section 214(d), the provision dealing with passports. It specifies, "For purposes of the registration of birth, certification of nationality or issuance of a passport in the City of Jerusalem, the Secretary [of State] shall, upon the request of the citizen or the citizen's legal guardian, record the place of birth as Israel."

The statute instructed the State Department in instances where an American citizen was born in Jerusalem to "record the place of birth as Israel" in consular documents and in their passports if they or their parents requested the designation. When President George W. Bush signed the measure into law, he issued a "signing statement," stating that he would not carry out the Jerusalem provision because it "impermissibly interferes with the President's constitutional authority to conduct foreign affairs." Such reservation did not affect the statute from becoming the law of the land, and it was probably unconstitutional as permitting the president to repeal or modify sections of the law he didn't agree with. Presidential "signing statements" started with James Monroe. The Constitution neither permits nor prohibits presidential use of signing statements. The *New York Times* reported that George W. Bush "broke all records," using signing statements to challenge about 1,200 sections of bills during his eight years in office, about twice as many as all of his predecessors combined. In 2006, a blue-ribbon task force of the American Bar Association said that signing statements "undermine the rule of law and our constitutional system of separation of powers." The Supreme Court has not spoken expressly on the matter.[5] In any event, Congress left it to the Jerusalem-born American citizen to decide what he or she wanted to list as place of birth in official documents.

The problem arose when the Obama administration, in direct defiance of the statute, took the position that it took no official position as to the status of Jerusalem, and that its future was to be resolved by negotiation between the Israelis and the Palestinians.

Accordingly, the Obama State Department ruled that an American citizen's passport may not state his or her place of birth as "Jerusalem, Israel," but only "Jerusalem." So what is the foreign policy of the United States? Who determines it? Must the political branches of the government always speak with one voice on foreign relations? They hardly do on domestic affairs, and the Constitution makes no distinction. As Council on Foreign Relations President Richard Haass, a seasoned veteran of the State Department, has reflected, "foreign policy begins at home."

The position on Jerusalem is a one-off double standard when compared with State Department regulations covering other areas of the world where questions are also among "the most difficult and complex in international affairs." For example, the State Department permits an Irish Republican to record his place of birth as "Belfast" rather than "United Kingdom." And even though the United States has not yet conceded to the Chinese that Taiwan is part of China but has not taken the provocative step of recognizing Taiwan as a state or country, the State Department records the birthplace of one born in Taiwan as either "China" or "Taiwan" at the option of the citizen and in accord with a law on which the law as to Jerusalem was modeled. The State Department has complied with the law, but states in its Foreign Affairs Manual, "The United States does not officially recognize Taiwan as a 'state' or 'country' although passport issuing officers may enter 'Taiwan' as a place of birth."[6]

Benjamin Netanyahu has said that Israeli sovereignty over Jerusalem is "indisputable." Palestinians believe that some or all of Jerusalem should be the capital of a Palestinian state, if such a state is ever established. De facto control of all of Jerusalem is beyond dispute within Israel's sovereignty, and many foreign-relations experts, except for some of the planners in the Obama administration, believe that the possibility of an agreed-upon partition is a train that may well have left the station. The lesson of history is that possession is nine points of the law. Illustrating the shifting situation on the ground, a 2015 Google search for "two state solution dead" yielded 22,900,000 hits. Mahdi Hasan, writing for Al Jazeera, recently posted that the "two state solution is dead" although "most of the West's leading politicians and pundits—especially of the liberal/left variety—continue to stick their heads in the proverbial sand, refusing to acknowledge this inconvenient truth."[7]

Obama reaffirmed his Jerusalem policy in a speech at the UN in 2011 when he stated, "Ultimately, it is the Israelis and the Palestinians, not us, who must reach agreement on the issues that divide them," including "Jerusalem."[8] As far as anyone can tell, he is the first president to make such a statement. Palestine may have been foremost in Obama's mind in 2011, but that was four years ago. There are many fault lines in the Middle East. Events in Syria, Iran, and the presence of ISIS in Iraq appear to have turned the president's attention elsewhere.

The Court's decision in favor of the Obama decision and against Zivotofsky was remarkable for the counterintuitive line-up of the Justices. The three Jewish Justices voted with Sotomayor and Thomas to reject Zivotofsky's suit. Kennedy, writing for the majority of six, declared, "Questions touching upon the history of the ancient city and its present legal and international status are among the most difficult and complex in international affairs."[9]

Whatever damage was done to U.S. foreign relations occurred with the enactment of Section 214(d). The statute of Congress did not sit well with the Palestinians. When Congress passed the bill in 2002, there were howls of protest on the West Bank and in Gaza. A cable from the U.S. consulate in Jerusalem noted that the Palestine Liberation Organization Executive Committee, the Fatah Central Committee, and the Palestinian Authority Cabinet had all issued statements claiming that the act "'undermines the role of the U.S. as a sponsor of the peace process.'"[10] In the Gaza Strip and elsewhere residents marched in protest.[11]

In dissent, Chief Justice Roberts jabbed back that to give weight to such protests is to subject an Act of Congress to an "international heckler's veto."[12] There was within the Court a deep separation-of-powers divide as to whether the executive branch enjoyed plenary authority over foreign affairs, including what goes into a passport. The scholastic debate over the recognition power was one that the Chief said "has not been necessary over the past 225 years" and "[p]erhaps . . . could have waited another 225 years."[13]

But the partisan subtext of the decision was how the Justices really felt about American foreign policy in the Middle East. Did they side with Congress's "bone to the Jews" that the United States should move toward recognizing the reality of Israeli sovereignty over Jerusalem? Or did they seek to bolster an all-but-abandoned foreign policy that harbored the vain hope for the partition of Jerusalem as an element of a two-state solution? It is difficult to see that *Zivotofsky* was more about the Constitution than about putting a judicial thumb on the scale of the Israeli-Palestinian dispute.

The majority sided with Obama's "head in the sand" view that the issue of Jerusalem remains on the table.[14] The six Justices rested their case on the president's purported power to "recognize" a foreign government, although Congress has legislated "irrespective of recognition by the United States" in a host of instances.[15] And where Congress has seen fit to legislate, the Constitution commands the president to "take Care" that the laws "be faithfully executed."[16] "Recognition" is a term of art under international law. It is a "formal acknowledgement" that a polity "possesses the qualifications for statehood" or "that a particular regime is the effective government of a state."[17]

Nowhere in the Constitution does it say that the president has the power to recognize a foreign government, much less the exclusive power to do so. The Court found such a power and authority in the president's ceremonial obligation to receive ambassadors in Article II. Indeed, in our history, recognition is a function that has been at times exercised by Congress. Some presidents have asserted an exclusive recognition power, but others, notably Jackson and Lincoln, have expressed uncertainty.

To cite an example marshaled in support of Scalia's dissent, Congress, not the president, legislated in 1934 to grant independence to the Philippines, then an American territory, and directed Franklin Roosevelt to "recognize the independence of the Philippine Islands as a separate and self-governing nation."

How the simple identifying statement in a passport, made at the request of an American citizen, that his place of birth be "Jerusalem, Israel" could conceivably undermine the president's power to recognize a foreign government or to make foreign policy boggles the mind. But there it is. Pure and simple, the statute has nothing to do with recognition. Full stop. Obama's State Department refused to use the words "Jerusalem, Israel" in Zivotofsky's passport or in the consular documents registering his birth as an expression of purported American neutrality on the subject of Jerusalem's status on the spurious basis that to do so would have undermined the president's recognition power. Of course, had Zivotofsky been born in Tel Aviv, his passport would have recited his place of birth as "Tel Aviv, Israel." This statement might have also outraged Fatah or Hamas, but Truman recognized Israel in 1948 and, for the time being, they are stuck with it. It is nothing short of amazing that such an inconsequential issue should have ever reached the Supreme Court.

When, without congressional authorization, Truman nationalized the steel mills in 1952 in the interests of "national security," the Court held 6-3 that the seizure was unconstitutional.[18] In that case, the Court said that if

> the President takes measures incompatible with the expressed or implied will of Congress . . . he can rely only upon his own constitutional powers minus any constitutional powers of Congress over the matter.[19]

To succeed in this third category, the President's asserted power must be both "exclusive" and "conclusive" on the issue.

Claims by the president to exclusive and preclusive power over Congress are inherently suspect. They stand "in the least favorable of possible constitutional powers," and such claims must be "scrutinized with caution."[20] As Chief Justice Roberts put it in his blistering dissent in *Zivotofsky*, "We have instead stressed that the President's power reaches 'its lowest ebb' when he contravenes the express will of Congress, 'for what is at stake is the equilibrium established by our constitutional system.'"[21]

The Constitution's text, history, and the precedents are unconvincing in their support for the arguments of the majority as to whether the president's power in the field of foreign relations is "exclusive" and "conclusive" when in defiance of a statute of Congress. The dissenters had the better part of the argument. When it comes to foreign relations, the powers of the political branches of our government are in many respects correlative and overlapping. The Constitution authorizes the president to appoint ambassadors, but with the advice and consent of the Senate.[22] The Constitution authorizes the president to negotiate treaties with other countries, but such treaties must be ratified by a two-thirds Senate vote.[23] The president can lead us into war, but only after Congress has declared it.[24] The president is bound to "take care that the laws be faithfully executed," but only after Congress has enacted them.[25] The president has the ceremonial obligation to receive ambassadors.[26] Nonetheless, Congress invited Israel's Netanyahu to address a joint session, presumably over the objections of the White House and the State Department. Nowhere does it say in the Constitution that the president or Congress has the authority to "recognize" another government. And, needless to say, there is nothing in the Constitution about passports or what they should contain or how the word "Israel" in the place-of-birth field in an American passport undermines presidential authority. The president can, without doing violence to his authority, disagree with Congress. And Congress, without undermining its own authority, can always disagree with the president.

The Court found, although it didn't need to, that the president has exclusive authority to recognize other nations. From this premise, they took a quantum leap and reasoned that the president has exclusive authority to determine what should be listed in a passport—even in defiance of an act of Congress. This finding was illogical, unprecedented, and without basis in the Constitution. For decades after the founding of the Republic states, cities and even notaries public issued passports alongside the federal government. The State Department took over the exclusive issuance of passports in 1856 when Congress gave it that authority.

The Constitution also gave Congress broad powers in the field of foreign relations, and the document is riddled with examples. These powers were previously in the exclusive preserve of the king of England. Aside from the war-making power, Article I, §8 authorizes Congress to appropriate money for the "common defense"; regulate international commerce; establish "an uniform rule of naturalization"; regulate the value of foreign coin; "define and punish Piracies and Felonies committed on the high seas" and "Offenses against the Law of Nations"; raise and support the army and navy; and "make laws necessary and proper for carrying into Execution" the powers of the government. Congress has declared that a child born outside the United States to parents who are U.S. citizens is deemed a citizen without naturalization and is entitled to a U.S. passport. Since a passport is proof of citizenship, the issuance of passports and their contents would appear to be well within a "rule of naturalization." At least eleven of the powers of Congress enumerated in Article I, §8 "deal in some way with foreign affairs."[27] There were no airplanes in 1789 either, but no one has ever suggested that Congress can't appropriate money to "raise and support" an air force. Had the Founding Fathers wished to give the president all the plenary powers of the king of England in the field of foreign relations, they easily could have said so. Instead, they visualized a delicate system of checks and balances so that too much power would not be vested in the president. After all, a president may be a master politician in raising money, campaigning hard, and energizing a political base. He may nonetheless be an inept statesman. In foreign as well as domestic affairs, the Constitution "enjoins upon its branches separateness but interdependence, autonomy but reciprocity."[28]

Scalia railed at the majority and particularly skewered the concurring opinion of Clarence Thomas, with whom he is usually in agreement: "Whereas the Court's analysis threatens congressional power over foreign affairs with gradual erosion . . . [the Thomas] approach shatters it in one stroke."

The Court by a vote of 6-3 gave the split decision to, as Scalia put it, a "presidency more reminiscent of George III than George Washington."[29] It held that a statute of Congress "impermissibly interferes with the President's constitutional authority to conduct the nation's foreign affairs."

The case is as interesting for which Justices voted how on the issue as for the result. Where the president was Barack Obama, three of the five Republican-appointed dissenting Justices (Roberts, Scalia, and Alito) voted with Zivotofsky and thought that there was nothing unconstitutional about Congress asserting its shared responsibility in foreign affairs in the matter of the contents of a passport. The majority voted for presidential primacy in the State Department's "neutrality" policy when it came to Jerusalem passports even though four of its members (Sotomayor, Breyer, Kagan, and Ginsburg) are normally wary of presidential power in wartime unless there is congressional authorization. The conservative Thomas, who normally votes to reaffirm presidential power, voted with them against the Congress. The three dissenting conservative Justices (Roberts, Scalia, and Alito) held that an act of Congress trumped a policy decision of the executive branch in the foreign policy field, but it was they who had voted in favor of presidential primacy when it came to military trials in Guantanamo.[30] Where the president was George W. Bush, three of the four liberals now sitting had held in that case that the president required congressional approval for such trials.[31] The wobbly "swinger," Kennedy, a moderate conservative, joined the conservatives in the Guantanamo case and the liberal majority in *Zivotofsky*. This left the bizarre vote of Clarence Thomas, who at least was consistent. He voted with the dissent in *Hamdan v. Rumsfeld*,[32] ready to grant extraordinary power to the president in a case of terrorist detention, but willing to "split the baby in half" with a tortured constitutional argument in *Zivotofsky*. Making a distinction without a difference, he said that Congress had validly trumped the president when it came to Jerusalem birth reports, but it lacked the power to trump the president when it came to passports.

There were interesting precedents on both sides of the issue, none of which seemed dispositive. The text and original understanding of the Constitution shed little light on the place-of-birth blank in a U.S. passport. No matter how any Justice explains his or her vote as an interpretation of the Constitution as to the separation of powers over foreign affairs, it is indisputable that the votes were driven by some nuanced policy choice between Israeli and Palestinian interests. Yes, the judiciary clearly must stay out of foreign affairs. The Constitution wisely leaves this arena to the political branches. This led Justice Breyer to duck the case entirely as presenting a "political question."

Courts are not supposed to answer political questions. But the able Justices who decided *Zivotofsky* had to have known that by tilting the scales toward the executive branch, they not only kept on life support a failed foreign policy, but also created a dangerous precedent in ceding to the president a "Constitution means what I would like it to mean" primacy in the field of foreign affairs.

Notes

1. Remark to diplomat Evelyn Shickburgh. *Diaries 1951–1956* (London, 1986).

2. Congress's naturalization power, Art. §8, cl. 4, enables it to grant American citizenship to such a person born abroad. *United States v. Wong Kim Ark*, 169 U.S. 649, 702–3 (1898). This would include furnishing its citizens with official papers documenting their citizenship, such as a passport.

3. "Place of birth" may differentiate citizens with the same or similar names.

4. "What I Think About When I Look at My Passport," by Noah Goldberg, Huffington Post, June 11, 2015. Available at http://www.huffingtonpost.com/noah-goldberg/what-i-think-about-when-i-look-at-my-passport_b_7552042.html.

5. But see *Clinton* v. *City of New York*, 524 U.S. 417 (1998), holding unconstitutional the presidential line-item veto, which is of a piece with a signing statement.

6. 7 FAM §1300, App. D, §1340(d)(6).

7. "The Two State Solution Is Dead" by Mahdi Hasan, May 27, 2015. Available at http://www.aljazeera.com/indepth/opinion/2015/05/state-palestine-israel-zionist-150527070943455.html.

8. Remarks by President Obama in Address to the United Nations General Assembly (September 21, 2011), 2011 Daily Comp. of Pres. Doc. No. 00661, at 4.

9. *Zivotofsky v. Kerry*, 576 U.S. (2015). Slip op. at 1.

10. *Zivotofsky v. Kerry*, 576 U.S. (2015). Slip op. at 4.

11. See the Associated Press and Reuters, "Palestinians Stone Police Guarding Western Wall," *Seattle Times*, October 5, 2002, at A7.

12. *Zivotofsky*, Dissenting opinion of Chief Justice Roberts. Slip op. at 5.

13. *Id.* at 6.

14. National Security Adviser Susan Rice told the Arab-American Institute on April 30, 2015, that a "comprehensive peace between Israelis and Palestinians" was still "possible."

15. See e.g., 18 U.S.C. §§11, 1116(b) (2).

16. Art. II, §3.

17. Restatement (Third) of Foreign Relations Law of the United States §203, Comment a, at 84 (1986).

18. *Youngstown Sheet & Tube Co. v. Sawyer*, 343 U.S. 579 (1952).

19. *Id.*, at 637–38. Concurring opinion of Justice Jackson.

20. *Id.*, at 640.

21. Citing *Youngstown Sheet & Tube Co. v. Sawyer*, 343 U.S. 579, 637–38 (1952) (Jackson, J., concurring).

22. Art. II, §2, cl. 1.

23. Art. II, §2, cl. 2.

24. *Compare* Art. 2, §2, cl. 1 *with* Art. I, §8, cl. 11.

25. Art. II, §3.

26. Art. II §3.

27. By Lawrence Tribe, American Constitutional Law, §5–18, at 965.

28. *Youngstown*, 343 U.S. at 365 (Jackson, J., concurring).

29. Dissenting opinion of Scalia, J. Slip op. at 19.

30. *Hamdan v. Rumsfeld*, 548 U.S. 557 (2006).

31. Kagan, who voted with the majority in *Zivotofsky* was not on the Court at the time of the *Hamdan* decision. Roberts took no part in the consideration or decision of the *Hamdan* case.

32. *Hamdan v. Rumsfeld*, 548 U.S. 557 (2006).

9

THE FEMALE SEAT AND RUTH BADER GINSBURG

Anatomy is destiny.
—Sigmund Freud

Ruth Bader Ginsburg was not the first female Justice. That was Sandra Day O'Connor, appointed by Reagan in 1981. Nor was she the last. That was Elena Kagan, appointed by Obama in 2010. From 2006, when the moderate conservative O'Connor retired, until 2009, when Obama appointed Sotomayor, Ginsburg was the sole inhabitant of a "female seat." She complained she felt lonely as the only woman on a bench of nine.

Plagued by bouts of illness and eighty-two years of age, she is the oldest Justice. She is also probably one of the wealthiest, reporting in 2015 a net worth within a range of $5–20 million. Intellectually sharp as a tack, she has given no indication of retiring any time soon. Born in Brooklyn at the height of the depression, the daughter of a furrier, she graduated from Cornell, attended Harvard Law School, but switched to Columbia to be with her husband, Martin Ginsburg, a tax lawyer who later became a partner in Weil, Gotshal & Manges, a New York law firm. They had met on a blind date.

Upon graduation, like O'Connor before her, she found it difficult to gain employment as a lawyer. She clerked for Edmund Palmieri, a terrific trial judge in the iconic Southern District of New York, referred to as the "Mother Court," as it is the oldest federal court in the country.

Palmieri, it is said, was not happy about taking her, and only relented when pressured by one of her professors at Columbia Law School.

A wisp of a thing, five feet tall, and weighing in at about one hundred pounds, bent over, her hair pulled back in her severe signature style, everyone's quintessential grandmother, she gives the overwhelming appearance of frailty. Nevertheless, her opinions draw deep water, and she is often the first Justice to hurl a trenchant question from the bench.[1] As a lawyer, Ginsburg became a stalwart advocate of women's rights, cofounding the ACLU women's rights project. Her effective advocacy for women is of historic dimension.

Jeffrey Toobin, in the best profile ever written about the Justice, perhaps exaggerates when he says, "[H]er reputation as the Thurgood Marshall of the women's rights movement exceeds her renown as a Justice."[2] Ginsburg credits herself with the appellate victory as an advocate in *Reed v. Reed*, the landmark Supreme Court case holding that the Equal Protection Clause applies to gender as well as racial discrimination.[3] She actually coauthored the brief for Mrs. Reed, but did not argue the case. The facts in *Reed* were quite stark. The story began March 29, 1967, in Ada County, Idaho, when 19-year-old Richard Lynn Reed, using his father's rifle, committed suicide. His adoptive parents, Cecil and Sally Reed, had separated. Sally enjoyed custody of Richard during his tender years, but once he became a teenager, custody went to Cecil. After Richard's death, the parents filed dueling petitions to become the administrator of Richard's estate. The court appointed Cecil the administrator based on Section 15-314 of the Idaho Code, which required that "[o]f several persons claiming and equally entitled to administer, males must be preferred to females."

Sally complained, claiming that she had been denied the equal protection of the law. The *Reed* case was hardly complicated in terms of the facts and the applicable law. But in light of the powerful political issue at stake, the issue assumed colossal proportions. The text of the Fourteenth Amendment mentions neither race nor gender. Indeed, unlike the Declaration of Independence, drafted by slaveholder Thomas Jefferson, which mentions equality up front when it proclaims that "all men are created equal," the only place in the Constitution that mentions equality came seventy-one years after the ratification of the document. And the original understanding of the Fourteenth Amendment was that it dealt with race—not gender.

Ginsburg challenged this assumption, and the Supreme Court unanimously agreed. Writing for the Court, Chief Justice Burger unmistakably declared, "[W]e have concluded that the arbitrary preference established in favor of males by 15-314 of the Idaho Code cannot stand in face of the Fourteenth Amendment's command that no State deny the equal protection of the laws to any person within its jurisdiction."

Reed became the benchmark precedent for subsequent cases protecting both men and women from gender discrimination. In 1972, Ginsburg and her husband won a tax case in the Tenth Circuit styled *Moritz v. Commissioner*,[4] where a man, not a woman, had been the victim of gender discrimination. Charles Moritz was a single man who lived with his invalid mother, and took care of her. She was dependent on him for support. He incurred the expense of a caregiver so he could be gainfully employed. The Internal Revenue Code allowed a deduction for such expenditures to a "woman or widower, or to a husband whose wife is incapacitated," but not to a single man. If he had been female, he would have had a deduction for expenses, but as a man he was not so entitled. The Court found the statutory distinction between a man and a woman was an "invidious discrimination" "premised on sex alone." Under the principles established by the Supreme Court in *Reed*, the distinction could not stand.

Ginsburg rose to become general counsel of the ACLU. Championing women's rights, she argued six cases before the Supreme Court between 1973 and 1976, and won five of them. In 1980, Jimmy Carter appointed her to the DC Circuit. He said he wanted to see more blacks and women on the federal bench. This time, her husband moved with her. He transferred to Weil's DC office. He was quite a wit. Addressing a lawyers' group, he quipped, "I am president of the 'Denis Thatcher Society.' It is a society of men whose wives have jobs they wish to hell they had." Martin Ginsburg died in 2010.

Jeffrey Toobin reports that Ginsburg dresses often in "exotic shifts," projecting "a dowager's elegance."[5] She was a close personal friend, despite being a professional foe, of Scalia, with whom she shared a love of grand opera, but with whom she disagreed in about half the decided cases. Scalia and his wife often enjoyed an Italian dinner with Ginsburg lubricated with a glass or two of fine Chianti.

Scalia may not have squared with Ginsburg's passion for modern art either. While his chambers are decorated with portraits of former Justices, adorning the walls of her chambers are two original paintings by the abstract expressionist Mark Rothko; a painting by Max Weber, an American cubist who turned to figurative Jewish themes; and one by abstractionist Josef Albers.[6]

"It's amazing to think of me—an icon at 82," she told an audience of law students recently at the American Constitution Society's annual meeting in Washington.[7] There, her former law clerk Justice Goodwin Liu of the California Supreme Court, showed a slide portraying a woman with Ginsburg's likeness tattooed on her arm. She was Rachel Fink, a 23-year-old student at the University of Maryland, College Park, who said she chose Ginsburg as a "role model for women's rights and gender issues." Liu surmised that even though Scalia was a rock star celebrity, it is hard to conceive of someone with a Scalia tattoo, "not even at the Federalist Society."

Supreme Court Justices seem to have difficulty with getting her name straight. When she made a full argument before the Supreme Court, in 1976, Chief Justice Warren E. Burger addressed her. "Mrs. Bader? Mrs. Ginsburg?" he said. (Men of Burger's vintage seldom saw female lawyers, much less those with hydra-headed names). Later in the same case, Justice Potter Stewart erred by calling her "Mrs. Bader." Scalia only recently in the course of oral argument referred to her as "Justice Goldberg." When laughter erupted in the courtroom, he said, "Sorry, Ruth."

Ginsburg, like Scalia, believes that social change should come from the legislature or from the executive branch of government. Yet she has consistently voted for gay rights. She has a continuing hand on the pulse beat of social change. When the U.S. ambassador to Hanoi, Ted Osius, wanted to renew his vows with his husband in August 2015, Ginsburg officiated. She said, "Officiating over the renewal of [their] vows was a joy." The couple had adopted two children. Noting the tectonic shift in public opinion about gay rights, she told the American Constitution Society that when gays came out into the open, people "looked around" and awakened to the fact that friends and family members are gay. This has not been true in the field of race relations, she says, where there is still a "high degree of segregation" in schools and housing, diminishing meaningful contact between the races.

Ginsburg thinks the judiciary should elaborate the way a society ought to develop in narrowly drawn decisions rather than sweeping pronouncements. For this reason, she would approach the Constitution like two porcupines mating—cautiously. Conservative Professor Steven Calabresi of Northwestern University Law School told Toobin that she is a "common law constitutionalist." She believes the "Court should not go too far in any given case." For example, in her well-known Madison Lecture given at the New York University School of Law in 1992, she expressed concern that the Court in *Roe v. Wade* had gone too far in its sweeping abortion-rights decision, provoking the backlash that ensued. She thought that the Court should have only invalidated the Texas statute before it and invited the other state legislatures to accomplish the needed reforms. She plainly understands how dangerous it is for the Court to utter pronouncements that find no public support or consensus.

Toobin quotes Ginsburg as saying, "The one big change in the time I've been here has been the loss of [her (professional) "sister-in-law"][8] Justice O'Connor. I think if you look at the term when she was not with us, every five-to-four decision when I was with the four, I would have been with the five if she had stayed." When Alito replaced O'Connor, the Court lurched in a 180-degree turn to the right. After the 5-4 decision in the *Hobby Lobby* case, she told anchor Katie Couric that she believes the male Supreme Court Justices who voted with the majority have a "blind spot" when it comes to women. But while she has dissented in more than her share of cases, Ginsburg has left an indelible mark like none other on development of the law of gender equality.

In Ginsburg's view, her crowning achievement on the Court has been in a case she lost, the *Lily Ledbetter* case, another partisan 5-4 decision with the four liberals (Ginsburg, Breyer, Sotomayor, and Kagan) in dissent, voting for the employee, Lilly Ledbetter, and the five conservative Justices voting for her employer, Goodyear Tire.[9] Lawyers and judges usually don't like to mention cases they lost, but in this instance Ginsburg frequently refers to the case in appearances throughout the country.

Lilly Ledbetter did not involve the Constitution or even the coverage of Title VII, the employment discrimination statute at issue. Instead, the case turned on the procedural issue of the statute of limitations. Ledbetter worked as an area manager, a job normally occupied by men, for Goodyear Tire and Rubber Company at its Gadsden, Alabama, plant from 1979 until 1998. In March 1998, shortly before her retirement, she received an anonymous note that she was being paid less than men in her position. Ledbetter had started with the same pay as male employees, but by retirement, she was earning $3,727 per month compared to fifteen male managers who earned anywhere from $4,286 to $5,236 per month. She sued under Title VII for gender discrimination. The evidence at trial indicated that Ledbetter's salary initially was similar to those of male employees, but over time her pay was discriminatory, and the disparity widened. The jury awarded her $3.8 million in damages.

The applicable statute of limitations provides that claims under Title VII for pay discrimination have to be brought within 180 days of the "violation." The issue was whether the suit was time barred because brought more than 180 days after the decision to discriminate and most of the discriminatory underpayments. Many of Lilly's claims went back for years. She conceded that discriminatory behavior occurred long before, but argued that it still affected her during the 180-day charging period. Was the period of limitations suspended each time that Lilly received a discriminatory paycheck? Alito thought not. He wrote for the Court that Lilly should have sued each time she received a paycheck. But how was she to know that she was the victim of unlawful discrimination when she didn't know how much anyone else earned? Often individuals do not know the salary of other employees in their workplace. Neither do partners in many large law firms. Ginsburg pointed out in a dry dissent that she read from the bench that "one-third of private sector employers have adopted specific rules prohibiting employees from discussing their wages with co-workers; only one in ten employers has adopted a pay openness policy." The holding was a very significant obstacle for many pay discrimination claims under Title VII. The decision was not based on the text of the law, and it was at odds with Congress's broad purpose of protecting workers. But *Lilly Ledbetter* was an employment case; and there the conservatives make their own rules.

In her dissent, Ginsburg invited Congress to rectify the decision as it had done in other instances of gender discrimination decisions by the Rehnquist court that were, in her view, wrongly decided. Congress acted quickly to reverse the decision. In 2009, just nine days after taking office, President Obama signed the Lilly Ledbetter Fair Pay Act. The act reinstates prior law and makes clear that pay discrimination claims on the basis of sex, race, national origin, age, religion, and disability "accrue" whenever an employee receives a discriminatory paycheck, as well as when a discriminatory pay decision or practice is taken, when a person becomes subject to the decision or practice, or when a person is otherwise affected by the decision or practice. This is important because women today are paid, on average, only seventy-seven cents for every dollar paid to white men.[10] On average, African American women earn only 64 percent and Latino women earn only 54 percent of the income of Caucasian, non-Hispanic males.[11] The Court's decision in *Ledbetter* is only one of a number of partisan decisions of the Roberts court that favor employers over employees bringing discrimination or sexual harassment claims.

So where is Chief Justice Roberts's "umpire," fairly calling balls and strikes? Discarded in the dustbin of partisan ideology. Meanwhile, Natalie Portman stars in a forthcoming biopic, titled *On the Basis of Sex*, depicting Ginsburg's struggles as a champion of women's rights.

Notes

1. In the October 2013 Term, Ginsburg asked the first question 37 percent of the time; Sotomayor, perhaps more inquisitive, asked the most questions of all the Justices, averaging more than 21 in each hour-long argument. See Liptak, note 6. Available at http://www.nytimes.com/2013/07/02/us/bound-together-on-the-court-but-by-beliefs-not-gender.html.

2. By Jeffrey Toobin, "Heavyweight—How Ruth Bader Ginsburg Has Moved the Supreme Court," *New Yorker*, March 11, 2013. Available at http://www.newyorker.com/magazine/2013/03/11/heavyweight-ruth-bader-ginsburg.

3. 404 U.S. 71 (1971).

4. 469 F.2d 466 (10th Cir. 1972).

5. Toobin, note 2, *supra*.

6. By Marisa M. Kashino, "Ruth Bader Ginsburg's Love of the Arts," October 10, 2012. Available at http://www.washingtonian.com/articles/people/stage-presence-ruth-bader-ginsburgs-love-of-the-arts/.

7. Reported by Tony Mauro in the *Legal Times*, "Ruth Bader Ginsburg 'Amazed' at Icon Status at 82." Available at http://www.nationallawjournal.com/legaltimes/expert-columns/id=1202729413008/Ruth-Bader-Ginsburg-Amazed-at-Icon-Status-at-82?mcode=1202619327776&curindex=0&back=NLJ&slreturn=20150520063048.

8. Linda Hirshnan, *Sisters in Law: How Sandra Day O'Connor and Ruth Bader Ginsburg Went to the Supreme Court and Changed the World*, New York: Harper (2015).

9. *Ledbetter v. Goodyear Tire & Rubber Co.*, 550 U.S. 618 (2007).

10. The figures on this are all over the lot. The White House puts the figure at 77 percent, while Pew puts it at 84 percent. http://www.pewresearch.org/fact-tank/2015/04/14/on-equal-pay-day-everything-you-need-to-know-about-the-gender-pay-gap/.

11. Statistics compiled by the American Association of University Women. Available at http://www.aauw.org/2014/09/18/gender-pay-gap/.

10

THE BLACK SEAT

Finding the "Best Qualified"

Two roads diverged in a wood, and I— / I took the one less traveled
by, / And that has made all the difference.
—Robert Frost, "The Road Not Taken"

The most supremely partisan of the Justices is the Court's only black
Justice, Clarence Thomas, successor to the iconic Thurgood Marshall.
Thomas is a polarizing figure, detested by liberals and beloved by conservatives. The liberal rap on Thomas is that he votes against black
interests every time the issue is presented. He even thinks *Brown v.
Board of Education* was poorly reasoned. He writes in his best-selling
memoir, *My Grandfather's Son*, of his having travelled the "road not
taken." "[I am] an ordinary man to whom extraordinary things happened."[1]

Clarence Thomas is an angry man with not much to be angry about.
He rose from an emotionally and economically impoverished background in the rural Georgia town of Pin Point to the highest echelon of
the nation's judiciary. Venerated by conservatives (including the Tea
Party, of which his wife is a member), trashed by the liberal media he
despises, sitting in high judgment on issues he cares deeply about, he
should be exactly where he wants to be. Yet possibly because of his
stormy confirmation hearings, he seethes with anger, largely against
what he calls liberal "elites." What Thomas means by "elites" is unclear.
Used as a noun, an elite is defined as a person of status or wealth. It is

hard to conceive of a personage with more status in American society than a Justice of the Supreme Court of the United States.

In *My Grandfather's Son*, Thomas recounts a troubled and difficult childhood. Deserted by his father shortly after birth, his mother known as "Pigeon" made a painful decision. She sent Thomas and his brother Myers to live with his maternal grandfather, Myers Anderson, whom he called "Daddy." Absent fathers were nothing new to Thomas's family. His grandfather and great-grandfather had also deserted their families. Anderson, who had only a third-grade education, ran a small fuel oil delivery business out of his home. A convert to Catholicism, Anderson raised Thomas sternly on "tough love," sent him to Catholic schools, and wanted him to go into the priesthood. "The damn vacation is over," Daddy said the morning the brothers Thomas moved into his house. Today, Thomas has a bust of Myers Anderson in his chambers.

The "most vivid childhood memories of the Supreme Court" Thomas said he could recall were the "Impeach Earl Warren" signs that lined Highway 17 near Savannah. When George H. W. Bush introduced him to the nation at Kennebunkport, Thomas reflected, "I didn't quite understand who this Earl Warren fellow was, but I knew he was in some kind of trouble."[2]

Thomas broke with "Daddy" when he decided to abandon the road to the priesthood and pursue secular studies. Thomas's adult personal life was also troubled—by divorce, alcohol, and financial instability. He tells of a humiliating incident when he was Equal Employment Opportunities Commission chairman where an airport rent-a-car clerk, after Sears declined to approve his credit, cut up his credit card in front of him. He portrays himself as a "man more sinned against than sinning," Richard Wright's *Native Son* and *Black Boy*, and Kafka's Josef K., all baked in together on steroids.

My Grandfather's Son avoids mention of Thomas's overarching judicial philosophy. Indeed, he rejects "futile academic debates" over what should inform judging. Instead, he says he asks himself, "What is my role in this case—*as a judge*?"[3] "In the legislative and executive branches, it's acceptable . . . to make decisions based on your own personal opinions or interests. The role of the judge is to interpret and apply the choices made in those branches, not make policy choices of his own."[4] Nothing could be further from the truth. On the Court, Thomas proved to be a hardline partisan conservative.

Nina Totenberg reported on *Morning Edition* of NPR:

> He is the only Justice willing to allow states to establish an official religion; the only Justice who believes teenagers have no free speech rights at all; the only Justice who believes it is unconstitutional to require campaign funders to disclose their identity; the only Justice who believes that truthful tobacco advertising and other commercial speech may not be regulated, even when aimed at minors; the only Justice who voted to strike down a key provision of the Voting Rights Act; the only Justice to say that the Court should invalidate a wide range of laws regulating business; and the only Justice who voted to allow the President to hold American citizens in prison indefinitely without charge and without review by the courts.[5]

Although he voted with Scalia in about 91 percent of the cases, he is unlike Scalia anything but a "faint-hearted" originalist.[6] Speaking of Thomas, Scalia famously told a synagogue audience, "I may be an originalist, but I am not a nut."[7] Indeed, while Scalia said that he is not about to overrule volumes of jurisprudence in the *United States Reports*, Thomas is spoiling to overrule any decision he does not agree with or which he deems contrary to the Constitution or to "natural law." This would appear to include "super-precedents" such as *Roe v. Wade*, which have been repeatedly reaffirmed, but with which he disagrees. Contrasting the two, premier Supreme Court advocate Tom Goldstein says, "Scalia has his foot hovering over the brake pedal. Justice Thomas' is firmly planted on the gas."[8]

But Clarence Thomas is a man of many paradoxes. His autobiography reveals a highly intelligent, driven man trapped in his own skin, anxious to break out of a racial stereotype, seeking recognition for some feature of his talented personality other than his race. Ironic it is that at every stage of his adult career, at Holy Cross; at Yale Law School; as an aide to Senator Jack Danforth when Danforth was attorney general of Missouri, which brought him to Washington when Danforth was elected to the Senate; as a junior in the legal department of Monsanto; as a middle-management official in the Reagan administration; and as the recipient of two judicial appointments, Thomas benefited from being black. Another paradox may be that his sister, Emma Mae Martin, was a welfare recipient. In a 1980 interview with Juan Williams, then of the *Washington Post*, he said,

I was opposed to welfare because I had seen its destructive effects up close in Savannah. Most of the older people among whom I had grown up felt as I did, sharing Daddy's belief that it would be the "ruination" of blacks, undermining their desire to work and provide for themselves. I added that my own sister was a victim of the system, which had created a sense of entitlement that had trapped her and her children.[9]

He also told Williams, "Now her kids feel entitled to the check too." One may wonder, with his professed love of family, his philosophy of natural law, and his opposition to blacks seeking help from the state, why he had not offered some form of help to his sister who was on welfare.

When Lyndon Johnson in 1967 named Thurgood Marshall as the first African American to sit on the Supreme Court, he said it was "the right thing to do, the right time to do it, the right man, and the right place." On July 1, 1991, when George H. W. Bush appointed Thomas to a "black seat" on the Court when Marshall retired, it was undoubtedly an "affirmative action" appointment. With respect to race, the Constitution may be "color-blind," but the appointing authority clearly is not. In appointing Thomas, George H. W. Bush denied an affirmative action strategy. Joe Biden, certainly not an unsavvy politician when it came to such matters, chaired the Senate Judiciary Committee hearings, which reviewed Thomas's qualifications. He gave a more candid appraisal of the appointment, saying that the "only reason Thomas is on the Court is that he is black."[10] Race matters.

The written text of Bush's remarks in introducing Thomas to the nation stated that Thomas was "the best man for the job on the merits." In the subsequent Q&A with reporters, however, Bush also put forward a different spin on why he had picked Thomas: "The fact that he is black and a minority has nothing to do with this in the sense that *he is the best qualified at this time*."[11] The appointment, however, was a political score. Over 50 percent of African-Americans applauded Thomas's nomination to succeed Marshall. Today, polls show that, in any cohort, he is the "least favorite" Supreme Court Justice.

In his autobiography, Thomas himself finds Bush's claim that he was the "best qualified" to be "extravagant."[12] Although he quotes White House Counsel Boyden Gray as telling him that his race in fact worked against him, his qualifications were gossamer thin. Forty-one years old, he had been for eight years the Reagan-appointed Chairman of the Equal Employment Opportunities Commission (EEOC), an under-funded and toothless agency, and a federal appeals court judge for only sixteen months. He had never tried a case or argued an appeal, much less been in a courtroom since his early days at the Bar. At the time of his nomination, he had written only 20 opinions as a circuit judge on fairly routine matters, as compared with Ruth Bader Ginsburg who had written 405. A white male with similar credentials would never have merited appointment to the nation's highest court.

Staffers in the Bush White House, assisted by Republican appa-ratchik Ken Duberstein, knew that Thomas would face a rough-and-tumble confirmation hearing in the Senate Judiciary Committee. Bork had gone down in flames by emphasizing competence, dismissing char-acter and constitutionalism as irrelevant. The Democratic senators on the committee had read Thomas's speeches and writings, and they knew well that Thomas believed in a right-wing ideology. It is unclear whether he expressed this ideology out of loyalty to the conservative patrons who put him in power or out of a recognition that his exception-alism would empower his driving ambition to succeed. Somewhere along the line, perhaps at Holy Cross with the Jesuits, he had become enamored of "natural law" and free-market economics, and he set about rejecting government intervention as the way forward for advancing the interests of African Americans. Channeling the views of his grandfather, he grew to regard welfare as the "ruination" of blacks, substituting total self-reliance.

The White House knew that senators would question Thomas close-ly about his ideology, particularly when it came to voting rights and abortion. This type of questioning is what had done in the case of failed nominee Robert Bork. So they had him evade and prevaricate. The handlers' approach, known as the "Pin Point strategy," was to have Thomas present himself as a man of exemplary character who had en-dured a lifetime of adversity and discrimination, and risen to the top of the heap through hard work and determination. Before the Senate Judi-ciary Committee, he testified to the grim poverty of his childhood, describing a "shared common bathroom, which was unworkable and unusable." In his opening remarks, he described his life in Pin Point as "far removed in space and time from this room, this day and this mo-ment."[13]

Confronted by a plethora of material in which, while in the executive branch, he had expressed an ultra-conservative ideology, the White House handlers had him disclaim that ideology not at the hearing, where he could be charged with a "confirmation conversion," but as of eighteen months earlier, the time he went on the federal bench, where he was sworn to be neutral and judicial. Repeatedly, he made professions of disavowal such as "I do not believe . . . that there is a role in judging for the expressions of the kinds of personal views . . . that you have in the executive branch."[14] This was how the handlers hoped to use his brief record of judicial service to meet the charge of confirmation conversion head-on. Of course, it was, to use some choice Scalia epithets, "pure applesauce" and "jiggery-pokery."

Thomas was not the first Supreme Court nominee in history to feel congressional heat. Brandeis and Thurgood Marshall faced tough confirmation hearings. During Lyndon Johnson's presidency, Fortas and Homer Thornberry met with successful opposition in the Senate, and early in Nixon's presidency the Senate rejected two nominees in a row, Haynsworth and Carswell. The Senate of course in 1987, only three years before Thomas's appointment, rejected Reagan's appointee, Robert Bork. Prior to 1894, the Senate rejected an average of one in four nominees. A Federalist Congress turned down one of George Washington's nominees, John Rutledge, a Justice whom Washington wanted to see as Chief Justice. There were rumors about Rutledge's mental stability. No Supreme Court nominees testified before the Senate until 1925 when Harlan Fiske Stone became the first to do so. Thereafter, it became quite customary. Until the "dead on arrival" Garland nomination, however, the Senate always held hearings on the qualifications of the candidate.

On abortion rights, Thomas particularly lacked candor. Senate Judiciary Committee member Patrick Leahy (D-VT) asked him whether he "ever had discussion of *Roe v. Wade.*" Thomas incredibly answered, "Only, I guess . . . in the most general sense." He said that he had never "debated" the opinion, and that he had not made a decision "one way or the other," even in his mind, as to whether *Roe* was "properly decided," leading committee member Paul Simon (D-IL) to quip, "If that is true, he is the only adult in the room who doesn't have an opinion on it."

In fact, the record showed that Thomas had given careful consideration to *Roe*. In 1986, he had participated in a White House working group report on the family that criticized *Roe* as "fatally flawed."[15] In 1989, he had cited *Roe* in a footnote to an article he wrote for the *Harvard Journal of Law and Public Policy*.[16] He repudiated before the committee his previous endorsement of a controversial 1987 *American Spectator* article by Catholic conservative political thinker Lewis Lehrman that called abortion a "holocaust" and argued that the Constitution gave fetuses a "right to life." Thomas had said that Lehrman's article was a "splendid example" of applying natural law. And also in 1987, he had referred to abortion in a column in the *Chicago Defender*.[17]

Evasive and disingenuous as Thomas's answers were, they made for good political strategy. Every nominee since Thomas, Republican or Democrat, has refused to tell the Senate what he or she thinks of abortion or privacy or any other hot-button issue on the basis that these were matters that might come before them.

Another example of Thomas's duplicity before the Judiciary Committee was the issue of prisoners' rights. His predecessor, Thurgood Marshall, wrote important decisions holding that certain kinds of prisoner maltreatment violated the Eighth Amendment's Cruel and Unusual Punishments Clause. At the hearings, Thomas seemed to be overcome with emotion, testifying that every day as a federal appeals court judge, he looked out the courthouse window and saw busloads of criminal defendants in custody brought to court. "And I say to myself every day," he testified, "but for the grace of God, there go I. . . . So I can walk in their shoes, and I can bring something different to the court." Two months later and on the Supreme Court bench, he failed to show the same empathy, joining Scalia in dissenting from a 7-2 decision upholding an $800 damage award to a black inmate of a Louisiana prison. Shackled, and held from behind, the prisoner had suffered facial injuries, his teeth loosened and his dental plate broken, as a result of a beating at the hands of "correction security officers." In a remarkably callous dissenting opinion, Thomas breezily held that the Cruel and Unusual Punishments Clause "should not be turned into a National Code of Prison Regulation."[18] Voting to dismiss the prisoner's claim, he wrote, "[A] use of force that causes only insignificant harm to a prisoner may be immoral, it may be tortious, it may be criminal, and it may even be remediable under other provisions of the Federal Constitution, but it is not 'cruel and unusual punishment.'" Apparently jesting over a serious issue, he mused, "Surely prison was not a more congenial place in the early years of the Republic than it is today."[19]

At the conclusion of the first phase of the hearings, it seemed that Thomas was headed for a speedy confirmation. He had testified for five days, and while many were unhappy about his abortion testimony, Democrats who held a majority in the Senate did not want to be seen as voting against a black nominee to succeed the iconic Justice Thurgood Marshall, particularly when they had been such strong proponents of diversity. Republicans and Democrats in Southern states, recognizing the gains in black voter registration as a result of the Voting Rights Act of 1965, also did not want to be seen as opposing a black candidate.

Then, the bombshell exploded. The hearings became up close and personal when Anita Hill, a black, 35-year-old law professor, came forward to allege that Thomas had sexually harassed her while she worked for him both at the Department of Education and the EEOC, where she had followed him in May 1982. Hill testified that Thomas had repeatedly pressured her to go out with him and had subjected her to sexually explicit conversations when the two were alone in the office. "He spoke about acts that he had seen in pornographic films involving such matters as women having sex with animals, and films showing group sex or rape scenes," she alleged. The pièce de la résistance was her assertion that Thomas had pointed to a Coke can from which he had been drinking and asked her, "Who has put pubic hair on my Coke?"

Before the first day of hearings ended, Thomas demanded to be heard. Seething with anger, he flatly denied the charges and accused the all-white committee panel of conducting a "high-tech lynching." It was a classic tale of "He said, she said," and to this day no one knows where the truth lies.

Conservatives defended Thomas, accusing Hill of being a "spurned lover," even suggesting erotomania. Former federal prosecutor and liberal Supreme Court pundit Jeffrey Toobin argues that what Hill alleged probably did happen because Thomas was single at the time and admitted that he was drinking heavily. But this speculation is highly unpersuasive.[20]

Testimony on the issue consumed three days, lasting one evening until past midnight. It is puzzling, however, why Hill waited a decade to make her charges, why she followed Thomas to EEOC if he had in fact harassed her at the Department of Education, and why she did not come forward when Thomas was up for a circuit judgeship in 1990. The explanation may lie in the fact that many victims of sexual harassment, particularly in the 1980s, were reluctant (and perhaps ashamed) to come forward with their charges for fear of damaging their reputations. *My Grandfather's Son* features a photograph of Hill at Thomas's side when he was sworn in as the agency's chairman. In the book, he calls Hill "my most traitorous adversary."

The committee divided 7-7 on Thomas's confirmation, and the Senate eventually confirmed Thomas by the closest vote in modern history, 52-48. Eleven Democrats, including seven Southerners, voted with 41 of the 43 Republicans to advise and consent to the nomination. Though Bush said, in announcing Thomas's nomination, that he was the "best man for the job on the merits" and the "best qualified," Charles Bowser, a distinguished African American lawyer from Philadelphia, said, "I'd be willing to bet . . . that not one of the senators who voted to confirm Clarence Thomas would hire him as their lawyer."[21]

Despite the fact that Thomas won the contest, and was promptly sworn in to a lifetime appointment, his anger at the liberal establishment over the Hill accusations continued to fester within him. It would hardly seem germane to mention the confirmation hearings in this book about the partisan nature of the Court except that Thomas continues to be angry with liberal "elites" over the entire episode, and his anger infects his policy decisions on many issues. Jeffrey Toobin reports that "his jurisprudence seems guided to an unusual degree by raw anger." Toobin quotes a "longtime friend" of Thomas saying of the hearings, "The real tragedy of this event is that his behavior on the Court has been affected. He's still damaged. He's still reeling. He was hurt more than anyone can comprehend."[22] Buttressing Toobin's assertion is that in October 2010, Thomas's wife, Virginia, left a voicemail on Anita Hill's answering machine asking Hill to "consider an apology sometime and some full explanation of why you did what you did with my husband." Hill's response was that she had testified truthfully and had nothing to apologize for. Thomas quite plainly has not gotten over the trauma of the confirmation hearings some twenty years after the fact. To this day, he wears his "heart upon his sleeve. For daws to peck at."[23]

Thomas took office with a well-honed political ideology. He had definitively concluded that only enumerated rights were to be found in the Constitution in conjunction with natural law, and that the very robust voting rights and affirmative action policies on race from which he had benefited his entire adult life were humiliating and detrimental to blacks.

Central to Thomas's ideology is his attitude toward race. He has it in for black civil rights organizations, such as the NAACP,[24] and civil rights advocates. He is even critical of the Warren Court and of his predecessor, Thurgood Marshall,[25] and of the decision in *Brown v. Board of Education*.[26] He rejects the notion that government and the courts should continue to coddle blacks as historic victims of oppression. His position, oddly enough, is not unlike that of Obama. African American thinker Ta-Nehisi Coates has repeatedly laced into Obama for pontificating in only the most general terms about what must be done to remedy ghettoized communities, while he comments with particulars about the alleged moral failure of blacks. What Thomas thinks is right for society in education, in employment, in prisoners' rights, and in social benefits is not to extend a helping hand to black people or for that matter to anyone else. As he wrote in *Fisher v. University of Texas*, "racial bigotry is an evil to be stamped out, not as an excuse for perpetual racial tinkering by the State" to fix racial imbalance.[27] The goal of diversity, he reasons, is an assumption of black inferiority. "[I]f separation is a harm, and if integration therefore is the only way that blacks can receive a proper education, then there must be something inferior about blacks."[28]

He has pointed approvingly to the fiery words of the nineteenth-century African American social reformer and abolitionist Frederick Douglass, who said,

> The American people have always been anxious to know what they shall do with us. . . . I have had but one answer from the beginning. Do nothing with us! Your doing with us has already played the mischief with us. . . . All I ask is, give him [the black man] a chance to stand on his own legs! Let him alone![29]

For Thomas, it would seem to be a case of "No need for a helping hand. I would have made it anyway." This means no affirmative action, no leg-up, no extraordinary measures, and no welfare. Nada. Just no bigotry. Conservative pundit Juan Williams, a black friend of Thomas who has followed him for thirty-five years, thinks he is the "most influential thinker on racial issues in America today" who is "now leading the national debate on race."[30]

THOMAS AND NATURAL LAW

Thomas bases his jurisprudence in large measure on natural law. He believes that the Court should look to Thomas Jefferson's Declaration of Independence in interpreting James Madison's Constitution. The Declaration states that "all men . . . are endowed by their Creator with certain inalienable Rights, that among these are Life, Liberty and the pursuit of Happiness." Since liberty is an inherent, God-given right, he reasons, it cannot be an unenumerated right to be found in the Due Process and Equal Protection Clauses of the Constitution. Liberty comes from God, he reasons, not from the government. His opinions, accordingly, are often spiced with references to Jefferson, natural law, or the Declaration of Independence.

Professor Tribe wrote two weeks after Thomas's appointment,

> [J]udging from his speeches and scholarly writings, [Thomas] seems . . . to believe judges should enforce the Founders' natural law philosophy—the inalienable rights "given man by his Creator"— which he maintains is revealed most completely in the Declaration of Independence. He is the first Supreme Court nominee in 50 years to maintain that natural law should be readily consulted in constitutional interpretation.[31]

Thomas's reliance on natural law has placed his stocky 5-foot 8.5-inch frame in the way of further development of "new" constitutional rights. Natural law should logically lead to maximum liberty for the individual, free of government interference, but in Thomas's world it does not. As Thomas sees it, there are no unenumerated rights imbedded in the Constitution—no right of privacy, no right to abortion, and certainly no right to same-sex marriage. Indeed, to push his libertarian thinking to its logical extreme, the Constitution would foreclose even a neutral stance on abortion, leaving the issue to the states, since the Declaration of Independence guarantees a right to life. In the gay marriage case, Thomas dissented on the ground that there was no unenumerated right to dignity. He sees this as a "distortion" of the text.

"Slaves did not lose their dignity (any more than they lost their human-ity)," he argues, because the government allowed them to be enslaved. The Japanese Americans held in government camps did not lose their dignity because the government confined them. And those denied government benefits certainly do not lose their dignity because the government denies them those benefits. The "government cannot be-stow dignity, and it cannot take it away."[32]

The love affair with natural law reached its climax in 2010 with his concurring opinion in *McDonald v. City of Chicago*,[33] where the Court, interpreting the Second Amendment's Right to Bear Arms Clause—"A well regulated Militia, being necessary to the security of a free State, the right of the people to keep and bear Arms, shall not be infringed"— considered whether the constitutional right to a gun, which it had elab-orated two years before in *District of Columbia v. Heller*,[34] applied to the states. It is well settled that the Bill of Rights limits only the powers of the *federal*, not the state governments.

The case was a slam-dunk for petitioners, who knew that the conser-vative majority was certain to vindicate state gun rights. But petitioners, joined at the hip with the gun lobby and a number of libertarian right-wing think tanks such as the Cato Institute, funded and founded by one of the ultra-conservative Koch brothers and the Institute for Justice, wanted the whole enchilada.[35] They sought to revive the Privileges or Immunities Clause of the Fourteenth Amendment—"No state shall make or enforce any law which shall abridge the privileges or immu-nities of citizens of the United States"—as the exclusive vehicle for "incorporating" the Bill of Rights and making it applicable to the states. If the last sentence makes your head spin, read it again. Should they be successful, it would be possible to make binding on the states only enumerated rights set forth in other provisions of the Constitution, as well as other unspecified "natural" rights derived from the Declaration of Independence or philosophical notions of natural law. Unenumerat-ed or "new" rights, born out of substantive due process or equal protec-tion, would be deemed *verboten*.

There are significant differences between Due Process and Equal Protection analyses on the one hand, and Privileges and Immunities on the other, mainly that the Privileges and Immunities Clause is much more limited in scope and application:

- The Privileges and Immunities Clause applies only to "citizens" while the Due Process and Equal Protection Clauses protect all "persons."
- The Privileges and Immunities Clause would be limited to rights set forth in the Bill of Rights and "natural rights," whatever those are, not new rights like abortion and gay marriage that are not found in the Constitution.
- The Privileges or Immunities Clause protects citizens from states making or enforcing bad laws, while the Due Process Clause protects all persons from "the unlawful exercise of governmental power" *of any kind.*[36]

In order to accomplish the petitioners' objective, it would have been necessary for the Court to overrule 137 years of jurisprudence, starting with the *Slaughter-House Cases*, which had essentially rendered the Privileges or Immunities Clause a dead letter for making the Bill of Rights or natural law principles binding on the states.[37] The *Slaughter-House Cases* involved challenges by butchers to a Louisiana law regulating the slaughtering of animals in New Orleans and restricting the location of abattoirs to a place on the outskirts of the city. The butchers claimed a natural right to "sustain their lives through labor" that could not be restricted by state law. Upholding the statute, the Court, 5-4, gave the Fourteenth Amendment's Privileges or Immunities Clause the narrowest of interpretations, holding that the clause only protected rights created by U.S. citizenship, not other rights that the "state governments were created to establish and secure" (*Id.* at 76). The decision established in Supreme Court doctrine the "police power" of the states to regulate conduct within their jurisdiction. As Brandeis famously articulated the police power, "It is one of the happy incidents of the federal system that a single courageous state may, if its citizens choose, serve as a laboratory; and try novel social and economic experiments without risk to the rest of the country."[38] After 1873, the Privileges or Immunities Clause went to the slaughterhouse as the pathway for applying the Bill of Rights to the states, and the clause became a virtual dead letter. While the Court in its 5-4 decision in *McDonald* predictably decided to apply the gun right to the states, it did so under the Due Process Clause of the Fourteenth Amendment, the well-settled vehicle it had invariably used for this purpose in constitutional interpretation.[39]

Opposed to the line of Court cases developing "new" rights under the Due Process and Equal Protection Clauses, Thomas bought into the libertarian, natural law argument hook, line, and sinker. Thomas likes to crib the language of the briefs of parties he agrees with. Using plagiarism software technology, Adam Liptak of the *New York Times* uncovered that Thomas's opinions had "the highest rate of overlaps with language in parties' briefs" than the opinions of any other Justice.[40] To be fair, judges with varied frequency do this all the time. Nothing wrong with it—just saves work.

Following the line taken in the amicus briefs of the Cato Institute and the other conservative think tanks, he wrote in *McDonald* that the "notion that a constitutional provision that guarantees only 'process' . . . could define the substance of those rights strains credulity for even the most casual user of words."[41] When it came to applying the gun right to the states, he saw the Privileges or Immunities Clause as the more "straightforward path . . . more faithful to the Fourteenth Amendment's text and history."[42] Parroting the reasoning, and perhaps even regurgitating the language, of briefs filed by the right-wing think tanks,[43] he was also fully prepared to get there by overruling the *Slaughter-House Cases*, the vitality of which he had previously questioned.[44] The right wing detests the *Slaughter-House Cases* because they believe the federal courts should be the "perpetual censor" of all state legislation.[45] Had this been accomplished, the decision would have wreaked havoc with 137 years of civil rights decision-making under the Due Process and Equal Protection Clauses.

The other conservatives on the Court, comprising the 5-4 majority, would have none of it. Alito, who wrote the opinion of the Court, said that the Court would not disturb 137 years of precedent, holding that there is "no consensus among the scholars that the *Slaughter-House* holding is flawed." He stressed, "For many decades, the question of the rights protected by the Fourteenth Amendment against state infringement has been analyzed under the Due Process Clause of that Amendment and not under the Privileges or Immunities Clause. We therefore decline to disturb the *Slaughter-House* holding."

Even Scalia made clear at oral argument in *McDonald* that while he had "misgivings" about substantive due process "as an original matter," he was not about to overrule well-settled law. The courtroom erupted in laughter when he characterized the *Slaughter-House Cases* argument as the "darling of the professoriat." He thus queried petitioners' lawyer, "[W]hy are you asking us to overrule 150, 140 years of prior law, when . . . you can reach your result under substantive due [process]. I mean, you know, unless you are bucking for a—a place on some law school faculty?"[46] It was all high theater.

The doctrinal debate over the *Slaughter-House Cases* was more than technical argle-bargle. It went beyond gun rights and had a distinct political flavor. I never said these guys weren't smart. The Constitution guards the liberty of our people through the Bill of Rights. As we have seen, the Bill of Rights is not binding upon the states, but only upon the federal government. The Court had long used the Due Process and Equal Protection Clauses of the Fourteenth Amendment not only to find the enumerated rights found in the Bill of Rights but also to develop "new" unenumerated constitutional rights in the future, using substantive due process, and applying them to the states. The "Due Process Clause and the Equal Protection Clause are connected in a profound way, though they set forth independent principles. . . . This interrelation of the two principles furthers our understanding of what freedom is and must become."[47]

If the *Slaughter-House Cases* were to be overruled, as Thomas, the right-wing think tanks, and the conservative members of the "professoriat" propose, all state legislation, including social and economic regulation, would be subject to censorship by the federal courts. State legislatures would be less free to "experiment" with social and economic measures, which Brandeis advocated in his famous dissent in *New State Ice Co. v. Liebmann*.[48] In short, the police power of states to legislate would also be limited.

It is significant that substantive due process has been the reasoning that led the Court to sustain such unenumerated rights as reproductive[49] and gay rights[50] or the right to teach one's children a foreign language,[51] to name a few. The libertarian think tanks and conservative law school professors had convinced Thomas that the revival of the Privileges or Immunities Clause would curtail the discretion of judges in finding new unenumerated rights under concepts of equal protection or substantive due process as they had in *Brown v. Board of Education*[52] or *Roe v. Wade*,[53] and it would curtail the states in experimenting with progressive legislation where they might "serve as a laboratory" and "try novel social and economic experiments." Brandeis thought that "[t]o stay experimentation in things social and economic is a grave responsibility. Denial of the right to experiment may be fraught with serious consequences to the nation."[54]

So it was important to the game plan of the conservatives to rein in the liberals by overruling the *Slaughter-House Cases* and do an end run around substantive due process. It was disingenuous of Thomas to argue that the Privileges or Immunities Clause was a "more straightforward path" to the Court's conclusion when he knew full well that the "more straightforward path," if taken, would make it much harder for future Courts to find "new" unenumerated rights and make it harder for states to enact progressive legislation of a social or economic nature deemed contrary to natural law.

As it happened, Thomas's "more straightforward path" was a "bridge too far" even for the conservative Justices, not one of whom agreed with his rationale. The effort failed, but it is certain that the conservative think tanks and Scalia's "professoriat" will not give up as long as Thomas is on the Court and there remains a conservative majority. In *McDonald*, Thomas cast the decisive vote but concurred only in the result, leaving the right wing to claim a Pyrrhic victory since it was Thomas's deciding vote that put *McDonald* over the top. For the time being anyway, the marginalized Privileges or Immunities Clause remains on life support in the Supreme Court as it has been for 140 years.

THOMAS AND THE VOTING RIGHTS ACT

The Thomas confirmation hearings began September 10, 1991. In the course of the hearings, the nominee promised committee member Senator Ted Kennedy that he would be aggressive in favor of voting rights. Yet no sooner was he on the Court than he voted in *Holder v. Hall*[55] to go far beyond the case in question, calling on the Court to overrule precedent, and stating that previous voting-rights decisions were those of "a centralized politburo appointed for life to dictate to the provinces the 'correct' theories of democratic representation." In doing this, he dismissed precedents so sweepingly that four liberal Justices (Ginsburg, Souter, Stevens, and Blackmun) rebuked him for his "radical reinterpretation of the Voting Rights Act" and rejection of *stare decisis*, a principle he had promised Kennedy he would hold in high regard.

The Fifteenth Amendment to the Constitution, one of the "Civil War amendments" ratified in 1870, guaranteed former slaves, as well as all other racial minorities, the right to vote, and it delegated to Congress the power to enforce that right on a state-by-state basis. The amendment was ignored for almost one-hundred years. Through the use of poll taxes, "white primaries," literacy or knowledge tests, "good moral character" requirements, voter IDs, special requirements for absentee ballots, and other subterfuges, Southern states effectively prevented African Americans and other minorities from voting.

Following voting rights demonstrations in Selma, Alabama, organized by Martin Luther King, Lyndon Johnson strong-armed Congress into passing the Voting Rights Act of 1965 (VRA). Congress found that discrimination against black voters in certain states was "pervasive," "flagrant," "widespread," and "rampant." It was only with the passage of the VRA that the majority of African Americans in the South registered to vote after almost a century of disenfranchisement. The policy divide over the interpretation of the VRA was dramatic. Conservatives, such as the young John Roberts, argued unsuccessfully in the Reagan administration that the purpose of the statute was limited to insuring ballot access only after a showing of an intent to discriminate (something difficult, but not impossible, to establish). Others, however, gave the law a broader interpretation each time the statute came up for renewal. Republicans and Democrats in Congress in overwhelming numbers, as well as Republican and Democratic presidents, saw the statute as policing "a much broader scope of the election system, which included encouraging greater representation for African Americans and other minority groups."[56] This interpretation would provide an election regime prohibiting discriminatory "effects," thereby insuring greater political influence for African Americans. The Supreme Court between 1969 and 2013, often by 5-4 votes, chipped away at the "effects" test, and repeatedly made the more restrictive policy choice.

A core provision of the VRA was §5 that prohibits certain "bad actor" or "covered" states, mainly in the South, from implementing changes in their election laws without receiving "preclearance" from the Justice Department or the federal district court in Washington that the change did not discriminate against protected minorities. The "coverage formula" of the statute, §4(b), named states that engaged in egregious voter discrimination in 1965. The "coverage formula" was originally set to expire five years after 1965; it lasted almost fifty years. There were also "bail-out" provisions so that a "bad actor" state or a covered entity could remove itself from coverage for good behavior if it had not used a discriminatory test or device in the preceding five years.

The issue was one of political power. Black suffrage presented a problem for Southern conservatives. Blacks tended to vote Democratic in overwhelming numbers, apparently forgetting that the Republican Party was founded as an anti-slavery party, and that it was Lincoln, a Republican, who had freed the slaves. The VRA was tremendously effective. In the decades following 1965, black voter registration in the South surged from 31 percent to 73 percent, and the number of black elected officials burgeoned from fewer than 500 to 10,500.

The VRA benefited blacks; it also benefited Republicans. Following the election of George H. W. Bush in 1988, Republican strategists, with the help of the Bush Justice Department, and an assist from black Democrats in the South, were able to create new black districts. But the black voters would be drained from adjoining white Democratic districts, leaving those districts predominantly white, and predominantly conservative. By reason of the statute, Southern black Democrats for the first time in history were elected to Congress in significant numbers, joining the Congressional Black Caucus, founded in 1971.[57] In 1992, seventeen African Americans were elected to Congress. Southern blacks were also elected to state court judicial positions and a variety of local offices. Notably, however, in 1994 Republicans gained fifty-four seats in the House and recaptured the lower chamber for the first time in forty years.

In 2006 Congress reauthorized the VRA, including the "coverage provisions," for another twenty-five years. The measure passed unanimously in the Senate, and with only thirty-three "nays" in the House despite conservative objections that the pre-clearance procedure was no longer needed. Congress had reviewed data that there were more Justice Department objections between 1982 and 2004 (626) than there had been between 1965 and the 1982 reauthorization (490). Between 1982 and 2006, Justice Department objections blocked over 700 voting changes based on a determination that the changes were discriminatory.[58] "Bad actor states" accounted for 56 percent of all discrimination cases brought under the law. In signing the reauthorization measure, George W. Bush said, "My administration will vigorously enforce the provisions of this law, and we will defend it in court." Everyone was on board with the 2006 re-authorization except the Supreme Court.

In 2008, Roberts, writing for the Court in an 8-1 decision narrowly holding that the bailout provisions of the VRA applied to a small Texas utility district, was prepared to declare, "Things have changed in the South. Voter turnout and registration rates now approach parity. Blatantly discriminatory evasions of federal decrees are rare. And minority candidates hold office at unprecedented levels."[59] Thomas, while concurring in the result, dissented in part in that he wanted to hold §5 unconstitutional. The handwriting was on the wall.

On June 25, 2013, the Court in a 5-4 decision, *Shelby County v. Holder*, struck down as unconstitutional the coverage provision of the VRA, and thereby extracted the teeth of the statute.[60] The Republican-appointed Justices, including Clarence Thomas, constituted the majority. Roberts, who had written memos seeking to water-down the VRA when he was in Reagan's Justice Department in the 1980s, authored the opinion of the Court striking down the coverage formula, which he called a "drastic departure from basic principles of federalism."[61] The decision effectively demolished the pre-clearance procedure established by Congress. Roberts noted changed conditions, with Census Bureau data indicating "that [s]ince 1965 . . . African-American voter turnout has come to exceed white voter turnout in five of the six original 'bad actor' states, with a gap in the sixth State of less than one half of one percent."[62] *Shelby County*, however, gave the "bad actor" states the green light for such black voter suppression techniques as skewed redistricting, voter ID requirements in Texas, and restrictions on eligibility for absentee ballots and early voting in North Carolina. The impact of black voter suppression has a double discriminatory whammy since jury pools are typically selected from voter registration lists. The result was highly favorable to the Republican Party.

In Thomas's concurring opinion in *Shelby County*, he went a step further than his four colleagues, adhering to his former views expressed in *Northwest Austin Municipal Utility District v. Holder*, and stating that, in light of changed conditions, he would further gut the statute and declare the entire coverage provision unconstitutional as well.[63] In other words, Congress to the contrary notwithstanding, he does not

believe there is any basis in the Fifteenth Amendment for special federal examination of voter registration laws in historically "bad actor"
states. Huh?

Thomas argues that black interests should not be defined by white
liberal "elites," and that blacks will do just fine if left to their own
devices.[64] Who knows where blacks would be politically without the
right to vote? At odds with Thomas's position is the organized black
community. The NAACP vigorously attacked the *Shelby* decision, declaring that June 25, 2013, was a "day that will go down in political
infamy"; that "[a]fter a black President had won two elections five Justices arrogantly said they knew more than the evidence considered by
98 senators"; and that "on June 26, 2013, we had less voting rights than
they had on August 5, 1965."[65]

THOMAS AND AFFIRMATIVE ACTION

Thomas's other *bête noir* is affirmative action. The doctrine also originated with Lyndon Johnson. In a 1965 Howard University commencement address, Johnson unveiled one of his most controversial "Great
Society" initiatives:

> Freedom is not enough. . . . You do not take a person who, for years,
> has been hobbled by chains and liberate him, bring him up to the
> starting line of a race and say, "You are free to compete with all the
> others," and still justly believe that you have been completely fair. . . .
> This is the next and most profound stage of the battle for civil
> rights.[66]

Thus was conceived the doctrine of affirmative action. As Johnson's
principal domestic adviser, Joseph A. Califano, Jr., has reflected, the
concept was born out of "Johnson's conviction that it was essential as a
matter of social justice to provide the tutoring, the extra help, even the
occasional preference, if necessary, to those who had suffered three
hundred years of discrimination in order to give them a fair chance to
share in the American dream."[67]

Affirmative action has not been an easy issue for the Court over the
years. As Califano puts it, the issue to this day "scratches like a finger-
nail on a blackboard and split the Supreme Court."[68]

Theoretically, the issue, of course, should not be whether any of the Justices believes that affirmative action is a good thing or a bad thing, or whether race-based distinctions have helped or hindered his or her career, but whether, based on its text, its history, and decided cases interpreting the Fourteenth Amendment, race-conscious distinctions drawn for totally benign purposes, largely in the context of state college admissions policies, pass constitutional muster. Thomas consistently votes against affirmative action programs because of his own feelings of being underestimated because of his race. He sees these programs as "nothing more than a façade, a cruel farce of continued racial discrimination that stamp minorities with a badge of inferiority."

It is presently the Court's position as elaborated in *Grutter v. Bollinger*[69] that race-based affirmative action such as what existed at the University of Michigan Law School is outlawed unless a state university can establish that it has a compelling interest in using race as a tool to achieve diversity. Unless *Grutter* is overruled, this will be the situation until 2028, an arbitrary line drawn by Justice O'Connor that presupposes the vestiges of segregation of blacks and Latinos will by then have disappeared, and there will no longer be a need for affirmative action. O'Connor has of course retired, having been replaced by Alito. The Court could of course advance the sunset date; and, if Thomas has anything to say about it, it will. Thomas dissented in *Grutter*, stating, "All the Law School cares about is its own image among know-it-all elites."[70]

Thomas's hatred for "know-it-all elites" has permeated his thinking. In *My Grandfather's Son*, he blames his confirmation difficulties on "America's elites . . . arrogantly wreaking havoc on everything my grandparents had worked for and all I'd accomplished in forty-three years of struggle." Who are these elites whom Thomas hates so much? Surely he thinks they are other than the large corporations, the fat cat political contributors, the jail wardens and executioners, the advertising hucksters, and the anti-Obamacare conservatives in whose favor Thomas so consistently rules.

There may be a number of alternatives to race-conscious admissions policies that may achieve the same result as affirmative action: doing away with legacies; accepting everyone in the state in the top X percent of the high school class; need-blind admissions; preferences based on economic status or place of residence; or strategic partnerships between universities and certain high schools. But if such approaches are shown to be proxies for race, the question is, Will they withstand close scrutiny? And will these ingenious "work-arounds" be successful in achieving the desired diversity?

For many of the Justices, affirmative action has had a personal impact on their careers; others oppose it on ideological grounds. Sotomayor readily admits that it played a role in her admission to Princeton and Yale Law School. "I am the perfect affirmative action baby," she has said.[71]

Thomas admits it figured in his admission to Yale as well. Instead of being grateful for the helping hand, however, he bites the hand that feeds and claims he has said he is angry with Yale because despite a Yale diploma he couldn't get a job in a top law firm. By December of his senior year, he had yet to receive one job offer. He writes, "Now I knew what a law degree from Yale was worth when it bore the taint of racial preference. I was humiliated—and desperate. The snake had struck."[72] He believed he had graduated from one of America's top law schools, but racial preference had robbed his achievement of its true value.

Aggrieved, he writes,

> As much as it stung me to be told that I'd done well in the seminary *despite* my race, it was far worse to feel I was now at Yale *because* of it. I sought to vanquish the perception that I was somehow inferior to my white classmates by obtaining special permission to carry more than the maximum number of credit hours and by taking a rigorous curriculum of courses in such traditional areas as corporate law, bankruptcy, and commercial transactions. How could anyone dare to doubt my abilities if I excelled in such demanding classes? . . . But it was futile for me to suppose that I could escape the stigmatizing effects of racial preference, and I began to fear that it would be used forever to discount my achievements.[73]

But what Thomas omits to mention is that it was Dean (later Judge) Guido Calabresi of Yale who recommended him to Jack Danforth, like Calabresi a Yale Law graduate, who gave him a job, and who, when in the Senate, repeatedly sponsored Thomas for his appointments by the Reagan and Bush administrations. Had Thomas gone to a black law school in Georgia instead of Yale, he surely would have been denied the entrée necessary for his eventual advancement to the top.

The votes of other Justices on affirmative action are also predicated on their life experiences. Alito, like Roberts, wrote memos when he was in the Reagan Justice Department arguing that racial quotas designed to achieve diversity were unconstitutional. Indeed, in 1985 he wrote an essay as part of his government application, stating that "the greatest influences on my views were the writings of William F. Buckley, Jr., the *National Review*, and Barry Goldwater's 1964 campaign."

Ginsburg sees the affirmative action issue as bearing on gender as well, noting that there were a small number of women in her class at Harvard Law School, and precious few women with tenure when she taught at Columbia. In her *Gratz* dissent, she adopted Judge Wisdom's rationalization of the constitutionality of affirmative action: "'[A]ctions designed to burden groups long denied full citizenship stature are not sensibly ranked with measures taken to hasten the day when entrenched discrimination and its aftereffects have been extirpated. . . . [T]he Constitution is color blind. But the Constitution is color conscious to prevent discrimination being perpetuated and to undo the effects of past discrimination.'"[74]

The Court's ruminations over the matter of affirmative action are an orgy of split decisions laced with vituperation. Scalia, who would have declared all forms of affirmative action unconstitutional, in one of his characteristically mordant opinions, called the issue the Court's "sorry line" of "race based admissions decisions."

As a humorous aside to the debate, on the TV show *Seinfeld*, Jerry is told he has received a phone call from a Donna Chang, who is looking for a date. His friend, Kramer, hung up on her.

> Jerry: How could you hang up? I love Chinese women.
> Kramer: That's racist.
> Jerry: How could it be racist if I love Chinese women?

Eventually, the couple hooks up. Donna is Jewish. She explains that her family name was Changstein, and they changed it. Justice Kennedy observed in *Schuette v. BAMN* that in our society, race-based categories are "becoming more blurred."[75]

Such is the essence of the affirmative action debate. Affirmative action is a "benign" form of discrimination, giving preferences to blacks and other minorities in education, employment, and housing. Affirmative action is a tool to rectify the injustices of the past. There is an obvious difference, liberals like Sotomayor, Ginsburg, and even Breyer would argue, between the use of malignant, race-based criteria to discriminate against minorities and benign, race-based criteria to bring the races together. Thomas would see an evil in such distinctions. He writes about affirmative action as though he were writing about segregation. Once race-based decision making is legalized for benign purposes, he believes, it will be only too easy to use them for malignant purposes.

And there are other arguments against affirmative action that few will voice publicly. Scalia, however, was unabashed. In a law review article titled "The Disease as Cure," he railed at the Court's affirmative action decisions as "an historic trivialization of the Constitution."[76] He later said, "One cannot say . . . that the Constitution prohibits discrimination against minority groups but not against majority groups." At argument in *Grutter*, he said, "The people you want to talk to are high school seniors who have seen people visibly less qualified than they are get into prestigious institutions where they are rejected. And if you think that is not creating resentment you are wrong." And this "resentment" is directed toward blacks, not toward the faceless admissions officers who write the policies. This totally undermines the goal of desegregation. But, Sotomayor would argue, the majority has been spared her own unfortunate history and that of other minorities in America meriting a helping hand.

Affirmative action is a difficult issue under the Fourteenth Amendment for how is government to drag a reluctant society beyond racism without taking account of race? Desegregation was the goal of *Brown v. Board of Education*. But it cannot be accomplished with the stroke of a pen. Affirmative action is the vehicle, many would say, for getting there. Critics of affirmative action in education, however, argue that the race-based preferences are harmful to blacks and Hispanics as they assume inferiority and don't sufficiently take account of the achievement of the individual.

Roberts, who is more legalistic, said in 2013 that the "whole point of the Equal Protection clause is to take race off the table." He reasons that "racial preferences may reinforce the doubt about equality, and if so they may do more harm than good." As we have seen, Thomas is unalterably opposed to affirmative action. Referring to *Brown*, he has stated that "what was wrong in 1954 cannot be right today." He has also said that there is no reason to suppose that blacks learn more sitting beside whites in school than they would sitting beside other blacks. The Constitution is color blind, and this means no color consciousness even for remedial reasons.

Equal Protection prohibits the states from discriminating either against or in favor of racial minorities. Michigan, like Washington State and California, became a laboratory for pushing the affirmative action envelope. Broad-based affirmative action programs at the University of Michigan that used race as the sole determining factor in college admissions have been declared unconstitutional. Narrowly based programs, designed to achieve diversity at Michigan Law School, passed constitutional muster, at least, the Court said, for the time being (25 years from 2003, the date of the decision). Justices often grant adjournments when they don't know what better to do.

In 2006, Michigan voters became dissatisfied with any form of racial preferencing. They decided to get their state out of the affirmative action business, adopting an amendment to the state constitution, which provided that race-based preferences cannot be a part of the admissions process for state universities. Full stop. The constitutional amendment required that the state not discriminate or grant preferences on the basis of race. So the issue arose as to whether the Fourteenth Amendment permitted the majority of Michigan voters to ban all forms of affirmative action in their state. In *Schuette*, six Justices held that they could, with Sotomayor and Ginsburg dissenting, and Kagan taking no part.

Just as Chief Justice Charles Evans Hughes famously said, "[T]he only way to disarm is to disarm," Chief Justice Roberts said, in striking down Seattle and Louisville school district assignment plans that used race as the sole determining factor to achieve diversity and avoid racial isolation, "[T]he way to stop discrimination on the basis of race is to stop discriminating on the basis of race."[77]

Engrafted on this mind-boggling jurisprudence is the line of cases the Court refers to as the "political process doctrine." Scalia regarded it as anathema, as does Thomas. In a nutshell, the idea is to make it unconstitutional to alter procedures of state government to advantage racial or other minorities. This was the basis for the argument against Michigan in *Schuette*. This doctrine might have prevented Michigan from doing what it did. Earlier, some states took measures designed to get around desegregative programs set by local school boards or administrators. In California, in 1967, voters amended the state constitution to prohibit legislative interference with an owner's right to sell or rent residential property, even if the owner's choice discriminated on the basis of race. The Court, in a 5-4 decision, readily saw through this "design and intent" to constitutionalize the right to discriminate privately, and it struck down this provision of the California constitution.

Two years later, the Court considered a case where the City Council of Akron, Ohio, had enacted a fair housing ordinance. Voters amended the city charter to overturn the ordinance and to provide that all anti-discrimination legislation had to be first approved by referendum. Other ordinances that were supposed to regulate real property were not subject to this threshold requirement. The Court held that the charter amendment denied Equal Protection because it imposed a "special burden" on racial minorities, making it more difficult for them to obtain favorable legislation.

In 1996, the Court decided *Romer v. Evans* 6-3, with Scalia, Thomas, and Rehnquist dissenting.[78] *Romer* involved a Colorado constitutional amendment. The amendment, enacted in response to a number of local ordinances prohibiting discrimination against gay citizens, repealed these ordinances and effectively prohibited the adoption of similar ordinances in the future. Although the Court did not expressly apply the political process doctrine in *Romer*, the case rejected an attempt by the majority to transfer decision-making authority from localities where the targeted minority group could influence the process to state government where it had less ability to participate effectively. Rather than being able to appeal to municipalities for policy changes, the Court commented, the minority was forced to "enlis[t] the citizenry of Colorado to amend the State Constitution."

After the Court decided that the University of Michigan's undergraduate admissions plan's use of race-based preferences violated the Equal Protection Clause[79] but that the law school admission plan's more narrow race-conscious policy did not,[80] Michigan voters adopted Proposal 2, now Article I, §26 of the state constitution, which prohibits the use of race-based preferences as part of the admissions process for state universities. Affirmative action was now dead in Michigan. The Court approved Michigan's constitutional amendment.

Sotomayor, joined by Ginsburg, vehemently disagreed. And here's where Sotomayor's personal ideology trumps the law. In her sizzling fifty-eight-page dissent, she turned Roberts's words against him, writing, "The way to stop discrimination on the basis of race is to speak openly and candidly on the subject of race." She warned that her colleagues were "out of touch with reality" on racism in America. "Race matters," she jabbed back in an eloquent and emotional rejoinder, "race matters in part because of the long history of racial minorities being denied access to the political process."[81]

> [R]ace matters for reasons that really are only skin deep, that cannot be discussed any other way, and that cannot be wished away. Race matters to a young man's view of society when he spends his teenage years watching others tense up as he passes, no matter the neighborhood where he grew up. Race matters to a young woman's sense of self when she states her hometown, and then is pressed, "No, where are you *really* from?" regardless of how many generations her family has been in the country. Race matters to a young person addressed by a stranger in a foreign language, which he does not understand because only English was spoken at home. Race matters because of the slights, the snickers, the silent judgments that reinforce that most crippling of thoughts: "I do not belong here."

Speaking at an annual event for the liberal American Constitution Society in June 2014, Sotomayor was asked about the dissent and whether she couldn't separate herself from her life experiences. Her answer: "It's easy when precedent supports you. I was doing what I understood was the law."[82]

It has been fashionable for critics to beat up on Clarence Thomas. They may have good grounds. The most recent case in point is his sole dissent in *Foster v. Chapman*, decided May 23, 2016.[83] There, he voted to affirm the Georgia murder conviction of a black defendant by an all-white jury. The defendant, Timothy Foster, awaited execution on death row. The record was laced with overwhelming evidence that Georgia prosecutors had improperly used peremptory challenges to keep two blacks off the trial jury in violation of the rule in *Batson v. Kentucky*.[84] Seven white Justices had little difficulty finding a discriminatory motive, but Thomas cast his vote to affirm the lower court. In reversing the case, Chief Justice Roberts said: "Two peremptory strikes on the basis of race are two more than the Constitution allows."

Jeffrey Toobin takes him to task because February 22, 2016, marked ten years since he asked a question at oral argument.[85] "His behavior," Toobin writes, "has gone from curious to bizarre to downright embarrassing, for himself and the institution he represents."[86] But give him time. Perhaps Thomas asked no questions for such a long time because he felt he was in a kind of exile. "I think my exile saved my life," James Baldwin wrote in *Esquire* in 1961, "for it inexorably confirmed something which Americans appear to have great difficulty accepting. Which is, simply, this: a man is not a man until he's able and willing to accept his own vision of the world, no matter how radically this vision departs from that of others." To be clear, he added: "When I say 'vision' I do not mean 'dream.'" [87] How long will Thomas's "exile" last? Who knows? His contrarian, natural law notions and his peculiar opinions on important legal questions have failed to get traction with any of the other Justices.

Following Thomas's induction as the 106th Justice, the revered chief judge of the U.S. Court of Appeals for the Third Circuit, A. Leon Higginbotham, Jr., took the unprecedented step of writing an "Open Letter to Justice Clarence Thomas from a Federal Judicial Colleague."[88] Judge Higginbotham, who happens to be black, cited Thomas's avowed hostility to the Warren Court, *Brown*, Thurgood Marshall, and the NAACP. He recited how much Thomas had personally benefited from the gains Thomas's adversaries had achieved in racial justice, voting, housing, and privacy rights. Were it not for an effective NAACP, he wrote, "isn't it highly probable that you might still be in Pin Point, Georgia, working as a laborer as some of your relatives did for decades?" He said that President Bush had "vested in you the option to preserve or dilute the gains this country has made in the struggle for equality." Higginbotham concluded,

> No one would be happier than I if the record you will establish on the Supreme Court in years to come demonstrates that my apprehensions were unfounded. You were born into injustice, tempered by the hard reality of what it means to be poor and black in America, and especially to be poor because you are black. You have found a door newly cracked open and you have escaped. I trust you shall not forget that many who have preceded you and many who follow you have found, and will find, the door of equal opportunity slammed in their faces through no fault of their own. . . . And so, with hope to balance my apprehensions, I wish you well as a thoughtful and

worthy successor to Justice Marshall in the ever-ongoing struggle to assure equal justice under law for all persons.

Equal Justice Under Law. The implications of these four words, engraved on the west pediment of the Supreme Court Building in Washington, are profound. In Jacob Lawrence's "Migration Series," the African American artist pictures two black defendants standing before a white judge on an extra-wide bench. The picture is intended perhaps to depict the race-based miscarriage of justice dispensed from a wide bench in Scottsboro. "Who is this white judge," the viewer wonders. "How did he get here?" "Can he conceivably administer equal justice under law to these two black men?" If it had been a black judge, would the disposition have been any different at Scottsboro? If Posner is right that changing judges changes law, it makes you wonder what law is. Does "equal justice" come from the law? Or does it come from the judge? Does Clarence Thomas dispense a different quality of justice from the justice administered by his predecessor, Thurgood Marshall? One hopes it wouldn't be. Judge Higgenbotham hoped it wouldn't be. Only time will tell.

Thomas has a lifetime appointment. He will be only 68 when Obama's successor takes office.

Notes

1. Clarence Thomas, *My Grandfather's Son*, New York: Harper (2007).

2. Transcript of presidential news conference of July 1, 1991. Available at http://www.presidency.ucsb.edu/ws/?pid=29651; *My Grandfather's Son* at 14.

3. Emphasis his.

4. Emphasis his. *My Grandfather's Son* at 204.

5. Nina Totenberg, "Clarence Thomas Retrospective," October 11, 2011. Available at http://www.npr.org/2011/10/11/141213260/thomas-confirmation-hearings-had-ripple-effect.

6. By Jeremy Bowers, Adam Liptak, and Derek Willis, "Which Supreme Court Justices Vote Together Most and Least Often," *New York Times*, July 3, 2014. Available at http://www.nytimes.com/interactive/2014/06/24/upshot/24up-scotus-agreement-rates.html?_r=0&abt=0002&abg=0.

7. See By Jeffrey Rosen, "If Scalia Had His Way," *New York Times*, January 8, 2011. Available at http://www.nytimes.com/2011/01/09/weekinreview/09rosen.html.

8. Quoted by Nina Totenberg, "Clarence Thomas Retrospective," note 5, *supra*.

9. *My Grandfather's Son* at 132.

10. Jules Witcover, *Joe Biden: A Life of Redemption*, New York: William Morrow (2010).

11. Transcript of presidential news conference of July 1, 1991. Available at http://www.presidency.ucsb.edu/ws/?pid=29651.

12. *Id.* at 216.

13. Thomas Hearings, quoted in the *New York Times*, September 11, 1991, at A1 (opening statement of Clarence Thomas).

14. Thomas Hearings, part 1, at 183, 190, 224, 267, 352, 473, and 483.

15. David G. Savage, "Democrats Skeptical on Thomas Testimony: Court: He Denies Ever Discussing Roe vs. Wade with Friends or Reading Anti-abortion Article He Once Praised," September 12, 1991. Available at http://articles.latimes.com/1991-09-12/news/mn-2960_1_supreme-court.

16. By Clarence Thomas, "The Higher Law Background of the Privileges and Immunities Clause of the Fourteenth Amendment," 12 Harvard J. Law & Pub. Pol. 63 (1989), n. 2.

17. By Clarence Thomas, "How Republicans Can Win Blacks," *Chicago Defender* February 21, 1987.

18. *Hudson v. McMillan*, 503 U.S. 1, 28 (1992).

19. 503 U.S. at 19.

20. By Jeffrey Toobin "Why Is Clarence Thomas So Angry?" *New Yorker*, November 12, 2007. Available at http://www.newyorker.com/magazine/2007/11/12/unforgiven.

21. Peter Binzer, "Bowser Is An Old Hand at Playing the Political Game in Philadelphia," *Philadelphia Inquirer*, November 13, 1991, at A11 (quoting Charles Bowser).

22. By Jeffrey Toobin, "The Burden of Clarence Thomas," *New Yorker*, September 27, 1993. Available at http://www.newyorker.com/magazine/1993/09/27/the-burden-of-clarence-thomas.

23. *Othello* 1.1.

24. The NAACP opposed Thomas's nomination to the Supreme Court. Juan Williams, "EEOC Chairman Blasts Black Leaders," *Washington Post*, October 25, 1984 ("These guys [black leaders] are sitting there watching the destruction of our race. . . . The lack of black leadership is the problem"). Available at http://www.washingtonpost.com/archive/politics/1984/10/25/eeoc-chairman-blasts-black-leaders/1f7fe039-e807-48ca-a92c-fd7bfcba3345/.

25. Clarence Thomas, "Black Americans Based Claim for Freedom on Constitution," *San Diego Union-Tribune*, October 6, 1987, at B7 (arguing that Marshall's "sensitive understanding of the Constitution's inherent defects" was

"exasperating and incomprehensible" and "alienates all Americans, and not just black Americans, from their high and noble intention").

26. See e.g., Clarence Thomas, "Toward a 'Plain Reading' of the Constitution—The Declaration of Independence in Constitutional Interpretation," 30 How. Law J. 983, 990–92 (1987) (*Brown* rested on "feelings" rather than "reason and moral and political principles"); Clarence Thomas, "The Higher Law Background of the Privileges and Immunities Clause of the Fourteenth Amendment," Speech to the Federalist Society, University of Virginia School of Law, March 5, 1988, in 12 Harvard J. Law & Pub. Policy 63, 68 (suggesting that *Brown* lacked the higher law foundation for a "just, wise and constitutional decision").

27. 570 U.S. (2013).

28. *Missouri v. Jenkins*, 515 U.S. 70 (1995).

29. *See Grutter*, 539 U.S. at 349–50 (Thomas, J., concurring in part and dissenting in part; first omission in original; quoting Frederick Douglass, "What the Black Man Wants": An Address Delivered in Boston, Massachusetts, on 26 January 1865, *in* 4 *The Frederick Douglass Papers* at 59, 68 (John W. Blassingame and John R. McKivigan, eds.) [1991]).

30. By Juan Williams, "America's Most Influential Thinker on Race," *Wall Street Journal*, February 20, 2015. Available at http://www.wsj.com/articles/juan-williams-americas-most-influential-thinker-on-race-1424476527.

31. By Lawrence H. Tribe, "Clarence Thomas and Natural Law," *New York Times*, July 15, 1991. Available at http://www.nytimes.com/1991/07/15/opinion/clarence-thomas-and-natural-law.html.

32. *Obergefell v. Hodges* 576 U.S. (2015). Slip op. at 17.

33. 561 U.S. 742 (2010).

34. 554 U.S. 570 (2008).

35. The right-wing Cato Institute frequently files briefs in the Supreme Court advocating partisan libertarian positions. Its watchword is "Individual liberty, free markets and peace." According to its website, Cato expects the judiciary to be the "'bulwark' of our liberties, as James Madison put it, neither making up nor ignoring the law but interpreting and applying it through the natural rights tradition we inherited from the founding generation." Available at http://www.cato.org/research/law-civil-liberties.

36. *Schuette v. BAMN*, 572 U.S. (2014). Slip op. at 15.

37. 83 U.S. 36 (1873).

38. *New State Ice Co. v. Liebmann*, 285 U.S. 262, 311 (1932) (Dissenting opinion of Brandeis, J.).

39. *Palko v. Connecticut*, 302 U.S. 319, 325 (1937) (Cardozo, J.). Incorporation is necessary where "a fair and impartial system of justice would be impossible without the right sought to be incorporated" or, in addition, where the

right is "rooted in the traditions and conscience of our people so as to be ruled as fundamental."

40. By Adam Liptak, "Clarence Thomas, a Supreme Court Justice of Few Words, Some Not His Own," *New York Times*, August 27, 2015. Available at http://www.nytimes.com/2015/08/28/us/justice-clarence-thomas-rulings-studies.html?action=click&pgtype=Homepage&version=Moth-Visible&module=inside-nyt-region&region=inside-nyt-region&WT.nav=inside-nyt-region&_r=0.

41. *McDonald v. City of Chicago, supra*, slip op. at 7.

42. *Id.* at 1.

43. Thomas, more than any of the other Justices, lifts language wholesale from lawyers' briefs filed in Court. See by Adam Liptak, "Clarence Thomas, a Supreme Court Justice of a Few Words, Some Not His Own," *New York Times*, August 27, 2015. Available at http://www.nytimes.com/2015/08/28/us/justice-clarence-thomas-rulings-studies.html?_r=0.

44. Dissenting opinion in *Saenz v. Doe*, 526 U.S. 489 (1999) ("We should also consider whether the Court should displace, rather than augment portions of our equal protection and due process jurisprudence").

45. Kevin R.C. Gutzman, *The Politically Incorrect Guide to the Constitution*, Washington, DC: Regnery Publishing (2007) at 134–37. Professor Gutzman's book was listed among the "10 Top Conservative Books of 2007" by *Human Events*, a politically conservative periodical.

46. Transcript of oral argument in *McDonald v. City of Chicago*, March 2, 2010.

47. *Obergefell v. Hodges*, 576 U.S. (2015) (Kennedy, J.). Slip op. at 19.

48. 285 U.S., *supra*, at 311.

49. *Griswold v. Connecticut*, 381 U.S. 479 (1965); *Roe v. Wade*, 410 U.S. 113 (1973).

50. *Lawrence v. Texas*, 539 U.S. 558, 572 (2003) [homosexual sodomy between consenting adults]; *Obergefell v. Hodges*, 576 U.S. (2015) [gay marriage].

51. *Meyer v. Nebraska*, 262 U.S. 390, 399–403 (1923).

52. 347 U.S. 483 (1954).

53. 410 U.S. 113 (1973).

54. *New State Ice Co. v. Liebmann, supra.* (Dissenting opinion of Brandeis, J.) "To stay experimentation in things social and economic is a grave responsibility. Denial of the right to experiment may be fraught with serious consequences to the nation."

55. 512 U.S. 874 (1994).

56. Ari Berman, *Give Us the Ballot: The Modern Struggle for Voting Rights in America*, New York: Farrar, Straus & Giroux (2015).

57. The 13 founding members of the CBC came from states other than the South. They were Parren Mitchell (MD), Charles B. Rangel (NY), Bill Clay, Sr. (MO), Ron Dellums (CA), George Collins (IL), Louis Stokes (OH), Ralph Metcalfe (IL), John Conyers (MI), Walter Fauntroy (DC), Robert Nix, Sr. (PA), Charles Diggs (MI), Shirley Chisholm (NY), and Gus Hawkins (CA). All were Democrats. The present chair is G. K. Butterfield (D-NC).

58. Dissenting opinion of Ginsburg, J. in *Shelby County v. Georgia*, 570 U.S. (2013). Slip op. at 13.

59. *Northwest Austin Municipal Utility District Number One v. Holder*, 557 U.S. 193 (2009).

60. *Shelby County v. Holder*, 570 U.S. (2013). Although the Court declined to declare the coverage provision, §5, unconstitutional, its ruling on §4(b), the formula, cut the heart out of the statute.

61. *Id.* Slip op. at 1.

62. *Id.* Slip op. at 2.

63. See note 61, *supra*; *Id.* Slip op. at 1.

64. Thomas apparently borrows his frequently angry reference to "elites" from Dan Quayle's statement in the 1992 presidential campaign when he noted a "cultural divide in our country." Referring to differences over such issues as abortion, homosexual parents, and sex education in elementary schools, Quayle said, "It is so great a divide that it sometimes seems we have two cultures, the cultural elite and the rest of us."

65. Statement of Reverend William Barber II, president of the North Carolina chapter of the NAACP, made at evening prayer service in Winston-Salem, July 12, 2013.

66. "To Fulfill These Rights," Commencement Address at Howard University, June 4, 1965, in *Public Papers of the Presidents of the United States: Lyndon B. Johnson*, 1965 (Washington, DC: Government Printing Office, 1966), 2:635–40.

67. Califano, note 160, *supra*, at xix.

68. *Id.* at xviii.

69. *Grutter v. Bollinger*, 539 U.S. 306 (2003).

70. *Grutter v. Bollinger*, 539 U.S. 306 (2003), n. 11.

71. http://www.cnn.com/2009/POLITICS/06/11/sotomayor.affirmative. action/index.html?iref=24hours.

72. *My Grandfather's Son* at 87.

73. *Id.* at 75. Emphasis is Thomas's.

74. Dissenting in *Gratz v. Bollinger*, 539 U.S. 244 (2003), quoting Wisdom, J. in *United States v. Jefferson County Bd. of Ed.*, 372 F.2d 836, 876 (CA5 1966). Slip op. at 5. The phrase "color blind" crept into constitutional law from Justice Harlan's dissent in *Plessy v. Ferguson*, 163 U.S. 537 (1896). "But in

view of the constitution, in the eye of the law, there is in this country no superior, dominant, ruling class of citizens. There is no caste here. Our constitution is color-blind, and neither knows nor tolerates classes among citizens. In respect of civil rights, all citizens are equal before the law." Ironically, Harlan was a former slaveholder from Kentucky.

75. *Schuette v. BAMN*, 572 U.S. (2014). Slip op. at 12.

76. Scalia, "The Disease as Cure," *Washington University Law Quarterly* (1979): 154.

77. *Parents Involved in Community Schools v. Seattle School District No. 1*, 551 U.S. 701 (2007).

78. 517 U.S. 620.

79. *Gratz v. Bollinger*, 539 U.S. 244, 270 (2003).

80. *Grutter v. Bollinger*, 539 U.S. 306, 343 (2003).

81. 99 *Schuette v. BAMN*, Slip op. at 45.

82. http://www.msnbc.com/msnbc/sonia-sotomayor-supreme-court-justice-going-backwards.

83. 578 U.S. ___ (2016).

84. 476 U.S. 79 (1986).

85. Thomas broke his silence February 29, 2016, two weeks after Scalia's death, when he questioned a government attorney in a low-profile case.

86. Jeffrey Toobin, "Clarence Thomas's Disgraceful Silence," *New Yorker*, February 21, 2014. Available at http://www.newyorker.com/news/daily-comment/clarence-thomass-disgraceful-silence.

87. Quoted by Benjamin Wallace Wells in "The Hard Truths of Ta-Nehisi Coates," *New York Magazine*, July 12, 2015. Available at http://nymag.com/daily/intelligencer/2015/07/ta-nehisi-coates-between-the-world-and-me.html.

88. Judge Higginbotham's letter is set out in its entirety at 140 Univ. Pa. Law Rev. 1005 (1992).

11

ANTONIN SCALIA (1936–2016)

"More Catholic Than the Pope"

I'll tell you that much. [The Supreme Court] has become politicized, but the reason it has become politicized is that for, oh, maybe 35 years, 40 years the Supreme Court has been making more and more political decisions that are not resolved by the Constitution at all.
—Antonin Scalia, interview with Maria Bartiromo, October 10, 2005

The most scintillating writer on the modern Court was undoubtedly Antonin Scalia. Possessed of an overpowering legal intellect, a mordant wit, and an uncommon flare for language, he was the pied piper of originalist doctrine. He believed that the Constitution is "enduring," if not dead. This means you look at the text and the original understanding, not some liberal notion of an evolving "living" Constitution that means whatever the Justice would like it to mean. As a friend of mine, a professor of Near Eastern Studies at Princeton, remarked to me once, "Scalia interprets the Constitution the same way that ISIS interprets Sharia."

Not infrequently his cogent and provocative opinions, grounded in logic, rich in the power of words, go beyond what Kennedy calls "the formal discourse of the law.[1] In fact, he often soared "over the top," and then some, to prove or punctuate a point. Scalia will remain the most-quoted Justice for decades to come. He was the greatest recipient of media attention. His antics on and off the bench were the most fun to watch. Their elegance aside, many of his statements were so outrageous, they would give Donald Trump a run for his money.

Scalia was a champion college debater and a Shakespearean actor, and the skills he then acquired were not lost. Agree with him or not, he was Punchinello, Rigoletto, Voltaire, all embodied in a consummate constitutional advocate. Scathing, irreverent, outspokenly opinionated, possessed of a sharp tongue and a sharper quill, he did not hesitate to critique the opinions of his sisters and brethren on the Court in a direct and personally confrontational fashion.

Of his favorite piñata, Justice Kennedy, Scalia wrote that he had produced a "tutti-frutti opinion."[2] Dissenting in the gay marriage case, he wrote that Kennedy's opinion of the Court was a host of "mummeries and straining to be memorable passages," an opinion "couched in a style that is as pretentious as its content is egotistic"; that it was "lacking even a thin veneer of law"; that its "showy profundities are often profoundly incoherent"[3]; and that "[i]f even as the price to be paid for a fifth vote, I ever joined in an opinion that began: 'The Constitution promises liberty to all within its reach, a liberty that includes certain specific rights that allow persons, within a lawful realm, to define and express their identity,' I would hide my head in a bag."[4] Of Justice Blackmun's approach to the death penalty, "false, untextual and unhistorical."[5] Of Justice Sandra Day O'Connor, one of her opinions was "irrational" and "not to be taken seriously."[6] Of the majority opinion in the Defense of Marriage Act case, "legalistic argle-bargle."[7] Of Justice Sotomayor, she had set herself up to be the "obfuscator of last resort."[8] Of the majority opinion in the Obamacare case, "pure applesauce"[9] and "jiggery-pokery."[10] Of the majority opinion in the gay marriage case, "The Supreme Court of the United States has descended from the disciplined legal reasoning of John Marshall and Joseph Story to the mystical aphorisms of a fortune cookie."[11] Then, the rhetorical flourish which came back to bite him, "It is one thing for separate concurring or dissenting opinions to contain extravagances, even silly extravagances, of thought and expression; it is something else for the official opinion of the Court to do so."[12] In saying this he proved himself ever the actor "whose end, both at the / first and now, was and is, to hold, as 'twere, the / mirror up to nature; to show virtue her own feature, / scorn her own image, and the very age and body of / the time his form and pressure."[13] For what Justice was guiltier of "silly extravagances of thought and expression" than Scalia himself?

Although the Senate confirmed Scalia in 1986 by a resounding 98-0 margin, he told MSNBC's Maria Bartiromo in 2005, "I wouldn't want to go through it today, I'll tell you that much."[14] The statement especially resonates today.

Scalia believed that the text of the Constitution, and the original understanding of its meaning at the time of ratification, and how courts have interpreted it, ought to be the decisive factors in interpretation, not the personal views of the individual Justice who wants the Constitution to mean what he or she would like it to mean.

He argued quite passionately that there is no such thing as a "living Constitution." At Princeton, he said of the Constitution, "Dead, dead, dead!" The Constitution, like the moral values he treasured, is neither living nor dead, but enduring. Confronted at Princeton, however, by a gay student who found offensive Scalia's comparison of homosexuality to murder in a judicial opinion, the jurist replied, "If we cannot have moral feelings against homosexuality, can we have it against murder?" "Can we have it against other things? I don't apologize for the things I raise." In other words, the Constitution meant exactly what *he* would like it to mean. Scalia's "originalism" was merely a tool for reaching desired policy goals by professing to rely on textual analysis and original understanding.

What the gay Princetonian was referring to was Scalia's dissent in a gay rights case coming from Colorado. There, he said that morality is not misplaced in judging, as though all citizens or all Justices will agree on what morality is or what it asks of us:

> The Court's opinion contains grim, disapproving hints that Coloradans have been guilty of "animus" or "animosity" toward homosexuality, as though that has been established as Un-American. Of course it is *our moral heritage* that one should not hate any human being or class of human beings. But I had thought that one could consider certain conduct reprehensible—murder, for example, or polygamy, or cruelty to animals—and could exhibit even "animus" toward such conduct. Surely that is the only sort of "animus" at issue here: moral disapproval of homosexual conduct.[15]

Scalia's view of "our moral heritage" was religiously informed. "You're looking at me as though I'm weird," he told an interviewer. "My God! Are you so out of touch with most of America, most of which believes in the Devil? I mean, Jesus Christ believed in the Devil! It's in the Gospels."[16]

The flaw in Scalia's originalism was its inconsistency. Justice Harry Blackmun stated that his approach seemed "to treat history as a grab bag of principles, to be adopted where they support the Court's theory, and ignored where they do not."[17]

"I am something of a contrarian, I suppose," Scalia told Jennifer Senior of *New York* magazine in October 2013. "I suppose I feel less comfortable when everyone agrees with me."[18] Scalia was *sui generis*. Funny, doctrinaire, endowed with a heretical, polemical worldview, Scalia left an indelible impact on the Court.

Professor Cass Sunstein, a liberally oriented professor at Harvard Law School, himself a law clerk to Justice Thurgood Marshall, blogged for Bloomberg View his favorite eight "greatest" as measured by their "historical significance" and "legal ability."[19] They are John Marshall, the fourth Chief Justice (for enunciating the broad regulatory power of Congress and the doctrine of judicial review); Oliver Wendell Holmes (for his "razor" mind, insisting upon a modest role for the federal judiciary—"If my fellow citizens want to go to Hell I will help them. It's my job"[20]); Brandeis (because "his eyes were on the heavens" in hallowing liberty as the "secret of happiness, and courage . . . [as] the secret of liberty"[21]); Frankfurter ("wise, deep, and . . . underrated"); Jackson (for being the "greatest writer in the history of the court"); Warren (for reforming American society and in this no Justice "had a larger impact"); Brennan (an "unfailingly kind and gracious man," who was the brains of the Warren court); and Rehnquist (for restoring what he believed to be the "right constitutional balance" in limiting the reach of Warren court rulings).

Judge Alex Kozinski of the Ninth Circuit, ideologically a libertarian,[22] would throw Scalia's hat in the ring for the Supreme Court Hall of Fame, and other liberal commentators would second the nomination. Kozinski compares Scalia, who was his friend, to Holmes, Brandeis, and Harlan, and he predicts he "will take his place among the Court's greats."[23] I do not subscribe to what was Scalia's conservatism on social issues or his originalist approach to constitutional interpretation, but I respect his courage and imagination, his illuminating advocacy for positions that were unpopular both on the Court and in the broader community, and for his "Hey, wait a minute" style. Let's remember, "it's a Constitution we are expounding." Formalism is important in legal discourse, but colloquialisms are one of many arrows in the advocate's arsenal of weapons.

Religion, ethnicity, and politics were undoubtedly factors in Scalia's 1986 appointment. Attorney General Edwin Meese had recommended to President Reagan two conservatives for the vacancy, Scalia and Robert Bork. Reagan said he chose Scalia because he wanted a Catholic and the first Italian American.

Scalia became the principal apostle of judicial conservatism. There has been no one quite like him on the Court. He was called "El Niño" after the weather phenomenon that wreaks devastation throughout the world. Born in Trenton, New Jersey, to an Italian immigrant father, he was an only child. His family moved to Queens. Later, he attended St. Francis Xavier High School and Georgetown University, both institutions of Jesuit education. Early in his formative years, Scalia found a hero in Saint Thomas More, a sixteenth-century English lawyer who refused to sanction the annulment of Henry VIII's marriage to Catherine of Aragon and to acknowledge that the king, rather than the Pope, was supreme. Tried for treason, More lost his head in 1535 on Tower Hill for his religious beliefs; his final words on the scaffold were that he died "the king's good servant, but God's first." Scalia wore a replica of the skullcap worn by More, as depicted in Holbein's famous painting, to Obama's second inaugural in 2013. The *New York Daily News* called it a "beret on steroids." More was once the patron saint of lawyers, but the Vatican recently demoted him to patron saint of politicians. Many saw Scalia's skullcap as a sign of religious protest against Obama's policies on abortion and other social issues.

According to his biographer Bruce Allen Murphy, Scalia's Catholicism took "center stage" in his life. He was a member of St. Catherine of Siena Church in Great Falls, Virginia. For many years, the congregation has been "traditionalist," named for the patron saint of unborn children.[24]

As Scalia elaborated the relationship between his religion and his judicial approach,

A religious person cannot divide his view of man. He can't separate religion from his own natural inclinations. Catholicism is not some superficial overlay. . . . It is who I am and how I see the world. . . . [R]eligiously motivated work is *not* un-American. . . . Official public expression of God and God's law distinguish us from most Western countries.[25]

Scalia reaffirmed that his Catholicism was who he was and how he saw the world when he sat in *Salazar v. Buono*,[26] a case involving a challenge under the Establishment Clause to a large cross situated on public lands and serving as a war memorial in a remote part of the Mojave Desert. During the oral argument of the case, Peter J. Eliasberg, a lawyer with the American Civil Liberties Union of Southern California, argued that the cross was the "predominant symbol of Christianity" that signifies that "Jesus is the son of God and died to redeem mankind for our sins."

Scalia was plainly skeptical of the claims of relatives of war dead, unaccepting of the divinity of Christ, that the government was preferring one religion over another.

Justice Scalia: It's erected as a war memorial. I assume it is erected in honor of all the war dead. It's the . . . cross is the . . . most common symbol of . . . the resting place of the dead, and it doesn't seem to me—what would you have them erect? A cross—some conglomerate of a cross, a Star of David, and you know, a Moslem half moon and star?

Eliasberg: Well, Justice Scalia, if I may go to your first point. The cross is the most common symbol of the resting place of Christians. I have been in Jewish cemeteries. There is never a cross on the tombstone of a Jew.

Clueless and angry, Scalia was quick to interject,

Justice Scalia: I don't think you can leap from that to the conclusion that the only war dead that the cross honors are the Christian war dead. I think that's an outrageous conclusion.

Eliasberg: Well, my . . . point here is to say that there is a reason the Jewish war veterans came in and said we don't feel honored by the cross.

Following his graduation from Harvard Law School in 1960, Scalia worked at a Cleveland law firm, taught at the University of Virginia, and held a variety of governmental posts. His widow is Irish-Catholic. He raised nine children, one of whom is a priest. Scalia remarked that his priest son, who was to preside at his funeral, had "taken one for the team." When Reagan elevated him from the DC circuit to the Supreme Court in 1986, a legal commentator said, "Scalia's conservative views on abortion, affirmative action, criminal procedure, and the limited role of the courts in setting public policy mirror those of the Reagan administration."[27]

Reagan hoped that Scalia would forge a new conservative consensus. In his first four years on the Court, however, before the appointment of Thomas in 1991, Scalia found himself a "voice crying in the wilderness,"[28] writing alone in major cases. On separation of powers, he wrote alone three times.[29] On whether to overrule *Roe v. Wade*, he was alone.[30] On the right to die—alone ("[F]ederal courts have no business in this field.").[31] On the death penalty, alone ("[O]ur jurisprudence and logic have long since parted ways").[32] As Ibsen said in *An Enemy of the People*, "The strongest man in the world is he who stands most alone."

In his epic dissent in *Morrison v. Olson*,[33] a separation of powers case involving the constitutionality of an independent prosecutor to take over some of the law enforcement responsibilities of the president, Scalia stood alone against his conservative Chief Justice William Rehnquist. In *Morrison*, what he describes as one of his best opinions, including his favorite one-liner, he wrote,

> That is what this suit is about. Power. The allocation of power among Congress, the President, and the courts in such fashion as to preserve the equilibrium the Constitution sought to establish—so that "a gradual concentration of the several powers in the same department," . . . can effectively be resisted. Frequently an issue of this sort will come before the Court clad, so to speak, in sheep's clothing: the potential of the asserted principle to effect important change in the equilibrium of power is not immediately evident, and must be discerned by a careful and perceptive analysis. But this wolf comes as a wolf.

As he told *New York Magazine* with not too little relish, "But my favorite one-liner is from *Morrison v. Olson*: 'But this wolf comes as a wolf.' . . . You gotta read the whole paragraph. Boom. [Punches the air]. . . . I say, 'God, that's a good opinion. I'm not sure I could write as good an opinion today.'"[34]

Scalia was "a confessed law-and-order social conservative."[35] He often stated that he saw "clarity, precision and predictability as essential elements of the law."[36] Professor Alan Dershowitz said derisively he had "[one] of the finest 19th century minds in America."

Scalia was an unabashed "originalist" for his opinions relying on the original understanding of the meaning of the Constitution at the time of ratification.[37] Originalism is an approach to constitutional interpretation that became the shibboleth of conservatives but was highly criticized and largely discredited in liberal circles even before Scalia's nomination.[38] Later on with the Roberts Court, it regained vitality in a number of cases with Scalia voting with the majority.[39] It is interesting that two ideological opposites, Scalia the "Constitution is dead" Justice and Sotomayor the "living Constitution" Justice, came out in exactly the same place with a rigid and unbending protection of Fourth Amendment rights in *United States vs. Jones* (government surreptitiously installs GPS on underside of car to track movements of drug dealer). The rest of the Court signed on for a more flexible approach that would protect "privacy" in some cases and not in others, punting the issue down the field for future interpretation.[40]

During oral argument in the video games case,[41] where the issue was whether violent video games were protected speech under the First Amendment, Alito appeared to poke fun at Scalia's originalism.

> Justice Alito: Well, I think what Justice Scalia wants to know is what James Madison thought about video games.
> (Laughter.)
> Justice Alito: Did he enjoy them?
> Justice Scalia: No, I want to know what James Madison thought about violence. Was there any indication that anybody thought, when the First Amendment was adopted, that there—there was an exception to it for—for speech regarding violence? Anybody?

Scalia also cast himself as a legal "positivist" for his views that statutory and constitutional text and precedent were the only legitimate reasons to offer in support of a decision, rejecting any reliance on policy or moral considerations (e.g., that a rule is unjust). "Fortunately," he said, "the overwhelming majority of issues of public policy do not rise to the moral level."[42]

Another feature of Scalia's style was his insistence upon eliminating balancing as the principal way to resolve constitutional issues. Balancing is the paradigm example of judicial legislation. If you want to favor an interest, call it "vital," if you want to discredit it, call it "trivial." In *Maryland v. Craig* (prosecutor presented to jury the testimony of a traumatized child, a sex abuse victim, on closed circuit TV), the issue was whether this satisfied the constitutional right to be confronted with witnesses against yourself. Scalia put it this way:[43]

> The Court today has applied "interest-balancing" analysis where the text of the Constitution simply does not permit it. We are not free to conduct a cost-benefit analysis of clear and explicit constitutional guarantees, and then to adjust their meaning to comport with our findings. The Court has convincingly proved that the Maryland procedure serves a valid interest, and gives the defendant virtually everything the Confrontation Clause guarantees (everything, that is, except confrontation). I am persuaded, therefore, that the Maryland procedure is virtually constitutional. Since it is not, however, actually constitutional, I would affirm the judgment of the Maryland Court of Appeals reversing the judgment of conviction.

As far as Scalia was concerned, balancing was out. Court decisions should enunciate or follow rules of general application. This would create certainty and prevent future courts from introducing their own personal policy preferences.

This is well and good except for the exceptions to neutral application of a decided rule when it comes to the polarizing social issues such as abortion, traditional family values, gay rights, and morality. There, his opinions might have paralleled more closely those of the Catholic Church. Of course, for many the Church altered course since Vatican II and then changed course again with the inauguration of the liberal Pope Francis in March 2013. Scalia insisted that the Pope hadn't backed off on the issues of homosexuality and abortion. "He's just saying, 'Don't spend all our time talking about that stuff. Talk about Jesus Christ and evangelize.' I think there's no indication whatever that he's changing doctrinally."[44] Undoubtedly, he was correct.

Of course, after reciting his originalist catechism, Scalia more often than not came to a conclusion welcomed by conservatives. At times, however, thanks to his originalist approach, he sometimes reached outcomes at odds with his conservative policy preferences.

In *Coy v. Iowa*,[45] he came down on the side of criminal defendants, holding that the Confrontation Clause of the Sixth Amendment did not permit measures to prevent two child witnesses from face-to-face encounters with the accused in a child abuse case, namely placement of a screen that prevented the witnesses from seeing the defendant as they testified against him at trial, stating, "It is a truism that constitutional protections have costs."[46] And in another Confrontation Clause case, *Maryland v. Craig*,[47] where the Court distinguished *Coy*, he joined the liberals—Brennan, Marshall, and Stevens—to dissent from the Court's judgment validating a Maryland procedure that permitted child molestation victims to testify over closed-circuit TV. The basis was vintage Scalia: "Seldom has this Court failed so conspicuously to sustain a categorical guarantee of the Constitution against the tide of prevailing public opinion."[48] To be confronted means to be confronted—face-to-face and eyeball-to-eyeball. The Court had come to an "anti-textual conclusion."[49]

> To quote the document one last time (for it plainly says all that need be said): "In *all* criminal prosecutions, the accused shall enjoy the right . . . to be confronted with the witnesses against him."[50]

In his best-known deviation from conservative expectation, he cast the deciding vote in the flag burning case, holding that free speech protected protestors who would burn the flag to make their point.[51] He gleefully told an audience of trial lawyers the story of a headline in the *Washington Post*, the morning after the decision, "Scalia Approves Flag Burning," recounting that when he came down the stairs to breakfast, his wife, Maureen, whistled George M. Cohan's "It's a Grand Old Flag," as she handed him the paper.

Scalia once called his originalism "faint-hearted," although he later pulled away from that description. If the original meaning of the text is too shocking to bear, it can be suppressed. This approach is what Holmes notoriously called the "puke" test: state action is unconstitutional only if it makes you want to puke.[52]

Here was Scalia in a 1989 law review article:[53]

What if some state should enact a new law providing public lashing, or branding of the right hand, as punishment for certain criminal offenses? Even if it could be demonstrated unequivocally that these were not cruel and unusual measures in 1791 [when the Eighth Amendment prohibition on "cruel and unusual punishment" was adopted], and even though no prior Supreme Court decision has specifically disapproved them, I doubt whether any federal judge—even among many who consider themselves originalists—would sustain them against an eighth amendment challenge.

But mostly his tortuous methodology led him to reject individual rights. In *Hudson v. McMillian*,[54] Scalia failed to invoke the "puke test," breaking with other conservatives and joining Thomas in dissent, to reach the conclusion that the Eighth Amendment's Cruel and Unusual Punishments Clause did not apply to prison guards arbitrarily beating a prisoner with punches and kicks that loosened the inmate's teeth, cracked his dental plate, and caused swelling of the face and mouth. He concluded that the Eighth Amendment reads only on the "punishment" imposed by the state, not how it was carried out.

In matters of family values and morality, Scalia's judicial utterances closely paralleled Catholic thought. *Michael H. v. Gerald D*[55] was a case in which a natural father sought parental rights in respect of his daughter, who was born of an adulterous relationship while the mother was cohabiting with her husband. Scalia, writing for the Court, affirmed the California courts' denial of parental rights and rejected the father's substantive due process arguments, stating his view that the Constitution protected only conformist people in conformist relationships, not adulterous fathers. There was a sharp dissent by Brennan—a spectacular example of two Catholic judges at opposite ends of the ideological spectrum, with Scalia quick to deny constitutional protections and liberty interests in an "unconventional relationship."

Our cases reflect "continual insistence upon respect for the teachings of history [and] solid recognition of the basic values that underlie our society." . . . Michael reads the landmark case of *Stanley v. Illinois*, 405 U.S. 645 (1972), and the subsequent cases of *Quilloin v. Walcott*, 434 U.S. 246 (1978), *Caban v. Mohammed*, 441 U.S. 380 (1979), and *Lehr v. Robertson*, 463 U.S. 248 (1983), as establishing that a liberty interest is created by biological fatherhood plus an established parental relationship—factors that exist in the present case as well. We think that distorts the rationale of those cases. As we view them, they rest not upon such isolated factors but upon the historic respect—indeed, sanctity would not be too strong a term—traditionally accorded to the relationships that develop within the unitary family. . . . As Justice Powell stated for the plurality in *Moore* v. *East Cleveland*, "Our decisions establish that the Constitution protects the sanctity of the family precisely because the institution of the family is deeply rooted in this Nation's history and tradition."[56]

As for Brennan's argument that due process extends to those in a nonconforming relationship, Scalia had this to say:

We do not accept Justice Brennan's criticism that this result "squashes" the liberty that consists of "the freedom not to conform." *Post* at 491 U.S. 141. It seems to us that reflects the erroneous view that there is only one side to this controversy—that one disposition can expand a "liberty" of sorts without contracting an equivalent "liberty" on the other side. Such a happy choice is rarely available. Here, to *provide* protection to an adulterous natural father is to *deny* protection to a marital father, and vice versa. If Michael has a "freedom not to conform" (whatever that means), Gerald must equivalently have a "freedom to conform." One of them will pay a price for asserting that "freedom"—Michael by being unable to act as father of the child he has adulterously begotten, or Gerald by being unable to preserve the integrity of the traditional family unit he and Victoria have established. Our disposition does not choose between these two "freedoms," but leaves that to the people of California. Justice Brennan's approach chooses one of them as the constitutional imperative, on no apparent basis except that the unconventional is to be preferred.[57]

And of course, he dissented in the consensual sodomy case, *Lawrence v. Texas*,[58] which struck down a Texas statute that criminalized "deviate" acts between consenting homosexuals (but not heterosexuals committing the same "deviate" acts). Finding "moral disapproval" a legitimate basis for government to act, he said that the Court had effectively decreed the "end of all morals legislation" and had called into question state laws regulating bestiality, bigamy, and masturbation. Heavens! *Mea maxima culpa.*

Summing up his "originalist-driven conclusion," he said in an expression of judicial homophobia unparalleled in modern jurisprudence,

> Today's opinion is the product of a Court, which is the product of a law-profession culture, that has largely signed on to the so-called homosexual agenda, by which I mean the agenda promoted by some homosexual activists directed at eliminating the moral opprobrium that has traditionally attached to homosexual conduct. . . . One of the most revealing statements in today's opinion is the Court's grim warning that the criminalization of homosexual conduct is "an invitation to subject homosexual persons to discrimination both in the public and in the private spheres." [citation omitted] It is clear from this that the Court has taken sides in the culture war, departing from its role of assuring, as neutral observer, that the democratic rules of engagement are observed. *Many Americans* do not want persons who openly engage in homosexual conduct as partners in their business, as scoutmasters for their children, as teachers in their children's schools, or as boarders in their home. They view this as protecting themselves and their families from a lifestyle that they believe to be immoral and destructive.[59]

And who are these "many Americans" but individuals influenced by ethnicity, background, and experience to have a negative view of homosexuals? If this be originalism, make the most of it. It strikes me as an unvarnished attempt at judicial legislation. But as Shakespeare said, "The devil can cite scripture for his purpose."[60]

Again favoring criminal defendants, he held that the Fourth Amendment prevented government examination of the underside of some audio equipment to detect its serial number, contrary to the contention of prosecutors that the item was in "plain view."[61] When it comes to the Fourth Amendment, Scalia was astonishingly liberal. In *Maryland v. King*,[62] a case involving the Fourth Amendment prohibition of "unreasonable" search and seizures, and the amendment's application to DNA testing of a person under arrest for one crime to find evidence of other unsolved crimes. Alito at oral argument called the case perhaps the most important criminal procedure case of the decade.

In 2009, Alonzo King was arrested in Wicomico County, Maryland, for menacing a group of people with a shotgun. He was subsequently convicted of second-degree assault. As a further incident to routine booking procedures, including photographing and fingerprinting, police after his arraignment applied a cotton swab to the inside of his cheeks to obtain a DNA sample. The procedure was quick and minimally invasive. The sample linked him conclusively to an unsolved crime he had committed in 2003 in Salisbury, Maryland, where, his face masked, he broke into a woman's home and raped her. The only clue in the 2003 crime was some genetic material the assailant had left behind.

Everyone agrees that it would have been constitutionally permissible to take a swab sample of King's DNA as an incident to his assault *conviction*, but the constitutional issue arises out of his rape conviction where the damning DNA evidence was obtained as an incident to his *arrest* on an unrelated assault charge. The Forensic Sciences Division of the Maryland State Police did not receive King's DNA sample until two weeks after King's arrest. The bureaucrats there did not get around to mailing the sample to a testing lab until two months after it was received, and nearly three months after the arrest. After the mailing, the test results were not available for several more weeks until they were entered in Maryland's DNA database. Maryland then forwarded the coded DNA sample to the FBI national database. It was not until four months after King's arrest that King's DNA sample, provided after his arrest on the unrelated charge, was matched with the DNA left at the scene of the cold case of rape that had occurred six years earlier. The delay in analyzing the DNA sample makes clear that the purpose of the test, unlike photographing and fingerprinting where the result is instantaneous, was not the identification of the arrestee, but the investigation of other crimes he may have committed.

In an alignment of five strange bedfellows consisting of Kennedy, Thomas, Roberts, Alito, and (would you believe it?) Breyer, the Court held that the sample, taken without a warrant as an incident to a lawful arrest, was a reasonable search as its purpose was to assure King's identity, not to rummage for evidence that he was guilty of unsolved crimes.

Scalia, certainly no friend of criminal defendants (except white collar criminal defendants), was an unbending guardian of Fourth Amendment values. He wrote one of his best dissents, which was joined in by Ginsburg, Sotomayor, and Kagan. The dissent promptly won the adulation of the liberal media. Jeffrey Rosen of the *New Republic* posted a piece the day after the decision titled "A Damning Dissent: Scalia's Smartest, Wittiest Ruling of all Time."[63] And liberal commentator Eugene Robinson of the *Washington Post*, never a fan of Scalia's jurisprudence, wrote a piece a week later titled "In the DNA Case, Scalia Was Right." "The words, 'Antonin Scalia was right' do not flow easily to me," Robinson wrote, "But the Court's most uncompromising conservative, who wrote a withering dissent, was correct when he issued a dire-sounding warning from the bench: 'Make no mistake about it: As an entirely predictable consequence of today's decision, your DNA can be taken and entered into a national database if you are ever arrested rightly or wrongly and for whatever reason.'"[64]

The majority in *King* in an opinion by Kennedy held the DNA testing of the arrestee, as opposed to a convicted criminal, to be reasonable under the Fourth Amendment as a minimally invasive procedure to verify King's identity since "[i]n every criminal case, it is known and must be known who has been arrested and who is being tried."[65] The problem is that the object of a search incident to a lawful arrest must be either weapons, or contraband that might be destroyed, or evidence relevant to the crime of arrest. The majority's reasoning that the search was justified by the need to "identify" the defendant drove Scalia into orbit.

Scalia went ballistic. "The Court's assertion that DNA is being taken, not to solve crimes, but to *identify* those in the State's custody, taxes the credulity of the credulous," he charged in a devastating critique of the Court's reasoning.[66] The DNA searches had nothing to do with identification. It was Scalia v. Kennedy, the art form—Scalia at his snarkiest. The original understanding of Madison and the other constitutional framers, he reasoned, was that, even with a warrant, a search must be "particular," that is to say "*individualized*" to the "place to be searched, and the persons or things to be seized." Although the Court had approved warrantless, suspicionless drug tests of railroad employees for reasons of safety or of student athletes to prevent teenage drug use, under no circumstances, with or without a warrant, had the Court ever approved a suspicionless search if its principal end was ordinary crime solving, namely, to solve cold cases.[67] So the Court must have had another method in its madness, namely its argument that the DNA testing was reasonable so as to identify the defendant.

This, Scalia might have aptly called "jiggery-pokery." It was clear from the record, he argued, that the DNA swab had nothing to do with identifying King. The Maryland law authorizing the DNA testing provided that testing might not begin prior to the first arraignment date. It was a criminal offense to do otherwise. In King's case the arraignment took place three days after his arrest. Surely he had been "identified" by that time. The test results were not known until three months after his arrest. Then and only then were authorities able to compare the results with the data in the FBI database of DNA samples taken from unsolved crime scenes. Scalia then reached the *coda* of his devastating argument:

> In fact, if anything was "identified" at the moment that the DNA database returned a match, it was not King—his identity was already known. (The docket for the original criminal charges lists his full name, his race, his sex, his height, his weight, his date of birth, and his address.) Rather, what the August 4 match "identified" was *the previously-taken sample from the earlier crime*. That sample was genuinely mysterious to Maryland; the State knew that it had probably been left by the victim's attacker, but nothing else. King was not identified by his association with the sample; rather, the sample was identified by its association with King.[68]

Scalia thereupon demolished what he called a "series of inapposite analogies" that he said the Court had used to "bolster its identification theory." These were well-established procedures used before the DNA era in criminal identification as an incident to arrest. Of photographing the defendant, he argued this is not a Fourth Amendment search because there is no physical intrusion; of noting "Bertillon" measurements of the arrestee's height, weight, shoe size, etc. on the back of a photograph, this is clearly a means of identification; and of fingerprints (perhaps the hardest analogy to attack), they are used primarily to identify arrestees (although they may incidentally lead to the solution of other crimes), while the entire point of DNA testing is to solve cold cases.

Scalia visualized a parade of horribles springing from the Court's opinion. He made a dire prediction of an Orwellian "brave new world" in which air travelers, public school children, or ordinary automobile drivers could be subjected to DNA testing ostensibly to verify their identity, but in fact to investigate cold cases and unsolved crimes. "Perhaps the construction of such a genetic panopticon is wise," he wrote, "but I doubt that the proud men who wrote the charter of our liberties would have been so eager to open their mouths for royal inspection."[69]

Scalia might well have said the same thing Brennan did before the Senate Judiciary Committee had he been asked the question about being "bound by his oath or by his religious obligations," and I would not contend that he reached the conclusions he did because they were inspired by pre–Vatican II doctrine. Doubtless, however, that his Catholic education and adherence to Catholic doctrine were important filters in his approach to constitutional interpretation, as was his moral stance on certain issues, as exemplified by his concurrence in *Michael H.*,[70] his dissent in *Lawrence*,[71] and his repeated calls for the overruling of *Roe v. Wade* as wrongly decided.[72]

Contrasting the judicial models of Murphy and Brennan for that matter on the one hand and those of Scalia on the other, we see liberal and conservative Catholicism at odds with each other. Murphy, wanting to carry out Christ's admonition to "Love thy neighbor as thyself," was quick to fashion and invent new judicial models such as "incorporation," "selective incorporation," and "balancing" to get there; and Scalia, being equally quick to seize upon Marshall's admonition that "it is a Constitution we are expounding," was equally quick to sacrifice "Love thy neighbor" (particularly if the issue was abortion or gay rights) on the altar of "originalism" and "text."

Which philosophy of constitutional law will win out, originalism or the living and evolving Constitution? Only time will judge. But the Court will surely miss Scalia's intellectual power. He was what he set out to be—a consummate partisan advocate.

Notes

1. Opinion of the Court per Kennedy, J. in *Obergefell, supra.* Slip op. at 8.

2. *Sykes v. United States*, U.S. (2011).

3. *Obergefell v. Hodges*, 576 U.S. (2015). Slip op. at 4, 7.

4. Dissenting in *Obergefell*, supra, the gay marriage case. Slip op. at 8, note 22.

5. *Callins v. Collins*, 510 U.S. 1141 (1994).

6. *Webster v. Reproductive Health Services*, 492 U.S. 490 (1989).

7. *United States v. Windsor*, 570 U.S. (2013). The *Oxford Dictionary* defines "argle-bargle," a British term, as nonsense. It is a rhyming reduplication of words, like "hocus pocus" or "mumbo jumbo."

8. *Michigan v. Bryant*, U.S. (2010).

9. *King v. Burwell*, 576 U.S. (2015). Slip op. at 10.

10. *Id.* Slip op. at 8.

11. Note 22 in dissenting opinion in *Obergefell v. Hodges*, 576 U.S. (2015). Slip op. at 7.

12. See slip op. in *Obergefell* at 7.

13. *Hamlet* 3:2.

14. Interview with Maria Bartiromo, MSNBC transcript, October 10, 2005, Lexis/Nexis.

15. *Romer v. Evans*, 517 U.S. 620 (1996).

16. Transcript of interview with Jennifer Senior of *New York* magazine, October 6, 2013. Available at http://nymag.com/news/features/antonin-scalia-2013-10/.

17. *Lucas v. South Carolina Coastal Council*, 505 U.S. 1003, 1060 (1992) Blackmun, J. (dissenting).

18. Note 17.

19. By Cass R. Sunstein, "Home-Run Hitters of the Supreme Court," BloombergView. Available at http://www.bloombergview.com/articles/2014-04-01/home-run-hitters-of-the-supreme-court.

20. Letter to Harold J. Laski (March 4, 1920); reported in Mark DeWolfe Howe, ed., *Holmes-Laski Letters* (1953), 1:249.

21. Concurring, *Whitney v. California*, 274 U.S. 357, 375 (1927).

22. I use "libertarian," as distinct from "liberal," to refer to the political belief in laissez-faire economics with minimal regulation, and minimal state limitation on the freedom of the individual.

23. Alex Kozinski, "My Pizza with Nino," 12 Card. Law Rev. 1583, 1591 (1991).

24. B. A. Murphy, *Scalia: A Court of One*, New York: Simon and Schuster (2014) at 281 (emphasis his).

25. B. A. Murphy, *Scalia: A Court of One*, New York: Simon and Schuster (2014) at 42.

26. 559 U.S. 700 (2010). The oral argument occurred on October 7, 2009. Available at http://www.oyez.org/cases/2000-2009/2009/2009_08_472.

27. Paul Marcote, "New Kid on the Block," 72 ABA J. (August 1986) at 20.

28. Isaiah 40:1–3.

29. *Morrison v. Olson*, 487 U.S. 654, 697 (1988); *Mistretta v. United States*, 488 U.S. 361, 413 (1989); and *Webster v. Doe*, 486 U.S. 592, 606 (1988).

30. *Webster v. Reproductive Health Services*, 492 U.S. 490, 532 (1989).

31. *Cruzan v. Director, Missouri Department of Health*, 497 U.S. 261, 292 (1990). Whether forcible measures should be taken to prevent suicide, "including suicide by refusing to take appropriate measures necessary to preserve one's life," should be left to state legislatures. "[T]he point at which the means necessary to preserve [life] . . . become 'extraordinary' or 'inappropriate,' are neither set forth in the Constitution nor known to the nine Justices of this

Court any better than they are known to nine people picked at random from the Kansas City telephone directory."

32. *Walton v. Arizona*, 497 U.S. 639, 656 (1990).

33. See note 30, *supra*.

34. Interview by Jennifer Senior, published October 6, 2013, note 17, *supra*.

35. By Adam Liptak, "Hints in New Scalia Book of Views on Health Law," *New York Times*, June 15, 2012.

36. Beschle, "Catechism or Imagination: Is Justice Scalia's Judicial Style Typically Catholic?" 37 Vill. Law Rev. 1329, 1335 (1992) citing Scalia, "The Rule of Law Is a Law of Rules," 56 Univ. Chi. Law Rev. 1175 (1989).

37. Scalia, "Originalism: The Lesser Evil," 57 Univ. Cin. Law Rev. 849 (1989).

38. See e.g., Ronald Dworkin, *A Matter of Principle*, Cambridge: Harvard University Press (1985) at 34–57.

39. Compare the right to bear arms cases *District of Columbia v. Heller*, 554 U.S. 570 (2008) and *McDonald v. Chicago*, 561 U.S. 742 (2010) making the Second Amendment binding on the states in virtue of the Due Process Clause of the Fourteenth. Horrors!

40. *United States v. Jones*, 565 U.S. (2012).

41. *Brown v. EMA*, 564 U.S. (2011). Available at http://www.supremecourt.gov/oral_arguments/argument_transcripts/08-1448.pdf.

42. Scalia, "Morality, Pragmatism and the Legal Order," 9 Harvard J. Law & Pub. Policy 123, 126 (1986).

43. 497 U.S. 836, 870 (1990).

44. *New York Magazine* interview by Jennifer Senior, note 17, *supra*.

45. 487 U.S. 1012 (1988).

46. *Id.* at 1020.

47. 497 U.S. 836 (1990).

48. *Id.* at 860.

49. *Id.* at 863.

50. *Id.* at 870.

51. *Texas v. Johnson*, 491 U.S. 397 (1989).

52. *Holmes-Laski Letters: The Correspondence of Mr. Justice Holmes and Harold J. Laski*, 2:1124 (Mark De Wolfe Howe, ed., 1953); see e.g., *Rochin v. Calif*, 342 U.S. 165 (1952).

53. Scalia, "Originalism: The Lesser Evil," 57 Univ. Cin. Law Rev. 849.

54. 503 U.S. 1 (1992).

55. 491 U.S. 110 (1989).

56. 491 U.S. at 123–24.

57. *Id.* at 130 (emphasis in the original).

58. 539 U.S. 558 (2003).

59. *Id.* at 602.

60. *The Merchant of Venice* 1.3.

61. *Arizona v. Hicks*, 480 U.S. 321 (1987).

62. 569 U.S. (2013).

63. Available at http://www.newrepublic.com/article/113375/supreme-court-dna-case-antonin-scalias-dissent-ages.

64. Available at https://www.washingtonpost.com/opinions/eugene-robinson-in-dna-case-scalia-was-right/2013/06/13/1bb1574a-d460-11e2-8cbe-1bcbee06f8f8_story.html.

65. *Hiibel v. Sixth Judicial Dist. Court of Nev., Humboldt Cty*, 542 U.S. 177, 191 (2004).

66. *Maryland v. King, supra*, 569 U.S. (2013). Slip op. at 1 (emphasis his).

67. *Id.* at 3–5. (emphasis Scalia's). Slip op. at 3.

68. *Id.* at 9 (italics Scalia's).

69. *Id.* Slip op. at 18.

70. *Michael H. v. Gerald D., supra*, note.

71. *Lawrence v. Texas, supra*, note.

72. *Webster v. Reproductive Health Services, supra*, note (concurring in part and concurring in judgment); *Planned Parenthood of Southeastern Pa. v. Casey*, 505 U.S. 833, 944 (1992) (concurring in part and dissenting in part).

12

SONIA SOTOMAYOR
The Wise Latina Woman and Identity Politics

I would hope that a wise Latina woman would more often than not
reach a better conclusion than a white male.
—Supreme Court Justice Sonia Sotomayor

When Obama sent the name of Sonia Sotomayor for Senate confirmation, he touted her "empathy" and potential for blazing a new historical
trail as the first Latina justice. She has been widely compared to Thurgood Marshall, the first African American Justice, and Sandra Day
O'Connor, the first female justice, both of whom made history by
breaking racial and gender barriers. She is the only Justice who has
been a judge in the trial court, and probably is the only sitting Justice
who ever tried a serious case.

Professor Lawrence Tribe, who taught law to both Obama and Roberts at Harvard, in his excellent book about the currents and crosscur-
rents of the Roberts Court, *Uncertain Justice*, describes Sotomayor as a
"'judge's judge'—steeped deeply in the logic of law and the context in
which cases arise." She may be more aptly described as a people's
judge. Tribe deems it significant that more than any of the other Justices, Sotomayor is "out there" and "with it," traveling around the country to flog her book, salsa dancing on Univision, appearing on *Sesame
Street* and *The Daily Show*, and even leading the Times Square count-
down to usher in the New Year. Tribe writes, "Sotomayor has bravely
engineered a different kind of public niche for a Justice—one that

embraces the humanity and experiences that guide her hand and allows her to serve as a respected role model to others facing tough challenges in life." She herself has said, as Tribe reports, "[T]he more important [measure of my life's meaning]" is not being a great Justice, but "my values and my impact on people who feel inspired in any way by me,"— a sentiment that her critics call "identity politics." Tribe's statement frames the issue in a nutshell. What is supposed to count more? A reasoned interpretation of the Constitution based on decided cases or the "humanity and experiences that guide her hand," however admirable?

A rigid legal construct, however, trumped Sotomayor's humanity in the case of Francisco Castaneda, a refugee from El Salvador, who died of cancer after he was denied adequate medical treatment while in federal custody. In March 2006, U.S. Immigration and Customs Enforcement (ICE) agents detained Castaneda, a lawful resident of the United States, at the San Diego Correctional Facility on drug charges. Upon his incarceration, he complained to prison authorities that he had an irregular, raised lesion measuring two square centimeters on his penis. Over the course of the next ten months, healthcare professionals advised that he needed a biopsy to ascertain whether the lesion was malignant. Castaneda had a family history of cancer. The government denied the request for a biopsy, reasoning that the procedure was "elective." Instead, he was "treated" with ibuprofen, antibiotics, and a change of underwear, the equivalent of no treatment at all. When a fourth specialist recommended a biopsy in January 2007, the government authorized the procedure but released Castaneda before the biopsy could be accomplished. A week later biopsy results confirmed a diagnosis of squamous cell carcinoma, which had metastasized to his groin. Doctors amputated Castaneda's penis and prescribed chemotherapy. The treatment was to no avail. Castaneda died in January 2008 at age 36.

When the estate sued the U.S. Public Health Services personnel and prison officials for failing to provide him with essential medical diagnosis and treatment, the case reached the Supreme Court. The government had conceded negligence while the case was on appeal. Writing for a unanimous Court, Sotomayor reversed the lower courts and dismissed the complaint against the individuals on grounds of the statutory immunity built into the Federal Tort Claims Act.[1] "Our inquiry in this case begins and ends with the text of [Section] 233(a)," she wrote, referring to the statutory provision granting immunity to the medical personnel involved. Castaneda's family had an "exclusive" remedy against the government under the Federal Tort Claims Act and no remedy against the individuals who accomplished the malpractice. Had Sotomayor become a textualist? We would hope not. She was of course correct on the law, but she apparently left her "humanity and experiences" in the Bronx. The failure to provide adequate medical care to a federal prisoner is an obvious denial of basic human rights and a "cruel and unusual punishment" under the Constitution. It failed to pass the "puke test." Over one hundred detainees have died in ICE custody since October 2003. California federal judge Dean Pregerson had held that the conduct of the healthcare professionals was "beyond cruel and unusual punishment" and "one of the most, if not the most, egregious" violations of constitutional rights that "the court has ever encountered." If liability does not extend to the individuals involved, who grossly neglected Castaneda's condition, how will we ever deter such an "egregious" deprivation of constitutional rights? Perhaps Congress can do something.

Latinos represent roughly 17 percent of the U.S. population, and they are a significant voting bloc. Many vote Republican, particularly in Florida, a key swing state, where Latinos feel that the Democratic Party betrayed them with a softer line on Cuba. Presidents since George H. W. Bush had wanted to appoint a Latino to the Court, but somehow the opportunity slipped away. No wonder that a Democratic president, Barack Obama, the nation's first African American president, sought in 2009 to appoint the first Latino. To nominate a sitting judge who happened to be a woman was undoubtedly a double, if not a home run.

Sotomayor tells her life story up until the time that she became a judge in her riveting and deeply personal memoir, *My Beloved World*, for which she reportedly received more than $3 million. Her background is a tale of the inner cities, as it is a story of the fulfillment of the American dream. She came from a Puerto Rican background, grew up in the housing projects of the South Bronx, worked hard, learned much, and achieved the prize. She says she was blessed with a "native optimism and stubborn perseverance" that overcame the adversity she encountered in her life. She tells us that her name Sonia is derived from the Greek name Sophia, meaning "wise woman."

One can only categorize Sotomayor as a "natural." She was born into what she calls "a tiny microcosm of Hispanic New York City" in 1954, the same year as the decision in *Brown v. Board of Education*,[2] which desegregated the public schools, and *Hernandez v. Texas*,[3] which accorded equal protection to Latinos to the same extent as blacks.

She grew up the daughter of Puerto Rican immigrants in an ethnic neighborhood of movie theaters, bodegas, drug dealers, and prostitutes, filled with the sound of the elevated subway train passing by and the pungent smells of onions and garlic cooked with meat over hot coals on a street corner stove. She describes her neighborhood as a "war zone" where gangs carved up the territory, and a "plague of arson" spread through the neighborhood as landlords of bombed-out buildings sought insurance dollars.

Her childhood had no want of adversity. Not yet 8 years old, she was diagnosed with Type 1 juvenile diabetes after she fainted in church. She learned to give herself daily insulin injections. She lived in crime-ridden surroundings, had an alcoholic father who died when she was 9, and for many years she found her mother, who worked nights as a practical nurse at a nearby hospital, to be "distant." She says she grew up in "material poverty." Her mother had only a high school education; her father was formally uneducated. Her mother's income was never more than five thousand dollars a year.

Although her mother made an effort to speak English at home after her father died, her family life was conducted largely in Spanish, but a Puerto Rican Spanish known as Nuyorcan. When a high school Spanish teacher tried to advance her and other Latinos to Spanish literature on the assumption that they already knew the syntax and conjugations of the language, she and others pushed back. The language spoken at home was anything but high Castilian. Later, in her well-known dissent in the Michigan affirmative action case, she wrote of the sense of isolation felt by a young first-generation American addressed in a foreign language when English was spoken at home.

From these humble and troubled beginnings, Sotomayor says she learned some tough lessons. Adults were unreliable. Existentially, she needed independence to survive. She survived, and more so.

Like Scalia, Thomas, and Roberts, she is a product of the Catholic parochial school system. She attended Blessed Sacrament where she was educated by black-bonneted Sisters of Charity wielding rulers to keep order. Later she attended Cardinal Spellman High School and won a scholarship to Princeton. She suggests that affirmative action affected her admission.

At Princeton, she came to realize during her freshman year that "many of the gaps in my knowledge and understanding were simply limits of class and cultural background, not lack of aptitude and application." She became in her sophomore year a "mover and shaker," a student activist, agitating for the inauguration of a Latin-American studies program and for the appointment of Latino professors and administrators. A complaint filed with the U.S. Department of Health, Education, and Welfare helped get things going. She opened a dialogue with Princeton's president Bill Bowen. The lawsuit led to the hiring of Princeton's first Latino administrator: the assistant dean of student affairs.

She joined Acción Puertorriqueña and the Third World Center, minority student groups; they served as a social and political hub and sought more opportunities for Puerto Rican and minority students. Her group also performed community service work at a nearby mental hospital, interpreting for the patients and advocating with the staff. She found this work to be satisfying, and she "began to think that public service was where I was likely to find the greatest professional satisfaction."

She wrote a 178-page senior thesis titled "La Historia Ciclica de Puerto Rico: The Impact of the Life of Luis Muñoz Marin on the Political and Economic History of Puerto Rico, 1930–1975." Marin was the first elected governor of Puerto Rico. The effort won honorable mention for the Latin American Studies Thesis Prize. She graduated from Princeton *summa cum laude* in history in 1976. She won the Pyne Prize, the highest award given to a graduating senior. She decided to attend law school and become a lawyer. "[T]hrough the law," she writes, "you could change the very structure of society and the way communities functioned."

She attended Yale Law School, where she made the *Yale Law Journal.* She published a law review note on the effect of possible Puerto Rican statehood on the island's mineral and ocean rights. "I had been admitted to the Ivy League through a special door," she wrote in *My Beloved World.* "For years," she wrote, "I lived the day-to-day reality of affirmative action." On a panel with two female judges in the early

1990s, she said, "I am a product of affirmative action. I am the perfect affirmative action baby."[4]

She became the protégée of Yale Law Professor (later Judge) José Cabranes, who recommended her to the legendary district attorney Robert M. Morgenthau, whom she had met at a chance encounter over a cheese table. He was at Yale recruiting students to join his office. In 1980, Morgenthau hired her out of law school to become a Manhattan prosecutor. She was intrigued with the idea of becoming a prosecutor and trying her own cases. She writes that she was confrontational growing up and lacked social graces. That's why she became a litigator. As an assistant district attorney, she quickly moved from misdemeanors to felonies and prosecuted a variety of cases, including shoplifting, prostitution, robberies, and assaults. She helped convict the "Tarzan murderer," whose signature was to swing into a victim's apartment on a rope affixed to the roof. She also worked on cases involving police brutality.

Three years later, Sotomayor was in private practice, first as an individual practitioner in Brooklyn, and later as a partner in Pavia and Harcourt, a New York boutique firm handling international trademark and copyright issues. A good deal of her practice involved going after counterfeiters of Fendi handbags. She also worked with a Puerto Rican civil rights organization and was a member of New York City's campaign finance board.

In a 1986 appearance on ABC's *Good Morning America* that profiled accomplished women ten years after college graduation, she said she had unrealistically expected the practice of law to be an "exciting life," such as people see on TV shows like *Perry Mason* and *Judd for the Defense*. She found, however, that the "vast majority of lawyering is drudgery work, sitting in a library, banging out a brief, [and] talking to clients for endless hours on not necessarily interesting topics." Many other lawyers would say that legal research is illuminating, brief writing is a creative process in the art of advocacy, and advising clients one of the real satisfactions of the profession.

Nevertheless, Sotomayor said that her expectations had been "greater" coming out of college. On the show, she made some perceptive comments about male and female professionals in the workplace, arguing that males have "different styles," and tend to promote themselves more than women, and therefore they get ahead faster. She did not suffer from a self-promotion deficit. Not naïve to politics, she made it her business to know the right people. As she observes in her memoir, "Sometimes, idealistic people are put off [by] the whole business of networking as something tainted by flattery and the pursuit of selfish advantage. But virtue in obscurity is rewarded only in heaven. To succeed in this world, you have to be known to people." She was about to fulfill her expectations meteorically.

George H. W. Bush appointed her a U.S. district judge for the Southern District of New York in 1992. Bill Clinton elevated her to the U.S. Court of Appeals for the Second Circuit six years later in 1998.

Sotomayor, quite commendably, is someone who has not forgotten where she came from. She deems it "wise . . . to count the blessings that have made me who I am, taking care not to lose sight of them, or my best self." Sotomayor undoubtedly learned tough lessons about race, gender, and income inequality along the way. She writes that she had some "darker experiences" growing up, but that her background furnished "sources of deep happiness and these bred . . . an optimism that proved stronger than any adversity." In her memoir, she asks the unanswered question, "How is it that adversity has spurred me on instead of knocking me down?"

She was certainly "spurred on" at her first annual Supreme Court party of Justices and their law clerks, celebrating the end of the 2009–2010 Term. The party took place in a formal room in the marble Supreme Court Building, festooned with formal portraits of past Justices. About 200 were in attendance. Customarily at the party, the clerks present musical skits delicately lampooning the Justices' foibles. Sotomayor signaled one of her clerks to play piped-in *salsa*, did a few steps by herself, swinging her hips, shoulders, and arms, her right arm bedizened with the ornate bracelets she often wears on the bench, to the distinctive Latin beat of trombones punctuated by Bongo drums, and then she danced with a few law clerks. Subsequently, she invited each of the Justices to join her on the dance floor. She started with the Chief Justice, who briefly followed her in a few steps and invited the other Justices to dance as well. They did so most reluctantly. As Scalia left, he joked to people he passed near the doorway, "I knew she'd be trouble."

And in Scalia's world, "trouble "she was.

Sotomayor applied her "with it" experiences as a New York City DA, and a federal trial judge, in a case involving law enforcement in the digital age, and actually came out much the same way as Scalia. In *United States v. Jones*,[5] the Court confronted a tracking device that federal agents, acting without a warrant, attached to the car of a major drug dealer in the District of Columbia. The intrusion, accomplished over a 28-day period, produced 2,000 pages of data that led them to a stash house where they seized $850,000 in cash, 97 kilograms of cocaine, and 1 kilogram of cocaine base. Much of the tracking followed Jones on public streets and in public areas. Nevertheless, the tracking data were sufficient to lead to Jones's conviction and sentence to life imprisonment with no possibility of parole.

The Court was unanimous in reversing Jones's conviction because of a violation of his Fourth Amendment rights. Scalia's approach, while recognizing a right of privacy, of course saw the whole thing through an originalist's eye darkly. This was old eighteenth-century wine in twenty-first-century digital bottles. He saw the warrantless installation of the GPS on Jones's vehicle as a "trespass" on Jones's "effects" (one of the protected items listed in the Fourth Amendment) and not very different from an eighteenth-century constable hiding in a suspect's horse-drawn coach and reporting to headquarters where the coach had been and what he had heard inside. This caused Alito to trash El Niño's analogy with the observation that it must have been some large coach and some thin constable—and probably both.

Six other Justices, rejecting Scalia's trespass analysis, concurred with Alito, and found eighteenth-century tort law to be irrelevant as there was a governmental invasion of an area where Jones had a reasonable expectation of privacy. Alito, keeping his powder dry, felt that an undefined "short-term" invasion might be upheld, but that a "long-term" invasion such as this was unconstitutional. Of course, the Constitution provides no light on when "short-term" surveillance becomes "long-term" surveillance. For Alito, twenty-eight days was too long. The majority left these and other issues for future case-by-case determination.

Sotomayor, unlike Scalia, took the privacy route, but, like Scalia, she refused to distinguish between "short-term" and "long-term" searches. She saw the issue in bright-line terms. More concerned with the obnoxious nature of the intrusion than how it was accomplished or how long it lasted, she wrote a paean to privacy in the digital age, which Professor Tribe calls "her most adventuresome opinion as a member of the Roberts court." It was enough for her that there was a violation of a "subjective expectation of privacy that society recognizes as reasonable." This she found a threat to liberty:

> GPS monitoring generates a precise, comprehensive record of a person's public movements that reflects a wealth of detail about her familial, political, professional, religious, and sexual associations. See, e.g., People v. Weaver, 12 N. Y. 3d 433, 441–442, 909 N. E. 2d 1195, 1199 (2009) ("Disclosed in [GPS] data . . . will be trips the indisputably private nature of which takes little imagination to conjure: trips to the psychiatrist, the plastic surgeon, the abortion clinic, the AIDS treatment center, the strip club, the criminal defense attorney, the by-the-hour motel, the union meeting, the mosque, synagogue or church, the gay bar and on and on"). The Government can store such records and efficiently mine them for information years into the future.

Then she blasted off into an area not necessary to decide the case before her. In a harbinger of how she might come out when the National Security Agency metadata spying program, laid bare by the Snowden revelations, comes before the Court, Sotomayor decided to take on the "third-party doctrine," elaborated in 1976 cases holding that there is no expectation of privacy where data is shared with third parties such as the phone company or a bank.[6] In an excursion from the facts of *Jones*, where there was a trespass, Sotomayor cast doubt that in the digital age where one necessarily reveals information to ATT Mobile, Google, or an Internet service provider, that person has no protected expectation of privacy:

> More fundamentally, it may be necessary to reconsider the premise that an individual has no reasonable expectation of privacy in information voluntarily disclosed to third parties. [citation omitted] This approach is ill suited to the digital age, in which people reveal a great deal of information about themselves to third parties in the course of carrying out mundane tasks. People disclose the phone numbers that they dial or text to their cellular providers; the URLs that they visit and the e-mail addresses with which they correspond to their Internet service providers; and the books, groceries, and medications they purchase to online retailers.

There is a difference, she wrote, between secrecy and privacy. "I for one doubt that people would accept without complaint the warrantless disclosure to the Government of a list of every Web site they had visited in the last week, or month, or year."

The Court decided two cases in June 2014 involving searches of data found on cellphones as an incident to a lawful arrest. Chief Justice Roberts wrote for a unanimous Court. The oral argument of the cases illustrated the "with it" approach of Sotomayor. Warrantless searches in such circumstances have long been upheld on the theory that the officer must necessarily search a suspect for weapons and prevent the destruction of relevant evidence. When the solicitor general argued that the defendant's confederates could "wipe" incriminating data from the cellphone, using a remote transmission, Sotomayor asked, "Why can't you [the government] just put the phone on airplane mode?" Then the phone would be secured while the officer obtained a search warrant.

During the oral argument in the same case, Chief Justice Roberts speculated why anyone other than a drug dealer would own two cellphones. "In a room full of government lawyers, each one of them has two cell phones," she said. "That's why it's important to have people with different life experiences," Sotomayor said. "Especially on a court like the Supreme Court, because we have to correct each other from misimpressions."

The Chief ultimately got it. In writing for a unanimous Court, he struck down the search and made an observation indicating where the Court might go in future surveillance cases:

> Cell phones, which are now such a pervasive and insistent part of daily life that the proverbial visitor from Mars might conclude they were an important feature of human anatomy.

In 1926, Learned Hand observed that it is "a totally different thing to search a man's pockets and use against him what they contain, from ransacking his house for everything which may incriminate him."[7] If his pockets contain a cellphone, however, that is no longer true. The search of a house may ascertain very little of relevance about an individual. The search of his cellphone might inform you about his entire life from contacts to books recently ordered from Amazon. A cellphone search would typically expose to the government far more than the most exhaustive search of a house.

Thanks in part to the savvy Sonia Sotomayor, the Court had its rude awakening in the digital age.

When Texas challenged the legality of Obama's immigration reform order, the Deferred Action for Parents of Americans and Lawful Permanent Residents program, there was no question about where Sotomayor stood on the issue. The program would defer from deportation about four million undocumented immigrants (most of them Latinos), who were parents of citizens or residents of the United States. The case came before the Court on April 18, 2016. At the oral argument, Sotomayor showed an admirable empathy, unparalleled by any other Justice, for the plight of the immigrants. She had the following exchange with Scott Keller, the Texas Solicitor General:

> Mr. Keller: But but, Justice Sotomayor, I think that's backwards. Congress has to grant the statutory authority first for the Executive to be able to act. And to do so, on a question that's of this deep economic significance, it would have to do so expressly.
>
> Justice Sotomayor: You know, you keep saying that, "deep economic significance." Those nearly 11 million unauthorized aliens are here in the shadows. They are affecting the economy whether we want to or not.[8]

She plainly had not forgotten those she knew on the way up struggling "in the shadows" of American society. The "people's judge" was at it again.

Notes

1. *Hui v. Castaneda*, 559 U.S. (2010).

2. 347 U.S. 483 (1954).

3. 347 U.S. 475 (1954).

4. By Bill Mears, "Sotomayor Says She Was 'Perfect Affirmative Action Baby,'" June 11, 2009. Available at http://www.cnn.com/2009/POLITICS/06/11/sotomayor.affirmative.action/index.html.

5. 565 U.S. (2012).

6. *Smith v. Maryland*, 442 U.S. 735 (1979); *United States v. Miller*, 425 U.S. 435 (1976).

7. *United States v. Kirschenblatt*, 16 F. 2d 202, 203 (CA2).

8. Transcript of oral argument of April 18, 2016, *United States v. Texas*, at 46, lines 11-20 available at http://www.supremecourt.gov/oral_arguments/argument_transcripts/15-674_h3dj.pdf

13

HOBBY LOBBY

Religious Freedom v. Reproductive Rights

The ability of women to participate equally in the economic and
social life of the Nation has been facilitated by their ability to control
their reproductive lives.[1]
—Justice O'Connor in re-affirming *Roe v. Wade*

What happens when reproductive rights conflict with religious freedom? If the Supreme Court can't make it illegal for women to avoid
being pregnant, it seems determined to make it as difficult as possible
for them to go freely about their reproductive lives. The Founding
Fathers formed the government, among other things, "to promote the
general welfare." In *Burwell v. Hobby Lobby*,[2] however, the Court's
five conservative Justices don't appear to have gotten the memo.

The owners of Hobby Lobby, a retail arts and crafts operation, ad-
herents of a fundamentalist Christian faith, oppose abortion as they
consider that life begins at the moment of conception.[3] At the heart of
their suit, invoking the Religious Freedom Restoration Act (RFRA),
was that FDA-approved contraceptive coverage available under the
Obamacare mandate included four measures that plaintiffs regarded as
abortifacients: two forms of emergency measures known as "morning
after" pills, and two forms of intrauterine devices (IUDs).[4]

Obamacare provides comprehensive healthcare to an estimated 18.7
million American women who previously had no form of health insurance. In the winter of 2013, when Obamacare kicked into gear, approx-

imately one in five women ages 18–64 were uninsured. For low-income women and minorities, the gaps were even starker, with four in ten uninsured as of the end of 2013. Nearly a quarter of black women and over one-third of Latino women were also uninsured. The law mandates all firms with more than fifty employees (except for not-for-profit religious organizations) to provide healthcare insurance that includes birth-control coverage, or else pay a fine. The government had exempted certain religious not-for-profit corporations, such as churches or associations of churches, from compliance with the mandate. It required, however, for-profit companies, such as Hobby Lobby, to provide contraceptive coverage.

The issue in the case was that Obamacare required Hobby Lobby to provide its female employees (and, presumably, the female family members of employees) with healthcare insurance coverage that included the cost of all forms of contraception approved by the FDA, including the four challenged devices. Hobby Lobby, a closely held for-profit corporation, sought to opt out of Obamacare, a law of general application, on the basis of religious scruple. The Supreme Court, in a 5-4 decision, answered that it could do so. It held that religious freedom trumps reproductive freedom, full stop.

Hobby Lobby is a chain of 575 retail outlets operating nationwide. It has roughly 23,000 employees. Presumably at least half are women, and many more are married to women. It is not known how many employees or employees' spouses, if any, had religious objections to coverage for the cost of contraceptive services. Most, if not all, may have even welcomed the benefit since women of childbearing age spend 68 percent more out-of-pocket on healthcare than men.

Measuring whether there was a justification for burdening free exercise of religion under RFRA, the Court was required to determine whether there was a "compelling governmental interest," the buzzwords used in RFRA in covering women for contraceptive services as part of healthcare, and the majority of the Justices "assumed" that one existed.

It's not just about a casual sexual encounter, resulting in pregnancy, that occasions second thoughts about carrying a child to term. Pregnancy, experts say, can be hazardous or life-threatening for certain women, particularly those with some congenital heart diseases, pulmonary hypertension, and Marfan syndrome. In some cases, pregnancy is associated with cancer, pelvic pain, or menstrual disorder. The two IUDs at issue were stated to be more effective, and also more costly, than other contraceptive methods as to which Hobby Lobby took no exception. As Justice Ginsburg noted in dissent, "[T]he cost of an IUD is nearly equivalent to a month's full time pay for workers earning the minimum wage."

Under the dangerous rationale of the Supreme Court's majority, a company could refuse to cover any form of contraception on religious grounds. On the same basis, it could engage in racial or gender discrimination. It could refuse to hire gays or provide HIV coverage. It could, like a health club company in Nevada, refuse to hire people living out of wedlock. While the Court appeared to carve the tax laws out of its ruling, the rationale would be the same: a fundamentalist Christian could withhold that portion of his federal income taxes that represents subsidies paid by the government under Obamacare for contraceptive services deemed abortifacient.

That human life, indeed formation of a soul (the immortal essence of a living thing), begins at the moment of conception is the accepted teaching of the Roman Catholic Church. Orthodox Jews, the Mennonite Church, and many fundamentalist Christian religions share this view. The Mennonite Church, which has 110,696 members in the United States and 950 congregations, categorically opposes abortion. This would create an issue for them as to the four contraception devices at issue, which may be abortifacients, that is, agents operating to destroy the zygote, a fertilized egg.

When a plaintiff makes a claim that something transgresses a tenet of his or her religion, the law is that the courts will assume that the belief is sincerely held. Furthermore, the courts will not pass on the plausibility of a religious claim. So the Court never went into the question of whether the four devices were in fact abortifacients, or that the plaintiffs were deluded in voicing their objection, any more than a court would go into the plausibility of a belief in the Immaculate Conception. Although there was nothing in the Court's opinion on it, medical experts say that the four devices at issue primarily operate to prevent conception and not to destroy a fertilized egg.

Scalia for one, voting with the majority, appeared eager to buy the abortifacient claim hook, line, and sinker. As he blurted out in oral argument after grilling the government attorney about the cost to the government of providing the services should the plaintiffs be exempted from furnishing the coverage, "You're talking about, what, three or four birth controls, not all of them, just those that are abortifacient." Unfortunately for Scalia, there was nothing in the record to show that the four "birth controls" at issue were in fact abortifacient. They were simply *claimed* to be so by the fundamentalist plaintiffs. And even if they were abortifacient, should the dissident religious beliefs of the Hobby Lobby employers place a burden on their employees' coverage that is distinct from the healthcare programs of employers throughout the country? The English jurist, Lord Ellenbourough, famously and rhetorically wondered in a case involving extraterritorial jurisdiction of a default judgment, "Can the island of Tobago pass a law to bind the rights of the whole world?"[5]

It is strange (or perhaps not so strange) that Scalia came down on the side of the religious dissenters in *Hobby Lobby*. In 1990, he had rejected the claims of fired employees for unemployment compensation when the employees had illegally ingested peyote for sacramental purposes at a ceremony of the Native American Church.[6] The employees claimed that the use of peyote was central to their religion. "What principle of law or logic can be brought to bear to contradict a believer's assertion that a particular act is 'central to his personal faith'?" Scalia wondered rhetorically. He cited with approval an 1879 case for the proposition that neutral laws governing actions and practices, as opposed to religious beliefs and opinions, must trump faith or every religious objector becomes "a law unto himself."[7] Seems like trite law. But as Scalia said in another context involving the free speech rights of anti-abortion protesters and counselors under the First Amendment, where he railed at the majority for allegedly ignoring a settled precedent in giving abortion rights advocates a free pass: "What has changed since then? Quite simple: This is an abortion case, and [the settled precedent] was not."[8] It was apparently the view of Scalia and the four other male Catholics voting with the majority in *Hobby Lobby* that laws of general application trump religious freedom, and religious dissidents cannot be a "law unto themselves"—unless of course "[it] is an abortion case." The peyote case, for example, was obviously not.

Justice Ginsburg and the other dissenters saw the majority decision as one of "startling breadth" that would allow corporations to opt out of almost any law that they find "incompatible with their sincerely held religious beliefs." The decision would "deny legions of women who do not hold their employers' beliefs access to contraceptive coverage." Could a corporation based on the religious beliefs of its owners now discriminate in its hiring practices on the basis of race? Could such a corporation refuse to hire individuals based on religion, sexual orientation, or immoral sexual conduct? Could it avoid environmental laws based on a sincerely held religious tenet? Could they end up being a "law unto themselves"? The majority says their ruling is not so broad as all that. Just abortifacients for the time being.

Ginsburg noted in dissent that Jehovah's Witnesses object to blood transfusions, Scientologists object to antidepressants, and Christian Scientists object to vaccinations. Some Muslims, Hindus, and Jews object to medications "derived from pigs, including anesthesia intravenous fluids and pills coated with gelatin." Remember, no employee of Hobby Lobby was required by the government to engage in contraception. That would be, as Ginsburg put it, "the woman's autonomous choice informed by the physician she consults." It was the religious fundamentalist employers (not the government) who objected to paying the freight for insurance *coverage* that included the cost of objectionable contraceptive services. Employers in the bedroom just as we are getting the government out? "We have to have the baby, Joe," she says to her husband. "It's our duty to the boss." Smacks of Orwell's *1984*.

The five Republican-appointed Justices upheld plaintiffs' claims to an exemption from the contraceptive mandate of Obamacare because the mandate "substantially burden[s]" the exercise of religion. As we have seen, the Court assumed the obvious without deciding that the mandate was "in furtherance of a compelling governmental interest," namely, guaranteeing cost-free access to the four contraceptive methods. But it then held that the "least restrictive" way to achieve the government's goal would be an "accommodation." The government itself could underwrite the cost of providing the four contraceptives to women who want them but can't obtain them because of their employers' religious objections. Alternatively, the government could treat the religious dissenters as it does a church, namely, allow the religious employer to send a piece of paper to the insurer certifying that it opposes funding contraceptive services on religious grounds, and then making the insurer cover these services separately at no additional cost to anybody. As Scalia said at oral argument, "[Abortifacient] that's not terribly expensive stuff, is it?"

Sounds reasonable enough—an accommodation so that Hobby Lobby's employees may receive the same healthcare benefits as those down the street. All that Hobby Lobby need do is fill out a simple form with name, rank, and serial number. Writing for the Court, Alito said, "The effect of the . . . accommodation on the women employed by Hobby Lobby and the other companies involved in these cases would be zero."

Unfortunately, there is more to the story. In an almost unbelievable sleight of hand, the Court, three mornings after the *Hobby Lobby* decision, granted a preliminary injunction in a separate case brought by Wheaton College, a nonprofit evangelical Christian institution of higher learning. Wheaton contended that its religious liberties were burdened by the requirement that it provide contraceptive coverage for its employees and asked the Court for permission to ignore the accommodation for the time being while challenging it in the courts. It was too much of a burden on religion, Wheaton claimed, to send a form to the insurer; all it wished to do is notify the government with a phone call. This sudden turnabout, which many have found baffling, was so out of line with the accommodation the Court had blessed three days earlier that it led Sotomayor to dissent. Writing for herself and her two women colleagues, she launched a broadside indictment of the majority position:

> Those who are bound by our decisions usually believe they can take us at our word. Not so today. After expressly relying on the availability of the religious-nonprofit accommodation to hold that the contraceptive coverage requirement violates RFRA as applied to closely held for-profit corporations, the Court now, as the dissent in *Hobby Lobby* feared it might . . . retreats from that position. That action evinces disregard for even the newest of this Court's precedents and undermines confidence in this institution.

The hostility of the Court's conservative majority to abortion rights could not have been clearer. The conservative Justices were just salivating for a case where they could overrule *Roe v. Wade*. There is also a new wrinkle. Anti-abortion activists have taken to demonstrating in the vicinity of abortion clinics. There, they pray the rosary, hand out leaflets, and even attempt to "counsel" women out of exercising their reproductive rights. In *McCullen v. Coakley*,[9] decided just a few days before *Hobby Lobby*, the Court unanimously struck down a Massachusetts law creating an exceedingly ample thirty-five-foot buffer zone around abortion clinics within which anti-abortion activists could not attempt to express their views.

The Court held the Massachusetts statute unconstitutional since the buffer zone could have been more narrowly drawn. Judging is often about drawing lines. The Court, in a strange departure from normal practice, "suggested" that Massachusetts could consider an ordinance such as that adopted in New York City that not only prohibits obstructing access to a clinic but criminalizes following and harassing "another person within 15 feet of the premises of a reproductive facility."[10]

Justices Alito, Thomas, Kennedy, and Scalia, however, took occasion in separate concurring opinions to note their dissent from favored treatment for abortion rights activists. They thought the whole set-up abridged free speech and was flat out unconstitutional. "Today's opinion carries forward this court's practice of giving abortion rights activists a pass when it comes to suppressing the free-speech rights of their opponents," Scalia thundered. With a pen dipped in the bile of sarcasm, he wrote, "There is an entirely separate, abridged edition of the First Amendment applicable to speech against abortion."[11]

The bottom line. Cases like *Hobby Lobby* and *Coakley* are not about law at all; they are about policy. The Court is trying to draw some practical lines (courts do that) that make sense for everyone. Thirty feet abridges free-speech rights; fifteen feet probably does not. Life begins at conception or three months after conception or six months after conception or whatever. And no one seems to know when a soul is born. Such lines are found nowhere in the Constitution, and the theological issues are beyond the competence of a judge to resolve, but it is for the judicial department to tell us what the law is, and you may draw your own conclusion as to whether it is doing a good job.

Politics and religious revivalism are alive and well in the Supreme Court. The interesting thing is that the terms "abortion," "'Obamacare mandate," "accommodation," "buffer zone," and "contraceptive" were all unknown at the time of the Constitution. And there probably isn't much that the Constitution has to do with any of it. What the Justices have not done is apply settled law to facts, but have spun out policy judgments that satisfy their particular personal leanings. And from all indications, they will continue to do so.

So I ask again, is the Supreme Court a partisan court? My answer: Of course, it is.

Notes

1. *Planned Parenthood of Southeastern Pa. v. Casey*, 505 U.S. 833, 856 (1992).

2. 573 U.S._____(2014).

3. The Court consolidated the Hobby Lobby suit with that of Conestoga Wood Specialties, a closely held for-profit corporation with roughly 950 employees. The owners of Conestoga, members of the Mennonite Church, also opposed mandatory Obamacare coverage for contraceptive services on the same grounds as those asserted by Hobby Lobby. Mennonites believe that "[t]he fetus in its earliest stages . . . shares humanity with those who conceived it." I use "Hobby Lobby" to refer to both plaintiffs.

4. Hobby Lobby claimed that the four demonized devices did not operate to prevent conception but prevented the fertilized egg, the zygote, from attaching to the uterine wall.

5. *Buchanan v. Rucker*, Hilary Term (1808).

6. *Employment Div., Dept. of Human Resources of Ore. v. Smith*, 494 U.S. 872, 887 (1990).

7. *Reynolds* v. *United States*, 98 U.S. 145, 166–67 (1879).

8. *McCullen v. Coakley*, U.S. (2014). Slip op. at 2.

9. *McCullen v. Coakley*, U.S. (2014).

10. N.Y.C. Admin Code §8-803(a)(3) (2014).

11. *Id.* Slip op. at 1.

14

THE OBAMACARE CASES

The Chief Rides to the Rescue

There is no surer way to misread any document than to read it literally. . . . As nearly as we can, we must put ourselves in the place of those who uttered the words, and try to divine how they would have dealt with the unforeseen situation; and, although their words are by far the most decisive evidence of what they would have done, they are by no means final.

—Learned Hand[1]

Somehow, Chief Justice John Roberts concluded he could not invalidate the 900-page Patient Protection and Affordable Care Act, popularly known as Obamacare, even though he thought it was a poor piece of legislation. His position rested on grounds so narrowly crafted that no other Justice joined in all of his opinion. Perhaps he secretly admired the statute's aspiration to affordable health care coverage for roughly 18 million uninsured Americans, however flawed the statutory scheme.[2] Probably, it was his desire to save the Court as an institution from invalidating Obama's signature piece of progressive legislation, the substance of which most of the Justices disagreed with politically, as they did in the case of social legislation in the discredited *Lochner* era. And so the umpire gave Congress a free pass, and Court watchers will argue forever about the momentary lapse that caused the Chief to become so untethered from his conservative moorings and take the one-off stance he did.

The purpose of Obamacare, which became law March 23, 2010,[3] was of course to reform health insurance markets by furnishing, through a series of interrelated provisions, low-cost healthcare coverage to virtually all Americans. What occasioned the need for legislative reform was that the cost of medical insurance had become prohibitive for millions of people. Many of those who could afford insurance were excluded if they were already sick. If sick people were insured, their premiums cost more than those charged to the healthy.

When states tried to force insurers to cover everyone, including those with pre-existing conditions, and to stop insurers from raising premiums of the sick, the result was mixed. The reform measures guaranteed that anyone could buy insurance at a cost unrelated to their state of health, but there was also an unintended consequence. The healthy waited to buy insurance until the hammer dropped. "Why buy insurance now when I am healthy," the 28-year-old, healthy Wall Street Quant might reason, "when I can buy it when I am sick at the same price?" As only sick people purchased insurance, premiums rose. As premiums rose, more and more healthy people dropped out of the pool, preferring to wait until they needed a doctor. This led to an unwanted economic "death spiral" as premiums rose as much as by 78 percent in Washington State, by way of example, with the number of insured falling by 25 percent. The program did not go far enough. Insureds cancelled their policies, and insurers left the market. But, reformers reasoned, if everyone, whether sick or healthy were *required* to buy insurance, the problem of the "death spiral" would go away.[4] And so, bring on Obamacare.

The first legal hurdle Roberts confronted was that the Obamacare mandate was clearly unconstitutional, and he knew it. In passing the bill Congress relied on the Commerce Clause, its power "to regulate Commerce with foreign Nations, and among the several States, and with the Indian Tribes."[5] The statute required almost everyone to buy health insurance or pay a stiff fine to the U.S. Treasury. Was it commerce or commercial foreplay when Congress ordered a citizen not having insurance to buy it or face a fine? The entire legislative scheme was a policy bridge too far.

Was the fine a penalty or a tax? A tax is thought of as a contribution to the revenue levied by the government on workers' income and business profits or added to the cost of some goods, services, and transactions. Congress never thought of the fine as a revenue-producing measure. So Roberts did a head fake, the "payment" was a penalty for certain purposes; a tax to save the statute.

On June 28, 2012, in a weird 5-4 decision, the Court decided *NFIB v. Sebelius*[6] with Roberts casting the decisive vote. The five conservative Justices held that Congress lacked the power under the Commerce Clause to enact the Obamacare mandate, but the Chief switched sides, and joined the four liberal Justices in the tenuous position that the statute was constitutional under the Taxing Power. As we all know, Congress has the power to tax even if it can't make us eat broccoli.

Roberts's opinion was highly questionable. Congress characterized the payment to be exacted upon non-compliance with the individual mandate as a "penalty" not a "tax." Likewise, on the threshold standing issue (whether the petitioner had the right to sue), Roberts had said that the Obamacare mandate with its attendant fine for non-compliance was not a tax, but a penalty. On the merits, however, he changed positions and held that the mandate was not a penalty, but a tax. Tweedledum he called tweedle-dee, and then tweedle-dee, tweedle-dum.

In upholding Obamacare, Roberts demonstrated an uncommon ingenuity in saving the statute. The fine was no longer a fine; it became a "payment to the IRS." There were rumors that Roberts switched his vote at the last minute to deflect criticism of the Court as a partisan institution, with five Republican-appointed Justices voting to invalidate the signature domestic achievement of a Democratic president. The contours of the opinion were so convoluted that White House staffers, reading the opinion quickly, at first thought they had lost the case, only to find that Roberts had snatched victory for Obama from the jaws of defeat.

The Court also addressed another provision of Obamacare. The statute provided that the states must expand their Medicaid coverage in certain ways or lose *all* existing Medicaid funding from the federal government. The administration defended this branch of the legislation under the Spending Clause of the Constitution.[7] Roberts, writing for the Court's majority, correctly saw this scheme as coercive as it "commandeers a state's legislative apparatus for federal purposes." The "federal government may not compel the states to enact or administer a federal regulatory program."[8] So to save the statute, he rewrote the law to withhold only the *additional* funds involved in the Medicaid expansion. But the core of the fragile statute, the universal mandate to buy health insurance, passed constitutional muster.

The legal challenges to Obamacare, fueled largely by conservative think tanks, continued. As Roberts conceded, in writing for the Court in *King v. Burwell*,[9] the statute "contains more than a few examples of inartful drafting." Republican lawyers pored over the statute, and its crazy-quilt provisions, in an effort to find a legal hole in the dike. The most pointed challenge came almost five years after Obamacare enactment as the last salvo by the anti-Obama right wing seeking to embarrass the Democrats just before the 2016 presidential election. The rightists had discovered what Professor Timothy Jost at Washington and Lee University Law School called "the secret bomb in the heart of the statute."[10]

King presented a fascinating issue of statutory construction as to whether Obamacare subsidies would be preserved for eligible providers irrespective of whether they bought on state or federally established exchanges. At stake was an issue that might result in the death knell of Obama's poster-child domestic accomplishment. If the challenge won in Court, studies predicted that healthcare premiums would rise by as much as 47 percent and enrollment would decline by as much as 70 percent—the very economic "death spiral" that Congress intended the statute to prevent. Speaking at a news conference in Germany, Obama seethed with anger that the Court had even taken the case. Oh, ye of little faith! Roberts again would ride to the rescue.

Having invested heavily in the constitutionality of Obamacare, Roberts next had to save the statute from Jost's "secret bomb at the heart of the statute." The statutory mandate was that all buy insurance on state-sponsored markets or "exchanges." If a state failed or refused to establish an exchange, the federal government, as a fallback, was to establish an "Exchange within the State." The law provided that those who could not afford insurance premiums would receive federal subsidies provided that they enrolled in "an Exchange established by the State." Initially, members of the Senate Finance Committee assumed that all states would set up exchanges. Later, they expected only a handful of states to opt out since local politicians could not be seen to deny their constituents millions in health benefits. In the event, as of 2015 only sixteen states and the District of Columbia had established their own exchanges,[11] with the remaining thirty-four states opting out. When

Congress set up federal exchanges in each state as a backstop, they totally failed to address the issue of whether subsidies would be available on the federal exchanges as well.

Roberts, writing for the Court in *King*, limned Obamacare's essential statutory scheme:

> First, [Obamacare] bars insurers from taking a person's health into account when deciding whether to sell health insurance or how much to charge. Second, the Act generally requires each person to maintain insurance coverage or make a payment to the Internal Revenue Service. And third, the Act gives tax credits to certain people to make insurance more affordable.[12]

"Tax credits," or federal subsidies for the poor, were the core of the statute. It was what made healthcare affordable. Six million Americans bought on federal exchanges in the thirty-four states. On the plain meaning of the statute, this would leave millions without subsidy for those who bought on federal exchanges in most states in the Union, cut the heart out of the legislation, and take us back to the very "death spiral" that Obamacare was intended to prevent. The Urban Institute estimated that a decision for petitioners in *King* would leave 8.2 million Americans without healthcare coverage in thirty-four states. This would include 6 million who would no longer have access to federal subsidies, 445,000 enrollees in the Children's Health Insurance Program, and another 300,000 in employer-based plans. Since so many people would be leaving the risk pools, the price of premiums would surge, forcing an additional 1.2 million Obamacare enrollees who didn't qualify for subsidies to drop their health plans.[13]

Obama by IRS regulation[14] (which could be changed by a subsequent administration) tried to save the statute by permitting subsidies for eligible persons buying insurance on federal as well as state-run exchanges. But the issue was, Did the IRS have the authority to do so when the plain meaning of the statute was so clear?

The words "established by the State" in various contexts appear at least seven times in the legislation, twice in Section 36B, the provision authorizing the subsidies. Congress did not repeat these words in lockstep throughout the statute. The measure uses at times the more general word "Exchange" or "Exchange established under [Section 18031],"[15] a contrast suggesting that the phrase "established by the State" was not inadvertent but intentional. In those contexts, the language of the statute is meaningless if federal exchanges count as state exchanges. No matter to the Chief Justice. Owning that the arguments of the challengers were "strong," he nevertheless ruled that federal exchanges are state exchanges only "for purposes of tax credits." He thereupon held that the subsidies are available on the federal exchanges, even though not "established by the State." The subsidies were at the core of the Obamacare program. As Scalia and the dissenters conceded in the original Obamacare case, "without federal subsidies Exchanges would not operate as Congress intended and might not operate at all."[16] This was the lynchpin of the *King* decision. A ruling for petitioners would result in a major policy defeat for Obama, and a catastrophe for the 8.2 million people who would lose their insurance.[17]

Roberts relied heavily on the "context" in which Congress had used the four words at issue. He used the word "context" eight times in his opinion. He effectively quoted Scalia who had said in another case that the "words of a statute must be read in their context with a view to their place in the statutory scheme."[18] "The devil may cite Scripture for his purpose."[19] But context was hardly a way around the plain meaning of the statute. Can context possibly provide a code that translates "established by the State" into "not established by the State"? Liberal Justice Elena Kagan had stressed in an earlier case that the "Court has no roving license, in even ordinary cases of statutory interpretation, to disregard clear language simply on the view that . . . Congress 'must have intended' something broader."[20] Judges are supposed to construe statutes according to their plain meaning, not edit them so they work. Plainly, "established by the state" does not mean "established or not established by the state." As Scalia argued in a *bravura* dissent, "Context always matters. Let us not forget, however, *why* context matters: It is a tool for understanding the terms of the law, not an excuse for rewriting them."[21]

Could the words "established by the State" conceivably mean "not established by the State"? Scalia declared, "[One] would think the answer would be obvious." The issue, he had said, is "not what Congress would have wanted, but what Congress enacted." The issue before the Court was really not technical, but political. Beneath the doctrinal divide on how to deal with contested statutory meaning was the fact that the textualists were all Republican-appointed, and presumably hated

Obamacare as much as the Republicans on Capitol Hill and elsewhere in the country. If striking down the subsidies on federal Exchanges gutted the Democrats' prize statute, it would only give the conservatives joy. Never mind the health benefits that would no longer flow to millions of Americans.

The partisan stakes in Obamacare were high. The program was the "Holy Grail" of the Democrats. Seven presidents from Truman on (Kennedy, Johnson, Nixon, Ford, Carter, and Clinton), both Republican and Democrat, had tried to introduce universal healthcare coverage. Their efforts had all met with failure. This eponymous statute was to be Obama's greatest domestic legislative legacy. Obamacare pleased progressives, and healthcare insurance companies as well; they would make a bundle in premiums on the newly covered insureds. More insureds should theoretically reduce premiums since, with many more healthy people in the pool, claims paid would be reduced. Don't hold your breath. The initial five-year experience with Obamacare was that while providing some benefit as to which there is consensus, for example, in requiring insurers to cover pre-existing conditions, the scheme proved to be just another "overpriced and underperforming governmental program."[22] Even many Democrats express dismay over how it has worked out. Americans saw their healthcare premiums rising dramatically with costs, particularly for hospital services, escalating beyond sustainability.[23]

Who drafted the bedeviling language "established by the State" remains shrouded in mystery. As noted, Roberts said that the statute "contains more than a few examples of inartful drafting." For example, Obamacare creates three separate Section 1563s. Success has many fathers, but failure is an orphan. The lawmakers in a position to know all ran for cover, and the drafters of the bill admit they used "inadvertent language" or "sloppiness in drafting."[24] The four little words, the Democrats claimed, were all a big mistake—a drafting error. But at least seven times defies credulity!

Brandeis famously observed, "The logic of words should yield to the logic of realities." Obamacare had a unique and checkered history. The Democrats in Congress hastily enacted the statute, which did not have even a smattering of Republican support, by a feat of legislative legerdemain. The House bill passed November 7, 2009, by a vote of 220-215 with 39 Democrats opposed. A similar but not identical bill passed the

Senate 60-39 on Christmas Eve 2009. Roberts noted that, "Congress wrote key parts of the Act behind closed doors, rather than through the traditional legislative process." It passed the bill without the requisite thoroughness of consideration, using a procedural ploy, a complicated budgetary procedure known as "reconciliation," which created no reconciliation at all. Reconciliation bypassed normal opportunities for debate and amendment for technical changes, as well as the Senate's sixty-vote filibuster rule. But the law is the law, whether enacted after years of discussion and debate or hastily or inartfully or irregularly.

As fate would have it, Teddy Kennedy died August 25, 2009, and the Massachusetts governor had appointed Paul Kirk, a Democrat, to fill his seat pending a special election set for January 2010. There was at first no rush on the part of the Democrats to reconcile the two bills in conference since they naïvely assumed that a Democrat would prevail in the special election, as no Republican had represented Massachusetts in the Senate in thirty-eight years when Edward Brooke held the office. Then came the stunning upset. Republican Scott Brown campaigned against Obamacare and won the Senate seat by 110,000 votes. This gave the Democrats a Senate majority of only 59 votes, one vote short of the supermajority of 60 desperately needed to conform the Senate bill to the House bill passed two months before.

So what happened? Brown's election left the Democratic leadership between Scylla and Charybdis: try to reconcile the two bills which wasn't going to happen as they lacked the necessary supermajority; or pass one of the two bills that had been voted in either House. In a precipitous move to save the legislation, they elected for the latter. Senator Harry Reid and House Speaker Nancy Pelosi cut a deal in which the House would pass the Christmas Eve Senate bill without changes. They did so by a vote of 219-212 on March 21. Obama signed the technically defective bill into law two days later, March 23, 2010, stating that the measure enshrines "the core principle that everybody should have some basic security when it comes to their health care."

Republicans hated the bill, viewed it as inept or socialistic or worse, and vowed to repeal it. They resented the arrogance of power with which the Democrats had ramrodded the bill through Congress. Obamacare became a political piñata, a touchstone for all that the right found loathsome in the president. John Boehner, the House Republican leader, said, "This is a somber day for the American people. By signing this bill, President Obama is abandoning our founding principle that government governs best when it governs closest to the people." Ironically, the Democratic Congress modeled Obamacare on a similar piece of legislation in Massachusetts accomplished by none other than Republican Mitt Romney. Romney claimed the program was successful. The failure of Congress to reconcile the two versions of the statute produced a legislative nightmare.

Petitioners, funded by the conservative think tank The Competitive Enterprise Institute, argued forcefully that the IRS exceeded its authority under the statute, which says clear as a bell that only persons purchasing on state-established exchanges are eligible for subsidy. Had Congress wanted coverage to apply in states that did not establish exchanges, they reasoned, it only had to say something like "established under the Act" instead of "established by the State." But it didn't do so. Had Congress intended subsidies under Obamacare to be available in fifty states, regardless of who built the exchange, it could not have chosen a poorer way to express its intention.

Kagan, a former law professor, and veteran of the Obama administration, had some fun with Michael Carvin, the lawyer for petitioners, at the March 4, 2015, oral argument in *King*:[25]

> Justice Kagan: Can . . . I offer you a sort of simple daily life kind of example which I think is linguistically equivalent to what the sections here say Justice Breyer was talking about? So I have three clerks, Mr. Carvin. Their names are Will and Elizabeth and Amanda, okay?[26] So my first clerk, I say, Will, I'd like you to write me a memo. And I say, Elizabeth, I want you to edit Will's memo once he's done. And I say, Amanda, listen, if Will is too busy to write the memo, I want you to write such memo. Now, my question is: If Will is too busy to write the memo, and Amanda has to write the memo, should Elizabeth edit the memo?
>
> Mr. Carvin: If you're going to create moneys to Will for writing the memo and Amanda writes the memo . . . then under plain English and common sense, no. . . .
>
> Justice Kagan: Because in my chambers, if Elizabeth did not edit the memo, Elizabeth would not be performing her function. In other words, there's a substitute. . . . I've given instructions: Elizabeth, you . . . edit Will's memo, but of course if Amanda writes the memo, the instructions carry over.

Then Alito got into the act, as though he were a "dueling diva," and deftly demonstrated the tyranny of analogy:

> Justice Alito: Well, Mr. Carvin, if I had those clerks . . . and Amanda wrote the memo, and I received it and said, This is a great memo, who wrote it? Would the answer be it was written by Will, because Amanda stepped into Will's shoes?
> Mr. Carvin: That was my first answer.
> (Laughter)
> Justice Kagan: He's good, Justice Alito.

The parties bringing the case had argued that their "literal interpretation" makes sense as Congress wanted the states to set up their own exchanges and presupposed that it would not have been politically tenable for the states to deny their citizens billions of dollars in tax credits. Congress offered the states a deal out of *The Godfather*—"an offer they couldn't refuse." They contended that Congress never thought about what would happen if some (or most) states opted out. The Obama administration argued the opposite, saying that in the broader purpose of the statute, it was self-evident that Congress intended to require almost every American to purchase healthcare coverage and would not have set up an insurance program that could be so seriously undermined. For example, Section 1312 provides that "[a] qualified individual may enroll in any qualified health plan available to such individual." A "qualified individual" is defined as one who seeks Obamacare enrollment and "resides in the State that established the Exchange." It is absurd, argued the government, that Congress would deny coverage eligibility to those who do not reside in states offering state-run exchanges. The answer, petitioners said, is that Section 1312 does not say that Americans residing in states with federally run exchanges cannot buy healthcare insurance. It just identifies those in the states with state-run exchanges who can.

The IRS regulations would permit coverage even in states that do not establish their own exchanges as it provides Obamacare coverage "regardless of whether the Exchange is established and operated by a State . . . or by [the federal government]."[27] The regs and the law would seem completely at odds. So what does the Court do about it?

The Court had held in *Chevron U.S.A. v. NRDC*[28] that Congress may delegate to an agency regulatory authority, and that the agency's regulations carry the force of law unless the contrary "intent of Congress is clear," in which case "that is the end of the matter . . . for the court as well as the agency must give effect to the unambiguously expressed intent of Congress." If, however, the Court determines that Congress has not addressed the precise question at issue, and the statutory language is ambiguous, the Court does not construe the statute, but accepts the agency's answer, provided it is reasonable.[29]

Scalia, the leader of the conservative wing, interpreted *Chevron* somewhat more narrowly.[30] If Congress, he said, has made its intent clear in the text of a statute, the Court must construe the statute using traditional methods of construction: plain meaning, case law, and policy considerations for, as Marshall put it, "[it] is emphatically the province and duty of the judicial department to say what the law is."[31] If, however, Congress failed to make its purpose clear, and there are two or more reasonable constructions, the court will accept the judgment of the administrative agency—even on a question of law—if the interpretation of the agency is reasonable. For him the rule was whether the "court concludes that the policy furthered by *neither* textually possible interpretation would be clearly 'better' (in the sense of achieving what Congress apparently wished to achieve)."[32] Only if it does will it yield to the agency's choice.

Chevron principles do not fit the *King* case neatly. The statute's natural meaning discloses no ambiguity that would license the IRS to make its own interpretation, much less to rewrite the statute. The statute says what it says. Coverage and subsidies are available only on exchanges "established by the State."

It is possibly for this reason that Roberts skirted a *Chevron* analysis. Although he found, and we wonder whether with a straight face, that the phrase "Exchange established by the State" was "ambiguous," he placed his refusal to defer to the IRS interpretation on another ground, reasoning that the availability of the subsidies on federal exchanges is a matter of deep "economic and political significance"—so much so that had Congress wished to delegate this issue to an agency, it would have done so expressly. Moreover, the Chief reasoned, as a makeweight argument, the IRS has no expertise in healthcare insurance policy. Here, Roberts was skating on thin ice. Under *Chevron*, once the Court has found that a statute is ambiguous, it *must* accept the agency's determination. It does not seek to divine whether Congress would have wanted it to defer to the agency's interpretation. This is perhaps why Roberts was unwilling to stake his all on *Chevron* grounds.

There may have been other reasons as well. *First*, the statutory language was clearly unambiguous even though he found it to be ambiguous. Judges can be ambiguous too, and their observations may be highly questionable. *Second*, it would have opened up the floodgates in future litigation to have held that such a clear provision was ambiguous so that agency interpretation could trump congressional expression. In every case to be filed, litigants would find some ambiguity, however tenuous, so they could get the court to defer to the agency. So he bypassed *Chevron* and ruled it is for the Court, not the agency, to construe Obamacare.

In no other case this past term was the partisan battle line more neatly drawn between the textualists and the "it means what I would like it to mean" factions on the Court. Text be damned. It was plainly unacceptable to Roberts that Obamacare would be gutted, leaving 8.2 million more uninsured and 35 percent higher premiums under a statute that Congress intended would provide affordable healthcare to all Americans.

The battle of words was over. The last word was that of the Chief Justice: "Congress passed the Affordable Care Act to improve health insurance markets, not to destroy them. If at all possible, we must interpret the Act in a way that is consistent with the former and avoids the latter."

Roberts drank the Kool-Aid and joined Kennedy and the partisans of the left willing to do anything to save the statute. Roberts's position on Obamacare has become anathema to the Republicans who appointed him. In the second Republican debate on September 16, 2015, Jeb Bush said that Court appointments are "the most important thing that the next President will do." He implied that as president he would not have appointed Roberts in light of his Obamacare opinions, saying, "Roberts has made some really good decisions, [but] he did not have a proven extensive record that would have made the [*sic*] clarity."[33] Scalia lamented that Obamacare had become "SCOTUScare."[34] He may as well have said that Obamacare had become "Robertscare."

The great jurist Learned Hand, whose words began this chapter, counseled, "[I]t is one of the surest indexes of a mature and developed jurisprudence not to make a fortress out of the dictionary."[35] The jurisprudence of the partisan Supreme Court was certainly "mature and developed" in *King v. Burwell*. It is said that the "British parliament can do anything, excluding changing a man into a woman." The decision in *King* establishes that the Supreme Court can do anything. And as will be seen in the ensuing chapter, the Supreme Court can do anything, *including* changing a man into a woman.

Notes

1. *Giuseppi v. Walling*, 144 F2d 608, 624 (2d Cir. 1944).

2. Obamacare did nothing to contain costs. On April 19, 2016, United Healthcare, the Nation's largest insurer, announced it was exiting from all but a handful of Obamacare markets, citing losses. United's withdrawal signaled higher premiums in many of the affected states. If other large insurers similarly exit, we might be left with the unappetizing prospect of a single payer (the government) and the failure of the program.

3. Obamacare is perhaps a misnomer since drafting of the bill originated not in the White House, but with Congress.

4. The statute exempted from the mandate those required to spend after subsidy more than 8 percent of income on health insurance. 26 U.S.C. §§5000A(e)(1)(B)(ii).

5. Article I, section 8, clause 3.

6. 567 U.S. (2012).

7. The Spending Clause grants Congress the power "to pay the Debts and provide for the . . . general Welfare of the United States." Art. I, §8, cl. 1.

8. *New York v. United States*, 505 U.S. 144, 188 (1992).

9. 576 U.S. (2015). Slip op. at 1.

10. By Timothy Jost, "Courts Won't Void the Affordable Care Act over Semantics," *Washington Post*, July 9, 2014. Available at http://www.washingtonpost.com/opinions/courts-wont-void-the-affordable-care-act-over-semantics/2014/07/09/5910c9d0-060b-11e4-a0dd-f2b22a257353_story.html.

11. The sixteen states are California, Colorado, Connecticut, Hawaii, Idaho, Kentucky, Maryland, Minnesota, New Hampshire, New York, Rhode Island, Vermont, and Washington, plus three states setting up their own exchanges, which use the federal website healthcare.gov: Nevada, New Mexico, and Oregon.

12. As noted, Roberts had previously saved Obamacare from constitutional attack by holding that the "payment to the [IRS]" was a tax not a penalty. The "tax credits" or subsidies would be paid directly by the government to the

insurers to reduce premiums for those with household incomes of 100 percent to 400 percent of the federal poverty line.

13. Available at http://www.urban.org/research/publication/health-care-spending-those-becoming-uninsured-if-supreme-court-finds-plaintiff-king-v-burwell-would-fall-least-35-percent.

14. U.S. Treasury regulation, 26 C.F.R. §1.36B-2(a)(1).

15. 42 U.S.C. §§18031(k), 18033; 26 U.S.C. §6055.

16. *National Federation of Independent Business v. Sebelius*, 567 U.S. ___, ___ (2012) (Scalia, Kennedy, Thomas, and Alito, JJ., dissenting) (slip op., at 60).

17. Of course, if that had happened, it is highly probable that the "opt out" states would have set up their own exchanges.

18. *Utility Air Regulatory Group v. EPA*, 573 U.S. (2014) (slip op. at 15).

19. *The Merchant of Venice* 1.3.

20. *Michigan v. Bay Mills Indian Community*, 572 U.S. (2014).

21. 576 U.S. Slip op. at 3.

22. "The Supreme Court Would Help Democrats by Killing Obamacare," Ed Rogers, *Washington Post*, June 11, 2015, available at http://www.washingtonpost.com/blogs/post-partisan/wp/2015/06/11/the-supreme-court-would-help-democrats-by-killing-obamacare/.

23. S. Brill, *America's Bitter Pill: Money, Politics, Back-Room Deals, and the Fight to Fix Our Broken Health Care System*, New York: Random House (2015).

24. Robert Pear, "Four Words That Imperil Health Care Law Were All a Mistake, Writers Now Say," *New York Times*, May 25, 2015. Available at http://www.nytimes.com/2015/05/26/us/politics/contested-words-in-affordable-care-act-may-have-been-left-by-mistake.html.

25. Available at http://www.supremecourt.gov/oral_arguments/argument_transcripts/14-114_lkhn.pdf.

26. Kagan did not make up the names. She had in fact clerks named Will, Elizabeth, and Amanda: Will Dreher, Harvard (2013); Elizabeth Wilkins, Yale (2013); and Amanda Rice, Harvard (2011).

27. 45 C.F.R. §155.20, by reference to 26 C.F.R. §1.36B-1(a) and (k) and 26 C.F.R. §1.36B-2(a)(1).

28. 467 U.S. 837 (1984).

29. *Id*. at 842–43.

30. Antonin Scalia, "Judicial Deference to Administrative Interpretations of Law," 511 Duke Law J. 511 (1989).

31. *Marbury v. Madison*, 5 U.S. (1 Cranch) 137, 177 (1803).

32. 511 Duke Law J. *supra*, at 515 (italics the author's).

33. George W. Bush appointed Roberts in 2005, and Senator Ted Cruz was one of the fifty-five Republicans, who voted to confirm his nomination.

34. For the uninitiated, SCOTUS is an acronym for the Supreme Court of the United States. What's a branch of government without an acronym?

35. *Cabell v. Markham*, 148 F.2d 737, 739 (2d Cir. 1945).

15

GAY MARRIAGE

"The Times They Are A-Changin'"

Marriage is the triumph of imagination over intelligence.
—Oscar Wilde

June 26, 2015, was a bad day at the office for Antonin Scalia. Five of his colleagues had just voted that there was a constitutional right to gay marriage. He knew it was coming. The considerations of new trends in contemporary society and just plain fairness in the gay marriage debate had played into the sweet spot of his colleague, Justice Anthony Kennedy, who had become the Thurgood Marshall of gay rights. The fifth vote had been there for the asking when the right case eventually came up. Dissenting in *Lawrence v. Texas*,[1] the criminal sodomy case, Scalia expressed alarm that the worst was yet to come.

Worse still for his treasured "originalism." The Court, when confronted with the undeniable fact that the Constitution doesn't even mention "marriage," much less what sexual orientation is required to enjoy its rights and privileges, had taken Scalia's hated "living Constitution" approach. Although it is beyond dispute that the "original understanding" of the Framers in 1787 and 1868 was that marriage is defined as the legal union between a man and a woman, the Court in *Obergefell v. Hodges*[2] chose to find a new right, a right no one ever thought was there, which they said was sewn into, but not expressed, in the Due Process Clause, namely the right to marry someone of the same sex. New unenumerated rights under the "liberty" value required by the

Due Process Clause should protect only those rights that are "deeply rooted in the Nation's history and tradition."[3] Use of substantive due process calls for judicial caution and restraint lest it undermine the credibility of the Court as a dispenser of "equal justice *under law*." In 1986, Kennedy himself had written,

> One can conclude that certain essential, or fundamental, rights should exist in any just society. It does not follow that each of those essential rights is one that we as judges can enforce under the written Constitution. The Due Process Clause is not a guarantee of every right that should inhere in an ideal system.[4]

He certainly changed his mind. In no case, with the possible exceptions of the discredited *Dred Scott* and *Lochner*-era decisions, had the Court gone so far to declare that the Constitution means not what it says but what a political action committee of five Justices would like it to mean. How could it plausibly be argued that the "right" of same-sex partners to marry was "deeply rooted in the Nation's history and tradition"? Any lawyer taking such a position would most certainly be laughed out of court. In 1972, *Baker v. Nelson*[5] raised the issue of the exclusion of same-sex couples from marriage. The Court's unanimous answer was a one-line summary dismissal, noting that the case did not even present a "substantial federal question." But forty-three years later in *Obergefell*, the four liberals, joined by Kennedy, found a new unenumerated right of "decency" in the Constitution that they said guaranteed same-sex marriage throughout the nation.

In Kennedy, the gay community found a "highly susceptible chancellor."[6] Kennedy had a profound personal investment in gay rights. He wrote the majority opinion in *Lawrence v. Texas*, striking down the criminalization of homosexual sodomy, and in *United States v. Windsor*,[7] where he cast the deciding vote striking down the federal Defense of Marriage Act. Besides, it appears that one of his closest friends and professional mentors, Gordon Schaber, who died in 1997, was a closeted gay man. Schaber had been dean of McGeorge School of Law in Sacramento where Kennedy taught part time for twenty-three years. Harvard Professor Lawrence Tribe, an advocate for gay rights, who in 1987 testified for Kennedy at his confirmation hearings, said that Schaber had enlisted Tribe's support, telling him that "Tony Kennedy was entirely comfortable with gay friends." Said Tribe, "He said he never

regarded them as inferior in any way or as people who should be ostracized, and I think that was a good signal of where he stood on these
matters." Kennedy has a gay law clerk, Joshua Matz, who wrote a 2012
law review article with Tribe titled "The Constitutional Inevitability of
Same-Sex Marriage." A former clerk, Paul T. Cappucio, openly gay
when he served Kennedy in the late 1980s, recently married. The *New
York Times* reported, "When Mr. Cappucio and his husband became
fathers in 2013, Kennedy sent his customary baby gift for clerks: an
inscribed pocket Constitution."[8]

Kennedy's opinion in *Obergefell* was based on the "Liberty Clause"
of the Fourteenth Amendment—in short, the notion of substantive due
process—that would grant gays the constitutional right to marry. For
Clarence Thomas, substantive due process is anathema. He thinks that
the meaning of "liberty" in the Fourteenth Amendment is "most likely"
limited to physical liberty, referring to the "power of loco-motion, of
changing situation, or removing one's person to whatsoever place one's
own inclination may direct; without imprisonment or restraint."[9] Thomas believes that even if liberty is something more than freedom from
physical restraint, it means "freedom *from* government action not as a
right *to* particular government entitlement"[10] —like a marriage license.
Rejecting such a narrow conception of "liberty," Kennedy, in the tradition of Brandeis who thought that the "law must protect a man from the
things that rob him of his freedom, whether the opposing force be
physical or of a subtler kind,"[11] found a new right of decency in the
"Liberty Clause" that would protect the right to same-sex marriage.

But the Constitution does not speak of decency, and if someone had
ever asked James Madison or the nineteenth-century drafters of the
Fourteenth Amendment whether they thought gay marriage was decent, well, you know the answer. The legal hurdles might be perceived
as insurmountable. Kennedy's eloquent answer was unvarnished sentiment. He wrote, "The nature of injustice is that we may not always see
it in our own times." To which, dissenting Chief Justice Roberts re-
sponded, "But to blind yourself to history is both prideful and unwise."[12] They're talking policy here, guys, not law.

Kennedy wrote one of the most eloquent and sentimental opinions
to come out of the Supreme Court. On a summer vacation in Stras-
bourg, he had advised the judges of the European Court of Human
Rights against cursory opinions: "If you're interpreting phrases like 'lib-

erty,' you have to do it in a way that commands the allegiance of the people."[13] The coda of his arresting opinion will surely live in the annals of great Supreme Court opinions:

> No union is more profound than marriage, for it embodies the highest ideals of love, fidelity, devotion, sacrifice, and family. In forming a marital union, two people become something greater than once they were. As some of the petitioners in these cases demonstrate, marriage embodies a love that may endure even past death. It would misunderstand these men and women to say they disrespect the idea of marriage. Their plea is that they do respect it, respect it so deeply that they seek to find its fulfillment for themselves. Their hope is not to be condemned to live in loneliness, excluded from one of civilization's oldest institutions. They ask for equal dignity in the eyes of the law. The Constitution grants them that right.

Heterosexual marriage goes back to the dawn of civilization. The book of Genesis tells of Adam and Eve, not Adam and Steve. The Proverbs recite, "Whoso findeth a wife findeth a good thing, and the favor of the Lord."[14] Solomon was not talking about a wife of the same sex. The Good Book condemns homosexuality as "an abomination."[15] As Chief Justice Roberts noted in a portion of his dissent that he might well have pulled from Google or Wikipedia, marriage is a "social institution that has formed the basis of human society for millennia, for the Kalahari Bushmen and the Han Chinese, the Carthaginians and the Aztecs."

The taboos on homosexuality were most likely grounded in community concerns about the propagation of the species. Heterosexual marriage, as originally understood, presented the possibility of children growing up in a supportive and nurturing family. Religion played a heavy role in it as well. Religious thinkers viewed the gay lifestyle as a sin—their sexual practices contrary to what nature intended. While interracial marriage had legal status at common law, Blackstone viewed homosexual sodomy as an "abominable and detestable crime against nature." Until 1973, the American Psychiatric Association considered homosexuality to be a "mental disorder."

Same-sex marriage is at most less than two decades old. It is not only modern, it is, as Alito put it in dissent, "post-modern." The Netherlands was the first country to legalize in 2000. Eighteen other countries soon followed, including Canada, France, Spain, the United Kingdom, and, quite astonishingly, in light of its predominantly Catholic population, the Republic of Ireland. This must have weighed heavily with Kennedy. In his *Lawrence* decision, Kennedy referred to a consensus in "Western civilization" against punishing homosexual sodomy. The first state of the United States, however, to legalize by judicial decision was Massachusetts in 2003—only twelve years ago. Voters and legislators in only 11 states and the District of Columbia, and judicial decisions in 5 other states, had opened marriage to same-sex couples, leaving 34 states that had not yet hopped on the bandwagon. This is hardly the consensus that Kennedy found so compelling in *Lawrence.*

Several factors influenced this convulsive move toward gay marriage. Pre-eminent was the strong desire of gays, once content to enjoy a single and clandestine lifestyle, to marry. Second was the increasing social and legal acceptance of homosexuals with the invalidation of laws that had long criminalized their sexual practices.

The cardinal game changer in societal attitudes toward homosexuals occurred in the 1980s with the scourge of AIDS. As we saw leading writers, artists, musicians and performers, and often friends and family members dying from this horrific disease, good-hearted Americans from all bands of the spectrum contributed millions to find a cure.

In 1993, Tom Hanks won an Academy Award for the film *Philadelphia*, the first big-budget, big-star film to come out of Hollywood tackling the issue of AIDS. The storyline poignantly depicted the agony and death of a sympathetic deeply closeted young lawyer who is outed in his law firm when a telltale AIDS lesion erupts on his forehead. The lawyer in the film is then fired because of his sexuality and his disease. Hanks's stirring Oscar acceptance speech raised the nation's consciousness to relate more strongly to homosexuals as human beings equal in the sight of God, and the eyes of the law.

That same year, Tony Kushner's play *Angels in America*, a gay fantasia depicting themes of AIDS and closeted gays, opened on Broadway to rave reviews. The play won the Pulitzer for drama, as well as the Tony and Drama Desk Awards for the outstanding play of 1993. The cultural shift had begun. TV shows began to feature gay themes and openly gay stars. TV star Ellen DeGeneres came out of the closet in 1997. Following a January 2002 appearance on the sitcom *Will & Grace* in which she played a lesbian mom, Rosie O'Donnell came out as a lesbian, announcing, "I'm a dyke!"

With the liberalization of societal attitudes, prominent celebrities, movie stars, athletes, and even politicians, such as Congressman Barney Frank of Massachusetts, publicly came out of the closet and took their rightful place in mainstream society, public service, commerce, and our artistic and cultural communities. Apple CEO Tim Cook came out in 2014, the first openly gay chief executive of a Fortune 500 company.

Another major breakthrough spurring gay marriage came from medical science. With scientific advances in the 1980s, there became an awareness of new possibilities for procreation never before dreamed of. Couples, who might have been childless in prior generations, could now have children by means of surrogacy, *in vitro* fertilization, artificial insemination, eggs frozen for a later occasion. Anonymous sperm donors could impregnate single women who desired to have children. With advances in artificial insemination, homosexuals could now have children, raise and nurture them together, and form a family unit similar to that achieved in traditional marriage. The prevalent myth that gays were different because they did not propagate and raise children evaporated. Homosexuals wanting children sought stable committed relationships with the same obligations and benefits available to married heterosexual couples.

And as more and more homosexuals elected to live in openly gay relationships, often having children through artificial insemination, many desired to marry as well.

There had been a sea change in public opinion on the issue. Some polls showed that 60 percent of Americans favor gay marriage. Even Dick Cheney, acknowledging that his daughter was gay, came out in favor. As Ruth Bader Ginsburg told the American Constitution Society, the situation changed when gays came out into the open, people "looked around," and awakened to the fact that friends and family members are gay. Spot on! When I was at Princeton University in the early 1960s, I could not have identified a single classmate as being gay. It was only in the 1980s when a number of my classmates died of AIDS that I realized that they had been there all the time, hiding their sexual identity from classmates, friends, and in some cases wives and children. But does this "awakening" justify finding a right to same-sex marriage in the Constitution?

Volumes have been written about the institution of marriage, and how it has evolved over time. Earlier in our history, families arranged marriages, often with great unhappiness. There was once upon a time the legal notion of "coverture," long since abandoned, that a man and woman in marriage became a single entity in the eyes of the law with no regard for the separate legal status of men and women. Then came the notion of romantic love, with sex reserved for the wedding night.

Marriage, however, was not invariably a "happily ever after." In 50 percent or more of American marriages, it was not a promise of "'til death do us part" but the reality of "'til one of us parts," with more and more marriages ending in divorce. Divorce of course bore a certain stigma. When Adlai Stevenson ran for president in 1952, there were whispers about his morals because he was a divorced man. It is said that Nelson Rockefeller's divorce disqualified him from the presidency. But these attitudes changed over time. When Ronald Reagan ran for the nation's highest office twenty-eight years later, there was hardly an objection that he had been previously married to actress Jane Wyman.

Marriage-like relationships replaced marriage for many. The stigma of a cohabiting, unmarried couple largely disappeared, as many heterosexual couples decided to cohabit before marriage formalized their relationships. Often cohabiting couples resolved not to marry at all. Gone was the condemnation that went with "living in sin." Some single women also chose to bear and raise children out of wedlock, and that was OK, at least in some corners of America. According to Alito's research, more than 40 percent of all children in America are born to unmarried women.[16] No longer a stigma, it had become the same kind of accepted fact as the weather.

By the millennium, America had embarked upon a social upheaval, a domestic-relations revolution more dramatic in many respects than the industrial, sexual, and civil rights revolutions combined, with the fallout yet to be determined. The very personal lives of the Justices of the Supreme Court reflect the changing cultural attitudes toward marriage of society at large. Two are divorced; one never married; and one is in an interracial marriage.

Whatever the deteriorated state of opposite-sex marriage, legal discrimination against homosexuals persisted. For immigrants, homosexuality was a ground for deportation. Gays, if identified, were denied employment as teachers or scoutmasters, could not serve in the armed forces, and could not hold sensitive positions in the government for fear of blackmail. Even if in a committed relationship, gays could not inherit as surviving spouses under laws of intestate succession, were barred from hospital visits to a loved one, and were denied spousal benefits. Socially ostracized, they became an underground culture, gathering in gay bars, bathhouses, and summer colonies on Fire Island and on Cape Cod.

In *Bowers v. Hardwick*, a 1986 case, decided the year before Kennedy was nominated to the Supreme Court, the Court, by a bare majority, upheld a Georgia law that criminalized homosexual acts.[17] Four liberal Justices, Blackmun, Brennan, Marshall, and Stevens dissented. Justice Powell, who wrote a separate concurring opinion, later said he thought he had never met a homosexual. Ironically, there was some suggestion that he had a gay law clerk at the time who was deep in the closet. In *Bowers*, the Court detailed the history of our outlawing of homosexual conduct, even if conducted in private between consenting adults:

> Proscriptions against [homosexual] . . . conduct have ancient roots. Sodomy was a criminal offense at common law and was forbidden by the laws of the original 13 States when they ratified the Bill of Rights. In 1868, when the Fourteenth Amendment was ratified, all but 5 of the 37 States in the Union had criminal sodomy laws. In fact, until 1961, all 50 States outlawed sodomy, and today, 24 States and the District of Columbia continue to provide criminal penalties for *sodomy* performed in private and between consenting adults.[18]

The Court overruled *Bowers* some seventeen years later in *Lawrence*, holding that *Bowers* was not correct when it was decided, and that laws criminalizing same-sex intimacy "demea[n] the lives of homosexual persons."[19] Kennedy viewed *Bowers* as a "cautious approach" that only perpetuated continued discrimination and humiliation. For this reason, he rejected the temporizing solution advocated by the dissenters in *Obergefell*.

In the Clinton years (1993–2001), homosexuals were still subjected to many forms of discrimination. Clinton announced a "Don't ask, don't tell" policy for the armed forces. If a soldier or sailor came out, he or she could be dishonorably discharged. Clinton signed the Defense of Marriage Act in 1996. The statute defined marriage for all federal purposes as the "legal union between one man and one woman as husband

and wife." The term "spouse" was to refer to a marital partner of the opposite sex. Conservatives in Congress knew what was coming 'round the mountain, and the purpose and effect of the legislation was to deny a gay spouse benefits under federal law, such as the spousal deduction for federal estate tax purposes, available to a person in an opposite-sex union.

The Court overturned the pertinent portions of the Defense of Marriage Act (DOMA) in *United States v. Windsor*, a 5-4 decision with Kennedy voting with the majority.[20] The Court held that DOMA was unconstitutional to the extent it precluded the federal government from treating gay marriages as valid even if legal where celebrated. The Court said DOMA impermissibly disparaged gays "who wanted to affirm their commitment to one another before their children, family, friends, and community."[21]

In *Obergefell*, Chief Justice Roberts found Kennedy's approach "to be dangerous for the rule of law."[22] Dissenting, the Chief was quick to stress the following:

> Understand well what this dissent is about: It is not about whether, in my judgment, the institution of marriage should be changed to include same-sex couples. It is instead about whether, in our democratic republic, that decision should rest with the people acting through their elected representatives, or with five lawyers who happen to hold commissions authorizing them to resolve legal disputes according to law. The Constitution leaves no doubt about the answer.

And Scalia, like the other dissenters in *Obergefell*, rested his gay marriage opinion on the footing that this is an issue to be left for the states to decide after a healthy debate, which is "democracy at its best." This was exactly what he had warned against in his *Lawrence* dissent in 2003 when he saw it all coming and cried aloud,

> One of the benefits of leaving regulation of this matter to the people rather than to the courts is that the people, unlike judges, need not carry things to their logical conclusion. The people may feel that their disapprobation of homosexual conduct is strong enough to disallow homosexual marriage, but not strong enough to criminalize private homosexual acts—and may legislate accordingly. The Court today pretends that it possesses a similar freedom of action, so that we need not fear judicial imposition of homosexual marriage, as has

recently occurred in Canada. . . . At the end of its opinion—after having laid waste the foundations of our rational-basis jurisprudence—the Court says that the present case "does not involve whether the government must give formal recognition to any relationship that homosexual persons seek to enter." . . . Do not believe it. More illuminating than this bald, unreasoned disclaimer is the progression of thought displayed by an earlier passage in the Court's opinion, which notes the constitutional protections afforded to "personal decisions relating to marriage, procreation, contraception, family relationships, child rearing, and education," and then declares that "[p]ersons in a homosexual relationship may seek autonomy for these purposes, just as heterosexual persons do." . . . Today's opinion dismantles the structure of constitutional law that has permitted a distinction to be made between heterosexual and homosexual unions, insofar as formal recognition in marriage is concerned. If moral disapprobation of homosexual conduct is "no legitimate state interest" for purposes of proscribing that conduct . . . and if, as the Court coos (casting aside all pretense of neutrality), "[w]hen sexuality finds overt expression in intimate conduct with another person, the conduct can be but one element in a personal bond that is more enduring," . . . what justification could there possibly be for denying the benefits of marriage to homosexual couples exercising "[t]he liberty protected by the Constitution"? . . . Surely not the encouragement of procreation, since the sterile and the elderly are allowed to marry. This case "does not involve" the issue of homosexual marriage only if one entertains the belief that principle and logic have nothing to do with the decisions of this Court. Many will hope that, as the Court comfortingly assures us, this is so.[23]

The flaw in the dissenters' argument is a pragmatic one. Once you allow a state to legalize same-sex marriage, what do you do about the couple legally married in that state that moves to another state where same-sex marriage is not recognized? Married or not married? Normally, the common law rule is that a marriage valid where celebrated is valid everywhere. If the common law rule is applied by the no-gay-marriage states, they will have to recognize gay marriage. If the common law rule is repealed by statute or judicial decision in a no-gay-marriage state, and the marriage is not recognized, you have a constitutionally unsustainable situation. As a practical matter, there has to be a uniform national rule, and this is precisely what the Court did.

Scalia came out with guns blazing. The worst fears he had expressed in *Lawrence* were realized. Lecturing to Kennedy as though he were a priest dressing down an acolyte, he raged that Kennedy's opinion, was "as pretentious as its content is egotistic"; it was "lacking even a thin veneer of law"; and its "showy profundities" were "often profoundly incoherent."[24] Unstated was his notorious antipathy toward homosexuals.

In his *Lawrence* dissent he had taken a more jaundiced approach:

> It is clear from this that the Court has taken sides in the culture war, departing from its role of assuring, as neutral observer, that the democratic rules of engagement are observed. Many Americans do not want persons who openly engage in homosexual conduct as partners in their business, as scoutmasters for their children, as teachers in their children's schools, or as boarders in their home. They view this as protecting themselves and their families from a lifestyle that they believe to be immoral and destructive.[25]

While his dissent in *Obergefell* was careful not to express any animus against gays, his earlier homophobic views hadn't changed. He told Charlie Rose in 2012, while "age may bring wisdom," "over the time he has been on the Court," "none of his fundamental views have changed."

Scalia's personal bias against homosexuality also came out of the closet (if it was ever in the closet) on April 28 in the course of an incident during the oral argument of *Obergefell*. As Mary Bonauto, the lawyer arguing against the marriage bans concluded her presentation, a spectator in the back row of the chamber rose and interrupted the proceeding: "If you support gay marriage, you will burn in Hell! It's an abomination," he screamed, as the marshals ejected him from the chamber.

In the hushed silence after the shouts quelled in the hallway, Scalia wisecracked, "It was refreshing, actually." What was so revealing about the incident was not so much the interruption of the proceedings by a crackpot homophobe, and not that Scalia, who said he believed in the Devil and in hell, personally agreed with the protester's view of morality, but that he might allow a biblically inspired vision of morality to guide his judicial view of marriage equality.

And while we are on the Bible, there is the further problem of free exercise of religion. Kennedy paid obeisance to people of faith who might disagree with his opinion. He stressed that they were of course free to teach and advocate the immorality of homosexual relationships. But the Constitution guarantees the free *exercise* of religion, and priests, rabbis, and ministers who do not approve of gay marriage may feel pressured into going along with it because it now has legal status.

The partisan Court had pushed the envelope to achieve its view of equal justice to homosexuals, but no one can seriously argue that the decision was under law. It was based on pure sentiment, surely the most hazardous and ephemeral basis for a judicial opinion.

They had rewritten the Constitution and made gay marriage legal and recognized in every state of the union. As Chief Justice Roberts epitomized in his dissent,

> If you are among the many Americans—of whatever sexual orientation—who favor expanding same-sex marriage, by all means celebrate today's decision. Celebrate the achievement of a desired goal. Celebrate the opportunity for a new expression of commitment to a partner. Celebrate the availability of new benefits. But do not celebrate the Constitution. It had nothing to do with it.[26]

Notes

1. 539 U.S. 558 (2003).
2. 576 U.S. (2015).
3. *Washington v. Glucksberg*, 521 U.S. 701, 720–21 (1997).
4. Kennedy, Anthony (July 24–August 1, 1986). "Unenumerated Rights and the Dictates of Judicial Restraint" (PDF). *Address to the Canadian Institute for Advanced Legal Studies, Stanford University. Palo Alto, California*, at 13. Archived from the original on June 27, 2008. (Also quoted at 443 of Kennedy's 1987 confirmation transcript.)
5. 409 U.S. 810.
6. Gilbert and Sullivan, *Iolanthe*.
7. 570 U.S. (2013).
8. By Sheryl Gay Stolberg, "Justice Kennedy's Tolerance Is Seen in His Sacramento Roots," *New York Times*, June 21, 2015. Available at http://www.nytimes.com/2015/06/22/us/kennedys-gay-rights-rulings-seen-in-his-sacramento-roots.html.
9. *Obergefell*, slip op. at 4 (internal quotation omitted).
10. *Id.* at slip op. at 7 (emphasis is Thomas's).
11. Quoted in the *Boston Journal*, February 3, 1916.

12. *Obergefell*, slip op. at 22.

13. Quoted by Jeffrey Toobin in "Swing Shift—How Anthony Kennedy's Passion for Foreign Law Could Change the Supreme Court," *New Yorker*, September 12, 2005. Available at http://www.newyorker.com/magazine/2005/09/12/swing-shift.

14. *Proverbs* 18:22.

15. "Thou shalt not lie with mankind, as with womankind: it is abomination," Leviticus 18:22.

16. *Obergefell*, dissenting opinion of Alito, J., slip op. at 4, note 2.

17. 478 U.S. 186.

18. Bowers v. Hardwick, *supra*, 478 U.S. at 192.

19. *Id*. at 575.

20. 570 U.S. (2013).

21. *Id*. at slip op. at 14.

22. Obergefell, 576 U.S. Slip op. at 22.

23. *Lawrence v. Texas*, *supra*, 539 U.S. at 604–5 (all citations and references within the quotation have been omitted; emphasis is Scalia's).

24. See a letter to editor of the *New York Times* dated July 3, 2015, by prominent lawyer William D. Zabel, arguing that Scalia was just a "sore loser." Available at http://www.nytimes.com/2015/07/03/opinion/after-a-historic-week-reflections-on-how-the-supreme-court-works.html.

25. *Lawrence v. Texas*, 539 U.S. at 602.

26. Slip op. at 29.

16

CAPITAL PUNISHMENT

Death Is Different

Our argument is essentially that death is different. If you don't accept the view that for constitutional purposes death is different, we
lose this case.
—Attorney Anthony Amsterdam, arguing in *Gregg v. Georgia* that
the death penalty is unconstitutional.

Is it ever constitutional in this day and age for the state to take a life? A
majority on the Supreme Court think so. Four cases before the Court in
the 2014–2015 Term tested the scope and application of the death
penalty, but none outlawed it altogether.

On April 23, 2015, a federal jury sentenced Boston Marathon bomber Dzhokhar Tsarnaev to death by lethal injection. The death penalty is
authorized in the federal system, although the federal government has
not executed anyone in twelve years. With the jury verdict against Tsarnaev, the judge was obligated to impose the ultimate penalty. The court
of appeals will have no discretion in the case; its power is limited to
determining whether the sentence imposed by the trial court is in accordance with law. The case will undoubtedly find its way to the Supreme Court in a matter of several years. Meanwhile, Tsarnaev awaits
execution on death row.

A federal jury convicted Tsarnaev in a savage attack that killed three,
including an eight-year-old child, and maimed and injured hundreds
more. He showed no remorse for the criminal acts, which tragically tore

asunder the lives of so many people. Attorney General Loretta Lynch said that the death penalty for Tsarnaev was "fitting punishment" for a "horrific crime." During her confirmation hearings, Lynch had said that the death penalty was "effective."

Some victims' families, like Bill and Denise Richard, parents of eight-year-old Martin who was murdered, and a daughter, Jane, dismembered in the attack, had publicly urged the government to take the death penalty "off the table." "We believe that now is the time to turn the page, end the anguish, and look toward a better future—for us, for Boston, and for the country," they said. Other victims' families were not so sure.

The possible injustice of the death penalty is starkly illustrated by a miscarriage of justice in Alabama in the 1930s in which nine African American men were convicted of the rape of two white women on a freight train near Scottsboro, Alabama. All of the defendants except thirteen-year-old Roy Wright were sentenced to death after a trial where they lacked the effective assistance of counsel. Blacks were systematically excluded from the jury. The Supreme Court reversed their convictions and ordered a new trial.[1] All defendants were eventually exonerated.

For sixteen years from 1972 to 1988, there was no federal death penalty. Since its re-instatement, eighty-one people, including Tsarnaev, have been sentenced to die in the federal system, but only three of those have been executed. Some were exonerated or had their sentences commuted. The rest, numbering fifty-nine, await their fate while they prosecute their appellate remedies. In 2014, there were thirty-five state executions, with most of them carried out in Texas, Missouri, and Florida. Only a fraction of death sentences have been carried out. In comparison to the thirty-five executions, there are roughly 3,000 defendants on state death row, including 743 in California, which hasn't executed anyone since 2006. As of April 1, 2015, there were 3,002 defendants on death row in the United States, mostly in California, Florida, Texas, and Alabama, 4.1 percent of whom are said to be factually innocent.[2]

Most Western countries, including England, France, and Germany, abolished the death penalty long ago as have nineteen American states and the District of Columbia. Indeed, 137 countries, a full 70 percent of member states of the United Nations, have abandoned death as a punishment. In 2013, the United States was one of only 22 countries to carry out any executions. Latest CBS/Pew polls show that 56 percent of Americans believe that the death penalty is sometimes just and appropriate, but that is the lowest level of support reported in the last forty years.[3]

In 1972, in *Furman v. Georgia*, the Supreme Court by a 5-4 vote came close to abolishing the death penalty as "cruel and unusual punishment" prohibited by the Eighth Amendment.[4] The case did not ban capital punishment altogether, but because the Court ruled it was cruel and unusual when inconsistently applied in the several states, it led to a *de facto* moratorium throughout the United States. The moratorium ended in 1976 when the Court decided *Gregg v. Georgia,* which tried to set uniform standards for administering capital punishment.[5] Now, with Scalia gone, a short-handed Court is at it again. The Constitution itself sets up the tension: the Fifth Amendment expressly authorizes the death penalty since it refers to answering to a "capital crime" and states that the government may deprive persons of life provided there is "due process of law," at the same time that the Eighth Amendment outlaws "cruel and unusual punishments." At the time of the Constitution, moreover, the death penalty was common not only for murder, but also for horse thieving, rape, and other less serious crimes. Thus it is hard to see that the Framers of the Constitution regarded the death penalty as either cruel or unusual.

Explaining his originalist position on the death penalty, Scalia observed that the Constitution, for example, forbids "cruel and unusual punishments." In 1789, punishments included days locked in stocks in a public square, pillorying, and ear notching. A conviction and sentence in Newport in 1771 was thus reported in the *Essex Gazette* (Massachusetts) of April 23:

> William Carlisle was convicted of passing Counterfeit Dollars, and sentenced to stand One Hour in the Pillory on Little-Rest Hill, next Friday, to have both Ears cropped, to be branded on both Cheeks with the Letter R, to pay a fine of One Hundred Dollars and Cost of Prosecution, and to stand committed till Sentence performed.

Hawthorne's scarlet letter A stood for "adultery," but history has failed to enlighten us as to what R stood for. Would such a punishment be deemed unconstitutional today? Scalia's originalist logic would say no since it was neither cruel nor unusual at the time of the Constitution. Stupid, yes. Politically untenable, most certainly. But unconstitutional, no.

Some Justices, however, have stated that the original scope of the prohibition on "cruel and unusual punishments" is not immutable but changing. Chief Justice Warren envisioned a Constitution that reflected "the evolving standards of decency that mark the progress of a maturing society"; in other words, a "living Constitution" that means what the individual judge thinks it ought to mean.[6] We once gave thieves thirty lashes. No more.

Acting under this principle, Justice Blackmun, shortly before his retirement in 1994, in a lonely dissent from the Court's refusal to hear the appeal of Bruce Edwin Callins, a Texas death-row prisoner, reversed himself, saying that after a twenty-year internal struggle with the issue of capital punishment, "the death penalty experiment has failed"; that the Court should abandon the "delusion" that capital punishment is constitutional; and that he would no longer "tinker with the machinery of death."[7] In *Furman*, Blackmun, a Nixon appointee, also lost out when he dissented with a four-Justice conservative minority to uphold the death penalty.

Blackmun's *Callins* dissent triggered a stinging rebuke from Justice Scalia:

> Justice Blackmun begins his statement [opposing capital punishment] by describing with poignancy the death of a convicted murderer by lethal injection. He chooses, as the case in which to make the statement, one of the less brutal of the murders that regularly come before us, the murder of a man ripped by a bullet suddenly and unexpectedly, with no opportunity to prepare himself and his affairs, and left to bleed to death on the floor of a tavern. The death-by-injection, which Justice Blackmun describes, looks pretty desirable next to that. It looks even better next to some of the other cases currently before us, which Justice Blackmun did not select as the vehicle for his announcement that the death penalty is always unconstitutional, for example, the case of the 11-year-old girl raped by four men and then killed by stuffing her panties down her throat. . . . How enviable a quiet death by lethal injection compared with that![8]

Two of the "four men" that Scalia referred to as meriting "a quiet death by lethal injection" were black. They were Henry McCollum, sentenced to death, and his half brother, Leon Brown, sentenced to life imprisonment as an accessory, in the 1983 North Carolina rape/murder of 11-year-old Sabrina Buie. McCullom was 19 at the time of his conviction; Brown was 15. The Supreme Court declined to review their convictions.

North Carolina had not gotten it right. In 2014, McCullom and Brown were exonerated by DNA evidence implicating another man, Roscoe Artis, who lived only a block away from where the victim's body was found. Artis had admitted to committing a similar rape and murder around the same time. North Carolina Governor Pat McCloy pardoned McCullom and Brown in June 2015. McCullom had served thirty years on death row. Both men were mentally challenged. Blackmun said McCullom had the mental age of a nine-year-old. Upon their release, they had served the majority of their lives in prison.

After McCullom's and Brown's exoneration, the blogosphere was atweet with comments trashing Scalia's concurrence in *Callins*, suggesting that he thought someone should be put to death who was later exonerated, as though he should confess error for his earlier views.[9] I read what Scalia said in 1994 as meaning that it was neither cruel nor unusual under the Constitution for a state to impose the death penalty on someone fairly convicted of such a horrific crime as the rape and murder of an eleven-year old girl. Obviously, he would oppose an innocent man being executed by lethal injection.

Since the advent of DNA exoneration, the possibility of "actual innocence" has revolutionized attitudes toward the death penalty. The first use of DNA evidence in a criminal case was in England in 1986.[10] The Court has noticed that "[w]ith the first use of forensic DNA analysis to catch a rapist and murderer in England in 1986 . . . law enforcement, the defense bar, and the courts have acknowledged DNA testing's unparalleled ability both to exonerate the wrongly convicted and to identify the guilty."

The English case also involved a rape/murder where DNA was used to incriminate the defendant. DNA may also be used to exonerate—often years after the sentence of execution is carried out. The specter of actual innocence dogs the death penalty. In July 2002, Jed S. Rakoff, an outstanding federal district judge, in a twenty-nine-page opinion that may prove prescient, held the death penalty unconstitutional. Noting that there had been twelve death-row inmates exonerated by DNA testing in the preceding nine years since 1993, the court stressed that "[w]hat DNA testing has proved, beyond cavil, is the remarkable degree of fallibility in the basic fact-finding processes on which we rely in criminal cases."[11] Where we impose the death penalty, the "fallible fact-finding process" of ours becomes irremediable once the sentence is carried out. In the narcotics/murder case before him, Rakoff threw out the death penalty counts. The appellate court promptly reversed his ruling.[12] Rakoff's imaginative argument was based on a Supreme Court case[13] holding that Leonel Herrera, a Texas death-row inmate who had exhausted his appeals in a murder case, was not entitled to a federal hearing based on the belated claim that he was "actually innocent." Chief Justice Rehnquist, writing for the Court in a 6-3 decision, made clear that Herrera did not appear to be innocent. He left open, however, the hypothetical possibility that "a truly persuasive demonstration of 'actual innocence'" would render an execution unconstitutional. Two of the concurring Justices, O'Connor and Kennedy, stated that they agreed with the fundamental legal principle that "executing the innocent is inconsistent with the Constitution."[14] Counting Kennedy, O'Connor and the three dissenters gave Rakoff the springboard for his argument. Rakoff's decision sparked heated criticism because, of course, it was not the law. A scathing editorial in the *Wall Street Journal* bore the headline "Run for Office, Judge." I wonder whether the *Journal* would say the same thing today.

Scalia believed that the Court since *Furman* artificially imposed, "under cover of the Constitution," limitations that did not exist when the Eighth Amendment was adopted, and that were not even adopted by a majority of states when the Supreme Court imposed them. Thus the Court at times has ruled out the death penalty for garden-variety murders as opposed to those evincing wanton brutality or depravity. It has ruled out the mandatory imposition of capital punishment and held that the ultimate penalty may only come following a jury recommendation after considering all factors, both mitigating and aggravating. It has ruled out death for the intellectually disabled (formerly the retarded) while it searches for a definition as to who is disabled and who is not; has prescribed an age limit at the time of the offense, at the moment seventeen; and has wrestled with what chemicals may be used in a lethal injection so that death might not be lingering or painful or botched altogether.

Scalia argued that there is ample room in our system for "evolving standards of decency." They must be reflected in the acts of the legislatures representing the American people. He argues that the Constitution, unless amended, says what it says. We have judges to tell us what the law is, not to re-make the law.

On no other issue, except perhaps abortion, has the partisan divide in the Court been so bitterly fought as it has on capital punishment. Some Justices influenced by Scalia see the Constitution as "enduring." On the other side are the liberal Justices who believe in a living and "evolving" Constitution. Scalia, often too clever by half, defended the ultimate penalty on the basis that it is consistent with Christian tradition. It is hard to see how he would rationalize under the "Christian tradition" the unjust execution of the icon he idolized, St. Thomas More, who lost his head in the Tower of London in 1535. King Henry VIII was angry with More for not attending the coronation of Anne Boleyn. Boleyn also lost her head the next year for failing to give Henry a son.

Strangely, the very conservative Justices who stress the sanctity of human life when it comes to abortion or assisted suicide see nothing inconsistent in their position on capital punishment. Explaining the apparent contradiction, Scalia distinguished between the morality of the state preventing one human being from taking her own life or the life of another (e.g., assisted suicide or abortion) and the morality of the state taking a life as a form of retribution. In his world, the state, provided (and this is the big provided) it "rules justly," enjoys "a scope of moral action that goes beyond what is permitted to the individual." Really? He surely would carve out Nazi Germany or Stalinist Russia or Henry VIII at the time of Thomas More since they didn't "rule justly." The state, in his view, is the emissary of God, the "powers that be are ordained of God." After all, the Good Book recites, "Vengeance is mine saith the Lord."[15]

Scalia saw capital punishment through a Catholic lens darkly. He concluded that the "more Christian a country is, the less likely it is to regard the death penalty as immoral." He argued that this is not the Old Testament retributive, "an eye for an eye," but a matter of Christian catechism. He contended that since the Christian believes in an afterlife, free will, the ability of men and women to resist temptation, heaven for those that do, and hell, fire, and brimstone for those who give in, Christians are doctrinally inclined not to view the death penalty as immoral.

The relevancy of religion to American law, in Scalia's view, came from, among other things, the Free Exercise of Religion Clause of the Constitution, the reference to God on our currency, in our Pledge of Allegiance, in the cry, "God save the United States and this Honorable Court" at the outset of Supreme Court proceedings, and in the dictum of Justice Douglas that "we are a religious people whose institutions presuppose a Supreme Being."[16]

Scalia rejected the *Evangelium Vitae* of Pope John Paul II, issued in 1995, that the death penalty is wrong. He would also reject the most forceful recent pronouncements of Pope Francis, reiterated in March 2015, inveighing against the death penalty "no matter how serious the crime committed." Pope Francis said capital punishment "contradicts God's plan for man and society" and "does not render justice to the victims, but rather fosters vengeance." According to the pontiff, "the traditional teaching of the church does not exclude recourse to the death penalty, if this is the only possible way of effectively defending human lives against the unjust aggressor," but modern advances in protecting society from dangerous criminals mean that "cases in which the execution of the offender is an absolute necessity are very rare, if not practically nonexistent."[17]

Scalia joined many Catholic thinkers in concluding that the Pope's stance was not the traditional Christian view. He argued that, unlike other Catholic doctrines such as prohibition of birth control and abortion, rejection of capital punishment was not a matter of faith and morals, which as a Catholic he was bound to accept; it was merely an exhortation to the faithful requiring careful consideration. After considering the Pope's encyclical, he decided to reject it.

The Supreme Court has still not gotten its act together on whether the death penalty is unconstitutional. On March 30, 2015, the Court granted review of three Kansas death-penalty cases and heard oral argument in a fourth—a Louisiana case presenting issues of whether a state prisoner who faces the death penalty has an intellectual disability that would preclude capital punishment. In the three Kansas cases, it granted review of the Kansas Supreme Court's decisions overturning the defendants' death sentences on the technical ground that their sentencing juries were not told that the defendant did not have to prove mitigating circumstances beyond a reasonable doubt.

In *Brumfield v. Cain*,[18] the Court heard argument in the case of a Louisiana man, Kevan Brumfield, sentenced to death before the Supreme Court ruling in *Atkins v. Virginia*[19] banning the execution of defendants with intellectual disability. The Court will determine whether the federal courts must defer to a decision of the state courts that rejected his claim of intellectual disability based solely upon the evidence presented at his trial or whether to credit a subsequent federal district court finding after a seven-day evidentiary hearing that Mr. Brumfield is intellectually disabled and may not be executed.

On April 29, 2015, the Court heard oral argument in *Glossip v. Gross*, a case challenging the use of an anesthetic known as Midazolam in lethal injections. Midazolam was used as the first drug in three botched executions in 2014. Prisoners on Oklahoma's death row argued that the drug Midazolam should not be used in executions because it could not reliably anesthetize the prisoner to prevent him from experiencing extreme pain when the second and third drugs in Oklahoma's execution protocol were injected. The Justices questioned both sides intensely, with the more conservative justices generally favoring the state, and the more liberal justices favoring the prisoner. Justice Elena Kagan compared the effects of potassium chloride, the third execution drug, to being burned alive, saying, "Suppose that we said we're going to burn you at the stake, but before we do, we're going to use an anesthetic of completely unknown properties and unknown effects." Conservatives criticized the case as a veiled attack on the death penalty itself. Horrors! On June 29, 2015, the Court in *Glossip*, by a 5-4 decision with the Justices divided along predictably partisan lines, upheld death. Richard Glossip was condemned to die by lethal injection even if the procedure inflicted severe pain. He had been on death row for eighteen years. At least two of the dissenters, liberal Justices Ginsburg and Breyer, questioned the constitutionality of the death penalty in any form. They lost, but the debate is unlikely to end there.

The lead defendant in *Glossip* had been one Charles F. Warner who was dead by the time the Court had a chance to grant review. Warner had been executed eight days before. The Court changed the style of the Warner case from *Warner v. Gross*, No. 14-7955 to *Glossip v.*

Gross, No. 14-7955 shortly after Mr. Warner was put to death. It is a glitch in Supreme Court procedures that it takes only four votes to grant review of a case, but five votes to stay an execution. Occasionally a Justice who did not vote to grant review casts a "courtesy fifth" vote in favor of a stay so as not to render the entire exercise academic. This is, however, a matter of convention, not statute or rule of court. Since August 2014, at least four prisoners have been executed over the objections of four Justices. Though Roberts at his confirmation hearing told the Senate that the "courtesy vote" practice "makes great sense," the Court continues to permit the executions of prisoners whose petitions have been granted *before* it has had a chance to review the case.

After the Supreme Court ruled that the lethal drug Oklahoma intended to use was not cruel or unusual punishment, Glossip did not fare so well in the courts. He had been convicted of murder in two separate trials of hiring one Justin Sneed to kill their boss. The murder occurred in January 1997. Glossip was not present. Sneed turned state's evidence in return for a promise of life imprisonment, and he was the sole witness against Glossip. Glossip made a claim of actual innocence, which was denied without a hearing in the Oklahoma courts. The Supreme Court thereafter denied a stay of execution. Then Oklahoma governor Mary Fallin granted a stay of execution because the department of corrections had received the wrong drug, potassium acetate instead of potassium chloride. You really can't make this up. The State of Oklahoma reset execution for November 6, 2015.

Where do I come out on the death penalty? Like Judge Rakoff, I am disturbed by the number of DNA exonerations, many coming after the ultimate penalty has been carried out, and the potential of actual innocence in a case even when there is no DNA evidence. And though I agree with Scalia that the evolving conscience of the American people generally should be expressed through their chosen representatives, and not the courts, the horrific prospect of executing the actually innocent implicates the Constitution, which only the courts may expound.

In addition, I am against the ultimate penalty because our society has moved on from the time it was generally accepted. I would argue, however, that in cases of terrorism or mass murder, where the evidence is overwhelming, the calculus is different just as death is different.[20]

As Hannah Arendt said in 1963, the year after Eichmann's execution, tion,

> Just as you [Eichmann] supported and carried out a policy of not wanting to share the earth with the Jewish people and the people of a number of other nations—as though you and your superiors had any right to determine who should and who should not inhabit the world—we find that no one, that is, no member of the human race, can be expected to want to share the earth with you. This is the reason, and the only reason, you must hang.

Arendt's moral logic, which applies equally, in my view, to terrorists of all persuasions, teaches that in cases of mass murder, such as Tsarnaev, the death penalty is not misplaced.

Meanwhile, the doctrinal debate rages on, and the Court is unlikely to strike down the death penalty any time soon. The votes, quite predictably, fall along partisan lines. The conservatives find support for the death penalty in the text and original understanding of the Constitution. The four current liberals believe in a "living" Constitution, which evolves with the standards of the community. The swing voter, Kennedy, appears to support the death penalty so long as there is "decency."

Although Kennedy is still prepared to uphold the death penalty, his preoccupation with a constitutional right of "decency" extends to solitary confinement. *Davis v. Ayala*[21] was a June 2015 case originating in California where it was claimed that state prosecutors impermissibly used racial criteria in excluding blacks and Latinos from the jury and then defended what they did at a hearing at which defense counsel was not present. The Court, in a 5-4 decision, predictably voted along partisan lines to deny the habeas corpus petition. A jury had convicted Ayala in 1989 of his involvement in a robbery resulting in the murder of three people. The court sentenced Ayala to death. He spent most of the next twenty-five years on death row in "administrative segregation," a euphemism for solitary confinement.

Concurring in the result, and noting that his views had "no direct bearing on the legal questions presented in this case," Kennedy went out of his way to question whether solitary confinement was a cruel and unusual punishment under the Eighth Amendment. He noted that Ayala resided in a windowless cell in a room "no larger than a parking spot." During the one-hour each day Ayala was permitted to leave his cell, he had little or no conversation or interaction with anyone. Kennedy estimated that there were 25,000 prison inmates in solitary in the United States. A disciple of using foreign sources as precedent, Kennedy cited eighteenth- and nineteenth-century English prison reformers, including Charles Dickens, who had told of prisoners going mad in solitary. He also referred to the June 2015 suicide of Kalief Browder, whom authorities had held in solitary on Rikers Island for three years without a trial.[22] The charge against Browder was stealing a backpack.

Kennedy's gratuitous reflections on solitary confinement brought only silence from the other Justices. Except one. In a sarcastic, one might say even callous, retort aimed at Kennedy, Clarence Thomas fired back that the "accommodations in which Ayala is housed are a far sight more spacious than those in which his victims . . . now rest. And, given that his victims were all 31 years of age or under, Ayala will soon have had as much or more time to enjoy those accommodations as his victims had time to enjoy this Earth."[23] Quoting Dostoyevsky, Kennedy had observed, "'The degree of civilization in a society can be judged by entering its prisons.' There is truth to this in our own time."[24] The observation must have somehow provoked Thomas's sense of outrage. Solitary confinement aside, public support for capital punishment is eroding. Yet pollsters tell us that most Americans favor the ultimate penalty.

Tony Amsterdam was right. Death is different.

Notes

1. *Powell v. Alabama*, 287 U.S. 745 (1932).

2. The *Guardian* reported the figure in a study by a team of legal experts purportedly using the latest statistical techniques. Available at http://www.theguardian.com/world/2014/apr/28/death-penalty-study-4-percent-defendants-innocent.

3. http://deathpenaltyinfo.org/national-polls-and-studies-Pew; CBS.

4. *Furman v. Georgia*, 408 U.S. 238 (1972).

5. 428 U.S. 153 (1976).

6. *Trop v. Dulles*, 356 U.S. 86, 101 (1958). Op. of Warren, Ch. J.

7. Dissenting from denial of writ of certiorari in *Callins v. Collins*, 510 U.S. 1141 (1994).

8. *Callins v. Collins*, n. 246, *supra*.

9. See e.g., http://www.newsweek.com/scalias-defense-death-penalty-tatters-342329; http://blogs.findlaw.com/supreme_court/2014/09/dna-sets-man-free-after-scalia-mocked-his-death-penalty-appeal.html.

10. *Maryland v. King*, 569 U.S. (2013). Slip op. at 3 (internal quotation marks omitted).

11. *United States v. Quinones*, 205 F. Supp. 2d 256, 264 (SDNY 2002).

12. *Id.*, 313 F. 3d 49 (2d Cir. 2002), cert. denied U.S. (2003). ("[I]f the well-settled law on this issue is to change, that is a change that only the Supreme Court is authorized to make.")

13. *Herrera v. Collins*, 506 U.S. 310 (1993).

14. *Id.* at 419.

15. *Romans* 12:19.

16. *Zorach v. Clauson*, 343 U.S. 306 (1952).

17. See report of the Pope's position on the death penalty dated March 15, 2015. Available at http://www.cruxnow.com/life/2015/03/25/pope-francis-takes-a-dim-view-of-the-death-penalty-but-not-all-catholics-are-convinced/.

18. No. 13-1433, cert. granted December 5, 2014.

19. 536 U.S. 304 (2002).

20. Neither Timothy McVeigh (the Oklahoma City bomber); Tsarnaev; the Nazi war criminals at Nuremberg; nor Adolph Eichmann ever disputed their responsibility for the mass murders of which they were accused.

21. *Davis v. Ayala*, 576 U.S. (2015).

22. By Michael Schwirtz and Michael Winerip, "Kalief Browder, Held at Rikers Island for 3 Years without Trial, Commits Suicide." *New York Times*, June 8, 2015. Available at http://www.nytimes.com/2015/06/09/nyregion/kalief-browder-held-at-rikers-island-for-3-years-without-trial-commits-suicide.html.

23. *Id.* slip op. at 1.

24. *Id.* slip op. at 4.

CONCLUSION

Just who do we think we are?—Chief Justice John Roberts dissenting
in the gay marriage case

Just what are we to take away from this glimpse of a supremely partisan
court? I hope we have made the case that there is more to judging than
a detached analysis of facts, text, precedent, and historical setting. John
Marshall said we are a government of laws, not of men. But it is men
and women, bringing to their daunting task the policy preferences of a
lifetime, who must tell us what the law is. From the dawn of the republic, we have been committed to the rule of law. The backbone of the
rule of law, for better or for worse, is the Supreme Court of the United
States. For it is its Justices who are the keepers of our sacred right to
justice.

The Supreme Court is a powerful court.

It has entered upon the field of faith and morals, influencing our
most intimate decisions, telling us when life begins, determining whether there is a constitutional right to assisted suicide, elaborating the
freedom of religion, and redefining an understanding of marriage,
which existed through the millennia. It has gone so far as to choose our
president and curb his awesome powers.

It has dabbled in foreign affairs, invalidated acts of Congress and of
the president, influenced race relations, drawn porous boundaries between church and state, set the rules for our elections, and imposed the
ultimate penalty of death, even regulating the machinery by which
death is carried out.

The Supreme Court is a political court.

It has to be more than a coincidence that the five Republican-appointed Justices were in the 5-4 majority in *Bush v. Gore*, disregarding Madison's admonition that allowing the judiciary to choose the presidential electors "was out of the question."[1] At the time, 554 law professors at 120 American law schools signed a letter reading, in part: "By stopping the vote count in Florida, the U.S. Supreme Court used its power to act as political partisans, not judges of a Court of law."[2] Sandra Day O'Connor, who was one of the Republican five, later said she regretted her vote.

It also has to be more than a coincidence that a decade later, five Republican-appointed Justices were in the 5-4 majority in *Citizens United v. Federal Election Commission*[3] where the Court struck down congressional limitations on campaign finance and opened the floodgates to unlimited corporate election spending. Ruth Bader Ginsburg deplored *Citizens United* as the "most disappointing" decision in her twenty-two-year tenure "because of what has happened to elections in the United States, and the huge amount of money it takes to run for office."[4]

Citizens United was the most politically partisan Court decision since *Bush v. Gore*. The ruling unleashed unlimited corporate and individual spending on behalf of political candidates, without disclosure in many cases of who the big money funders were. Clarence Thomas thinks that any disclosure requirement is unconstitutional since free speech presupposes a right to anonymity. Just as *Bush v. Gore* benefited the Republican candidate George W. Bush, *Citizens United* benefited Republican candidates in the 2012 and 2016 elections, with the lion's share of extravagant contributions to conservative Super PACS coming from such fat-cat donors as the Koch brothers and Sheldon Adelson. The ruling also benefited Democratic candidates to a lesser order of magnitude, with large contributions to liberal Super PACS from well-heeled luminaries like George Soros and James Simons. As a result of the decision, Republican apparatchik Karl Rove organized Super PACs that spent over $300 million in support of Republicans during the 2012 election cycle.

Thereafter, in *Shelby County v. Holder*, the Court, 5-4, once again with the Republican-appointed Justices in the majority, declared the end of history, and eviscerated the Voting Rights Act of 1965. Color-blind universal suffrage aside, the act insured that "bad actor" states would persist in barring black voters whom they knew were all but certain to vote for Democratic, not Republican, candidates.

If you are a Republican, you may agree with the political outcomes in *Bush v. Gore*, *Citizens United*, and *Shelby County*; if you are a Democrat, the opposite. But either way, undeniable is that these decisions smack of raw partisanship. And such decisions, if they continue, will only breed disrespect for the Court as an institution and for the rule of law as the normative standard of the commonweal.

At times the law in its Doric simplicity dictates a result at variance with what is in a Justice's heart. This probably happened to Sotomayor in the Castaneda case, where she denied recovery to an abused Latino prisoner, and to Scalia in the DNA-cheek-swab[5] and GPS-installed-in-the-vehicle[6] cases, where he sided with the rights of criminal defendants in deference to the Fourth Amendment, and in the flag burning case,[7] where he sided with the free speech rights of a hated war protester in deference to the First. At times a Justice's political savvy drives him to a result at variance with what he knows the law to be. This happened to Roberts in the Obamacare cases where, I argue, he concluded that the Court's institutional interests restrained him from making a *Lochner*-like legislative decision, which would repeal a major program of the Obama administration, which he didn't really like. At times a Justice's heart drives him to a position where there is little in the law to support him. This happened to Kennedy in the gay marriage case. Certainly, an able Justice finds a way to "discover" law or some handy language in a decided opinion to support his or her policy choices. And with 226 years of jurisprudence, there is a lot of law out there to discover on all sides of any question.

A key consideration, applicable to attempts to overrule *Roe v. Wade*, is the doctrine of *stare decisis*, requiring judges to stand by their decisions. There is more to applying the precedents of decided cases than meets the eye. It is not just a question of cribbing from a prior ruling a nice turn of phrase here or a sentence there that seems to have a surface application to a proposition at issue. Justices need to consider carefully the facts and rationale of a prior decision, as Kagan said at Princeton; "think hard" about whether they are applicable or distinguishable; and in a Constitutional case "think hard" about how the clause at issue was understood and interpreted by jurists or Founding

Fathers long gone from the scene. Justices have thought hard about recent precedents, and all too often, in my view, found a facile way to ignore or overrule them. We seem to have gone back to 1937 when Franklin Roosevelt told the nation in his ninth Fireside Chat that "the sound rule of giving statutes the benefit of all reasonable doubt has been cast aside. The court has been acting not as a judicial body, but as a policy-making body."[8]

Our judges are highly skilled in constitutional law, but their differences cannot be fully explained by doctrine. Like politicians, they tend to vote in predictable blocs for the liberal or conservative policy outcomes they hold dear. And their approaches are anything but consistent. Conservative Justices would strictly limit Congress to its enumerated constitutional powers, and strictly construe statutes in accordance with the plain meaning of their text. In the first Obamacare case, they did not believe that Congress had the constitutional power under the Commerce Clause to order us to buy health insurance any more than it has the power to order us to eat broccoli. The measure only passed constitutional muster because because, as I argue, the Chief Justice did not want to play Hamlet to the ghost of Justice Peckham in *Lochner v. New York*, and legislate from the bench. The conservative Justices in *Lochner* did not like social legislation or economic regulation coming out of the states or from Franklin Roosevelt's New Deal. New York's shorter working hours for bakers, it was claimed, interfered with freedom to contract and denied the employers "substantive due process." So they struck down the New York statute.

But two of the same conservative Justices upheld the poorly drafted statute in the second Obamacare case even though the text of the statute required the opposite result. Conservatives have not hesitated to strike down statutes of Congress they didn't like, such as portions of the McCain-Feingold campaign finance law in *Citizens United*. Liberal Justices stressed deference to the expertise of Congress when it came to the Voting Rights Act of 1965, but were happy to strike down congressional enactments when it came to re-defining marriage or what may appear on the passport of an American citizen born in Jerusalem. Conservatives would defer to a Republican president on issues such as questionable detention or interrogation of terrorist suspects in the interests of national security, but reel in a Democratic president when it comes to insulating from immediate deportation roughly four million undocumented immigrants who are the parents of citizens or of lawful permanent residents.

Just as we in a democracy have learned to accept the at times disappointing will of the majority, which we may hope to overturn at the first opportunity, the American people have largely accepted the decisions of the Supreme Court as the final arbiter of the Constitution even when they strongly disagree with the outcome, when the Court's rationale is inconsistent, when the decision is clearly partisan, or when there is little hope of overturning those decisions in their lifetime.

The Supreme Court, unlike the political branches of government, cannot declare war; raise, spend, borrow, or print money; conduct foreign relations; or command the army. It cannot even implement its own decisions. This is left to the executive branch. So what is the source of its awesome power? Does it come simply from the fact that we tend to obey people in office? As Frankfurter said, "The Court's authority possessed neither of the purse nor the sword ultimately rests on sustained public confidence in its moral sanction."[9]

Nevertheless, the Court loses that "sustained public confidence" when its decisions are partisan, based not on the text of the Constitution and a fair interpretation of how the precedents have construed its meaning, but on the ideological beliefs of the Justices. Gallup polls say that as of June 2015, only 32 percent of Americans (up from 30 percent last year), have either a "great deal" or "quite a lot" of confidence in the Court—save for the 2014 figures, the lowest ebb in over four decades. This is much lower than the high approval ratings of the "lame duck" President Obama, but unsurprisingly far better than that of newspapers at 24 percent, TV news at 21 percent, or our dysfunctional Congress, which has hovered around 8 percent.

Retired Justice David Souter stated in a 2010 commencement address at Harvard that he found merit in the "criticism that the Court is making up the law, that the Court is announcing constitutional rules that cannot be found in the Constitution."[10] Judge Richard Posner calls these political bases for decision "priors" (opinions formed prior to reading the briefs and hearing oral argument).[11] Other commentators agree. Justin Driver, a distinguished law professor at the University of Chicago who served as a law clerk to both Justices O'Connor and Breyer, has written, "An undesirable consequence of the Court's partisan divide is that it becomes increasingly difficult to contend with a straight face that constitutional law is not simply politics by other means."[12]

Political views have often hold sway in the Supreme Court, and this has not always been totally good or terribly bad. John Marshall took Hamilton's Federalist line on judicial review in writing *Marbury v. Madison*. Roger Taney, born into a slaveholder family, decided *Dred Scott* as in accordance with his inhumane political opinions about slavery. Brandeis, the advocate for the underdog, who hated "the curse of bigness," consistently looked after the little guy, whom Franklin Roosevelt would later call "the forgotten man at the bottom of the economic pyramid." Frank Murphy, with his rebellious Irish-Catholic background, dissented in the Japanese internment case. Kennedy, who developed profound insights into people from a lifelong friendship with a gay law professor, supported gay rights each time the issue was presented, and eloquently led the Court to recognize same-sex marriage as a constitutional right. Sotomayor, the "people's judge" and the very personification of "identity politics," who climbed the ladder of success to scale the ivied walls of Princeton and Yale, fought to preserve the last vestiges of affirmative action, the program that had given her a helping hand. As a divorced single woman, she had a "with it" awareness of smartphone privacy in the digital age unappreciated by the other Justices. And there is the "libertarian" Clarence Thomas who, based on his life experience, finds affirmative action "demeaning" to African Americans and holds unconstitutional all race-conscious decisions, however benignly intended, even including voting rights in "bad actor" states.

Whether the Supreme Court is a partisan court, a political court, or a court of law, it is the enduring bulwark of liberty in our system. Political humorist Finley Peter Dunne quipped, "No matter whether the Constitution follows the flag . . . the Supreme Court follows the election returns." Madison and Hamilton, the principal authors of the Constitution, saw grave potential dangers in democracy. If a demagogue is elected president by a populist majority, and seeks mass deportation of American citizens because their parents or grandparents are here illegally,[13] or advocates the exclusion of immigrants because of their religion or "punishment" for a woman or her doctor over an abortion, or wants to exclude immigrants or profile citizens because of their religion, we have to count on the Supreme Court, independently of the election returns, and based on law, not on popular sentiment, to restrain him, emphatically declaring what the law is, and that he has exceeded its bounds.

In the October 2015 Term, the Court, now without Scalia's fine Italian hand, may dispose of cases involving such hot-button issues as reproductive rights, apportionment of political districts, religious freedoms, affirmative action, fair-share fees payable to public-employee unions, criminal procedure, business issues, Obama administration efforts to cut power-plant carbon emissions, Obama's controversial immigration order, and certainly more death penalty cases. In such cases, the "usual suspects" will probably line up in accordance with their past predilections.

So what is the answer to the Chief Justice's rhetorical question, "Just who do we think we are?" Where do nine unelected and unrepresentative lawyers come off making these profound decisions based on ideology and not on law? And why do these awesome decisions continue to command, although often begrudgingly, the confidence of the American people?

Harvard's Cass Sunstein says that Robert H. Jackson was the best writer ever on the Court. Jackson was a great Justice, and he took a leave of absence from the Court to become the Nuremberg prosecutor after World War II. He dissented in *Korematsu*, where he wrote a brilliant opinion, warning that the Court, in backing the order of the military to intern Japanese Americans in wartime, was expanding a principle "to the limit of its logic" by making a racist order a "doctrine of the Constitution."[14] He was the very model of a supremely nonpartisan Justice.

"Just who do we think we are?" Jackson knew. With a bit of characteristic humility, he put it all in a nutshell when he stated, "[W]e are not final because we are infallible, but we are infallible only because we are final."[15]

Notes

1. Madison, July 25, 1787 (reprinted in 5 Elliot's Debates on the Federal Constitution 363 [2d ed. 1876]). Cited in dissenting opinion of Breyer, J. in *Bush v. Gore*, 531 U.S. 98 (2000).

2. New York Times, full-page ad, January 13, 2001.

3. *Citizens United v. Federal Election Commission*, 558 U.S. 310 (2010).

4. Remarks at an evening sponsored by Duke University Law School, July 29, 2015. New York Times, "FirstDraft. Jul30." Available at http://www. nytimes.com/politics/first-draft/2015/07/30/today-in-politics-polls-keep-bolstering-a-trump-seemingly-impervious-to-scrubbing/-post-mb-4.

5. *Maryland v. King,* 569 U.S. (2013).

6. *United States v. Jones*, 565 U.S. (2013).

7. *Texas v. Johnson*, 491 U.S. 397 (1989).

8. Franklin D. Roosevelt, Ninth Fireside Chat (March 9, 1937). (emphasis mine).

9. Dissenting opinion in *Baker v. Carr*, 369 U.S. 186, 267 (1962).

10. Commencement address delivered at Harvard, May 27, 2010.

11. By Richard A. Posner, "The Supreme Court Is a Political Court: The Republicans' Actions Are Proof," Washington Post, March 9, 2016. Available at https://www.washingtonpost.com/opinions/the-supreme-court-is-a-political-court-republicans-actions-are-proof/2016/03/09/4c851860-e142-11e5-8d98-4b3d9215ade1_story.html?hpid=hp_no-name_opinion-card-a%3Ahomepage%2Fstory.

12. Quoted by Adam Liptak, "The Polarized Court," New York Times, May 11, 2014. Available at http://www.nytimes.com/2014/05/11/upshot/the-polarized-court.html?abt=0002&abg=1.

13. It has long been unquestioned that anyone born in the United States, even of foreign parents who are here legally or illegally, is deemed an American citizen. U.S. Constitution, Amend. XIV, §1. Birthright citizenship is the law of the land since the Constitution provides that "[a]ll persons born or naturalized in the United States, and subject to the jurisdiction thereof, are citizens of the United States and of the State wherein they reside." United States v. Wong Kim Ark, 169 U.S. 649 (1898).

14. *Korematsu v. United States*, 323 U.S. 214, 225 (1944).

15. Justice Robert H. Jackson, concurring in *Brown v. Allen*, 344 U.S. 443, 540 (1953).

ACKNOWLEDGMENTS

Writing a book is a solitary, often soul-searching, exercise. The writer, however, rarely writes on a blank slate. This book has many godfathers and godmothers whose contributions are reflected in its pages.

First, I express appreciation to my two great professors of constitutional law, Alpheus Thomas Mason of Princeton and Paul Kauper at Michigan Law School, who over a half-century ago enkindled my interest in the Supreme Court and its Justices.

I am grateful generally to the peerless reportage of my sometime interlocutor Jeffrey Toobin, and of Adam Liptak of *The New York Times*, both of whose grasp of how the Court really works exemplifies the best intersection of law and journalism that we have in America today. Their superb body of work added fuel to the fire.

I am particularly appreciative of others who read and commented upon earlier versions of the manuscript or who furnished some invaluable ideas, including Dennis Suplee, Eamon Joyce, Thomas L. Pulling, Peter Dougherty, Josh Harlan, John Doyle, Frank Wisner, Peter Georgescu, and two brilliant and distinguished English jurists and close observers of the Supreme Court, Lord Jonathan Mance and his wife, Dame Mary Arden.

I very much thank my agent, Carol Mann, for her patience with me and her determination, as well as Jonathan Sisk for his fine editing, Christopher Utter, Alden Perkins, and the many others at Rowman & Littlefield who helped with this book.

Finally, I thank my talented and beautiful wife, Marlene Hess, to whom I again dedicate a book, not just for her unconditional love and encouragement (that would be gift enough), but for her reading the manuscript many times, thinking of the perfect title, and making so many wise suggestions. Without her, *Supremely Partisan* never could have been written.

INDEX

ABA. *See* American Bar Association
abortion. *See* reproductive rights and
 abortion
Abrams, Floyd, 95
Ackley, Gardner, 133
ACLU. *See* American Civil Liberties
 Union
Adams, Charles Francis, 122
Adams, John, 77
Adamson v. California (1947), 106
Adelson, Sheldon, 279
Adkins v. Children's Hospital (1923), 16
affirmative action, 40, 57, 161, 162, 167,
 178–186, 217, 283
African Americans: Murphy and, 105;
 Thomas's views on, 161–162, 163,
 167–168, 178, 179, 283; voting rights
 of, 175–178. *See also* affirmative
 action; Black seat
Agricultural Adjustment Act, 17
AIDS, 253
Albers, Josef, 154
Ali, Ayaan Hirsi, 89
Alito, Samuel: and abortion, 41, 45, 91,
 230, 231; and affirmative action, 181;
 appointment of, 21, 45, 52n25, 57, 70;
 Catholic religion of, 10, 45, 59, 64,
 111; on church-state separation, 61; on
 freedom of speech, 94; and gay
 marriage, 252; judicial opinions of,
 146, 156, 172, 205, 206, 220; judicial

questioning by, 242; judicial views of,
 10, 27, 200; personal background of,
 37; on precedent, 20
American Bar Association (ABA), 21, 115,
 123, 133, 140
American Civil Liberties Union (ACLU),
 86, 153
American Psychiatric Association, 252
American University Law School, 136
Amidon, Charles, 119
Amsterdam, Anthony, 263, 274
Anderson, George W., 121
Anderson, Myles, 160
appointments, to U.S. Supreme Court:
 criteria for, 21; ethnic politics in, 54,
 55–56; partisanship in, 1–2, 21, 27, 36;
 political nature of, 44; upon Scalia's
 death, 1–2; Senate rejection of, 37,
 164; suggestions for changing, 47;
 vetting of, 21. *See also* religious test;
 reserved seats; *under individual
 Justices*
Arendt, Hannah, 272–273
Artis, Roscoe, 267
Atkins v. Virginia (2002), 271

Baker v. Nelson (1972), 250
balancing, 201
Baldwin, James, 185
Beame, Abraham, 53
Becker, Charles, 101